WHY LEADERS CHOOSE WAR

WHY LEADERS CHOOSE WAR
The Psychology of Prevention

Jonathan Renshon

Foreword by Alexander L. George

PRAEGER SECURITY INTERNATIONAL
Westport, Connecticut • London

Library of Congress Cataloging-in-Publication Data

Renshon, Jonathan, 1982–
Why leaders choose war : the psychology of prevention / Jonathan Renshon;
 foreword by Alexander L. George.
    p. cm.
  Includes bibliographical references and index.
  ISBN 0–275–99085–0 (alk. paper)
  1. War—Causes. 2. Preemptive attack (Military science) 3. United
States—Military policy. I. Title.
  U21.2.R46 2006
  355.02'75—dc22   2006006636

British Library Cataloguing in Publication Data is available.

Library of Congress Catalog Card Number: 2006006636
ISBN: 0–275–99085–0

First published in 2006

Praeger Security International, 88 Post Road West, Westport, CT 06881
An imprint of Greenwood Publishing Group, Inc.
www.praeger.com

Printed in the United States of America

The paper used in this book complies with the
Permanent Paper Standard issued by the National
Information Standards Organization (Z39.48–1984).

10 9 8 7 6 5 4 3 2 1

This book is dedicated to my parents. Thank you.

Contents

Foreword *by Alexander L. George*   ix

Preface   xi

1. Preventive War: An Introduction   1

2. Preventing What? The Suez Canal Crisis   23

3. Israel's Preventive Strike against Iraq   41

4. How Real Was "Dr. Strangelove?" American Preventive
    War Thinking Post–WWII   59

5. To the Brink...India and Pakistan's Nuclear Standoff   87

6. Preventive War as a Grand Strategy? George W. Bush
    and "Operation Iraqi Freedom"   107

7. Conclusion: Preventive War in Perspective   143

Epilogue: Preventive War in the Age of Terrorism
and Rogue States   161

Notes   167

Bibliography   199

Index   219

Foreword

This book makes an important contribution to understanding preventive war. The major contribution is the author's emphasis on the critical importance of a top leader's role in considering preventive war.

A basic distinction is made between preventive war and preventive action. Five detailed case studies are presented, only one of which—the U.S. attack on Iraq in 2003—constitutes a preventive war. One case study considers President Eisenhower's rejection of preventive war against the Soviet Union. Two other case studies deal with preventive action: the British-French-Israeli action against the Suez Canal in 1956, and Israeli action in 1981 against Iraq's nuclear reactor. The fifth case study focuses on military conflicts and crises between India and Pakistan, 1982–2002, in which neither preventive war nor preventive action occurred.

The author provides impressive conceptual, historical, and theoretical analysis. At the same time, he emphasizes that "preventive war is a blunt instrument, not a panacea. If utilized unwisely, or without thought given to the likely consequences, its effects may be more detrimental than beneficial."

The impetus for the study was President George W. Bush's decision to wage war against Iraq. The author asks, "If the Iraq war was a 'test case' for preventive action, then did it pass the test? Will this preventive war be an isolated incident, an anomaly in the history of modern U.S. foreign policy? Or does President Bush's National Security Strategy signal a major and long-lasting change of 'grand strategy'? Will the policies of George W. Bush outlast his presidency?"

The author addresses the challenging task of developing "a theory of preventive war." He provides incisive elaboration of his thesis that the most significant variables in preventive war doctrine and decisions are individual leaders and their perceptions. This focus on the top leader of a country, he notes, "must necessarily take into account his perceptions of power, morality, stakes, reputation, and threats." Each of these perceptions is considered.

The author identifies five factors that may contribute to a decision to initiate preventive war or more limited preventive action. One: declining power in relation to an adversary; two: an inherent bad faith image of the adversary; three: a belief that war or serious conflict is inevitable; four: a belief that there is only a short "window" in which to act; and five: a situation that is believed to favor the offensive.

The presence or absence of these factors is discussed in the case studies. Was each factor present in the cases, and did it contribute to deciding on preventive war or preventive action? And were these factors present in the cases in which there was no resort to preventive war or preventive action? Analysis of these questions provides a first-cut causal analysis required for developing a theory of preventive war or preventive action.

The results can be summarized as follows: none of the five factors or combinations of them emerge as a necessary or sufficient condition for initiation of preventive war or preventive action. Presence of a "necessary" condition obviously does not suffice since it does not always make an important causal contribution to the decision. Most of these five factors, as the author notes, occurred in all five cases. They must be regarded, therefore, as factors that may contribute to decisions on preventive war. In other words, presence of a factor may favor the decision; it may be a contributing cause. A good way of summarizing this important first-cut theory of preventive war is the postulate the author provides that one or another, or some combination of the factors, may indeed influence a leader's decision without being "necessary" or "sufficient" conditions for it.

This study will stimulate much useful discussion of preventive wars and preventive action. A persuasive case is made for the critical importance of the psychology and thinking of the top leader. There are alternatives to preventive war or action. Particularly useful is the author's discussion of the possibility that preventive war may be regarded as relevant and perhaps necessary when deterrence is regarded as ineffective or irrelevant. Other alternatives exist, such as diplomacy, containment, coercive diplomacy, and even some type of careful appeasement. The research and policy agenda should address the question of whether preventive war or preventive action is relevant, and under what circumstances, for dealing with *non-state* terrorists or states that support them—questions that the author addresses.

Alexander L. George

Preface

In the wake of the devastating attack of September 11, 2001, the Bush administration committed the United States to a doctrine of preventive action against threats to the United States.[1] The 2002 National Security Strategy of the United States justified the new stance as a response to the changed circumstances of the world after the Cold War. The "Bush Doctrine," as it came to be called, stimulated sharp criticism and intense debate. Among the most controversial aspects of the doctrine was the elevation of preventive war to a fundamental part of strategic doctrine. Was preventive war ever justified? How would it be decided what magnitude of threat would require preventive action? What would be the effect of such a doctrine on other states?

These are critical questions to pose and to answer; however, they may not be as novel as many believed. Preventive war is not a new idea, and preventive action has been a mainstay of the international system since the days of the Peloponnesian War.[2] Yet, while preventive wars have been fought throughout history, there have been few dedicated attempts to analyze why states initiate preventive action. The "new" stance of the United States has focused attention on the issue of preventive and pre-emptive action, but there are still a relatively small number of analyses that make any attempt to systematically study preventive war. This book addresses that need.

The purpose of this book is to begin building a comprehensive theory of preventive war in order to better understand the motivations of those leaders who initiate preventive action, and the circumstances that bring it about. Such an understanding will not only better illuminate conflicts of the past, but also serve as a guide for the future. It also holds important implications for the conduct of American national security policy in the coming years.

The adoption by the United States of preventive war as a fundamental part of its grand strategy is unique in history. Because of the relative power and global role of the United States in the international system, its decisions and actions have large ramifications for the rest of the world. Preventive war as a strategy is fraught with questions of moral and legal legitimacy (*Should* it be done?), practicality (*Can* it be done?), and potentially devastating consequences (What will happen *after* it is done?). The purpose of this study is to provide a better understanding of these problems, as well as one other: *Why* do states initiate preventive action? These are questions associated with preventive war at any time, but the adoption of such a doctrine by the United States, a hegemonic power, makes this a particularly relevant issue for examination.

This book will focus on the motivations of states and leaders in initiating preventive action. There are many possible motivations for states' decisions to go to war preventively. It would be helpful to understand which of these, either alone, or likely in some combination, lead to these lethal decisions. Utilizing the case-study method, this work will examine the cognitive mechanisms and psychological heuristics and biases that lead decision-makers to initiate preventive action. The focus will be on why leaders act and the reasoning that underlies their decisions to do so.

However, historically there have also been circumstances when leaders might have chosen preventive war, but did not. These instances, too can tell us much about preventive action, and so this book will also examine cases in which states, after considering preventive action, decided against it. These will help to illuminate factors that might tend to dissuade leaders from preventive action, for example, international law, morality, risk assessment, and considerations of precedent and alliance stability. The ultimate goal of this work is to isolate the most important factors that incline leaders toward preventive war and the circumstances that favor such action.

Ultimately, the best avenue for understanding preventive war decisions is a close examination of the individual leader responsible for such decisions. Material factors matter, and are not ignored in this study. However, objective estimates of material capabilities are filtered through the beliefs, values, and perceptions of individual leaders. Accordingly, the case studies examined in this book focus to a large extent on individual leaders and their perception of material realities. In the end, each case study provides further evidence that individual leadership matters, and nowhere more so than in decisions involving preventive war.

This work took almost three years from inception to publication, and many people provided guidance and assistance during that time. At Wesleyan, Martha Crenshaw served as my advisor and helped to shape this work from the very beginning. Doug Foyle kindly offered to read an early draft and provided many helpful comments. Jack Levy and Ned Lebow both read early drafts and provided helpful critiques and notes. At the London School of Economics and Political Science, all of my professors and classmates helped to advance my thinking and pushed me to think about the issues from different perspectives. I would also like to thank all of my friends, who have supported me, and have endured the topic of preventive war for almost three years. I would also like to thank Hilary Claggett, my editor at Praeger Security International, for helping to get this book published. I would also like to thank Alex George, who has been an invaluable resource, reading and commenting on early drafts, and offering to write the foreword. Finally, I would like to thank my parents for the countless hours spent reading, editing, and discussing this book with me.

1

Preventive War: An Introduction

The Bush Doctrine, and most particularly its emphasis on preventive war, is among the most controversial national security policies that have emerged in the post–World War II period. President Bush has argued that "if we wait for threats to fully materialize, we will have waited too long."[1] He further promised that "to forestall or prevent such hostile acts by our adversaries, the United States will, if necessary, act pre-emptively."[2] Vice President Cheney argued that when it came to "deliverable weapons of mass destruction in the hands of a terror network, or a murderous dictator, or the two working together . . . the risks of inaction are far greater than the risks of action."[3]

For Bush's critics, this was seen as a dangerous escalation of American unilateralism and a policy more likely to create threats than to get rid of them. The *New York Times* headlined one of its editorials "Preventive War: A Failed Doctrine."[4] Democratic senator Edward Kennedy compared Bush's use of the doctrine in Iraq to the Japanese attack on Pearl Harbor and said that such a policy had little place in American national strategy.[5] Arthur Schlesinger argued that Bush's dangerous search for "monsters" abroad over-turned two centuries of American foreign policy doctrine, not to mention the wisdom of James Madison.[6]

Nor were criticism and concern about the doctrine limited to the left of the political spectrum. Even members of Bush's own party expressed reservations. In the debate that led up to the congressional action authorizing the president to confront Iraq, Republican senator Arlen Specter said, "Taking pre-emptive action against a nation-state would be a change in policy for the United States. It is my view that we ought to exhaust every alternative before turning to that alternative—economic sanctions, inspections, diplomacy."[7]

Some of the president's allies went much further. Paul Craig Roberts, a conservative commentator, penned an article about the administration's new doctrine entitled "Is the Bush Administration Certifiable?" and began the pundit piece by asking, "Has President Bush lost his grip on reality?"[8]

Yet other mainstream analysts opined that "the Bush administration challenged conventional wisdom when it proclaimed the concept of pre-emption as if it were an American invention. In fact, pre-emption is inherent in the structure of the new international order regardless of who serves in the White House."[9]

So the Bush Doctrine was either a necessary response to the 9/11 attacks or a reckless, dangerous, and needless search for enemies that has put American foreign policy on a par with the Japanese attack on Pearl Harbor. Sorting through these highly charged and conflicting views is a matter of both importance and urgency. The convergence of threats from "rogue regimes" and nuclear terrorism is unlikely to fade away for quite some time, if ever. This being the case, the questions—both theoretical and practical—surrounding the Bush Doctrine must be addressed head-on. Has the Bush administration really rewritten the rules of international conduct? Is the post–9/11 environment fundamentally different from its predecessor? Is a doctrine that has at its core the option of preventive action dangerous and irresponsible, or a necessary response to changed circumstances?[10]

In order to sort through these conflicting claims and arguments, one must begin with clear definitions. It is important to be clear about our terminology and concepts, and to examine the logic of the policies that spring from those understandings. For example, though used interchangeably, "pre-emption" and "prevention" are not synonymous. Pre-emption has a specific legal definition—which will be explored in depth later in this chapter—centering on a response to an *imminent* threat. Preventive action is in response to a threat, or a potential threat, farther in the future. Using the two concepts interchangeably, as some do, does little to advance our understanding or assessment of these very important theoretical and practical concepts.

What is the relationship of the Bush Doctrine to traditional understandings of international politics? What legal standing, if any, does this doctrine have, and when may it be used, if ever? These and other questions addressed in this book will help us to define and understand the dynamics of this policy, but conceptual analysis will take us only so far.

In addition to understanding the concepts and their relationship to other bodies of international relations theory, it is important to carefully examine cases in which preventive action was initiated—or could have been but was not—and why these decisions were made. Such cases can help us to understand why nations have decided to utilize preventive action—or why they have decided against such an action—and help us to explore the consequences and implications of both.

DEFINITIONS

Before undertaking an analysis of the motivations behind preventive war, it is imperative to clearly distinguish between pre-emption and prevention. Consider two countries, Country A and Country B, between which there is an adversarial relationship.[11] Let us imagine that Country B has received intelligence that Country A is preparing to launch a military strike against it. If Country B then takes military action to make sure that Country A can no longer attack them (as planned), it has *pre-emptively* attacked. According to Lawrence Freedman, a pre-emptive action "takes place at some point between the moment when an enemy decides to attack—or, more precisely, is perceived to be about to attack—and when the attack is actually launched."[12] *True* pre-emption can be thought of as defensive in motivation, and offensive in effect. However, since it is primarily defensive, it is generally perceived to be more morally legitimate, as well as having a more solid standing in international law, than prevention.[13]

There is the tendency to rely on the term "imminence" in definitions of pre-emptive war. However, there is also the tendency to confuse the true meaning of the word, and to equate it with the time period in which a threat resides. Consider the following terms: "imminent," "impending," "looming," and "gathering." All can refer to threats that are days or weeks away. Because of this, relying on the term "imminent" in definitions of pre-emptive war can, and often does, lead to considerable confusion. "Imminence" carries with it the implicit assumption that an attack might happen at any second, and that events have been *set in motion*. An imminent threat is one that must be pre-empted without delay. Conversely, preventive wars are waged when the threat is in the distance, but that is merely a descriptive comment, not a "key" defining characteristic. Threats are *always* in the distance—where else could they be? What defines a preventive war is not where in time the threat is, but rather the prime motivation of the decision-maker in initiating the war.

In another situation, imagine that Country B's capabilities are increasing relative to Country A's. That is, B is still weaker than A, but the power differential between the two countries is shrinking. If Country A acts militarily to prevent B from continuing to increase its relative power, then A has launched a preventive war. This is a preventive war in the classic sense of the term, a war fought to preserve the status quo balance of power.

Most previous explanations of preventive war have focused on this particular aspect. For example, Samuel P. Huntington described preventive war in 1957, as "a military action initiated by one state against another for the purpose of forestalling a subsequent change in the balance of power between the two states which would seriously reduce the military security of the first state."[14]

Jack Levy argues that the "preventive motivation" for war arises from the "perception that one's military power and potential are declining relative to that of a rising adversary, and from the fear of the consequences of that decline."[15]

Michael Walzer, coming from a notably different perspective than both Huntington and Levy, also describes preventive war as one "fought to maintain the balance, to stop what is thought to be an even distribution of power from shifting into a relation of dominance and inferiority."[16]

Thus, conventional explanations of preventive war focus on the balance of power, and define preventive war as a war to prevent a change in that balance.[17] In fact, what these scholars describe is only one possible motivation for preventive war, not its defining characteristic.[18] In defining preventive war as one fought to maintain the balance of power, these scholars have conflated a motivation *for* war with a *type* of war. Thus, the War of Spanish Succession (one of Walzer's examples) was, in fact, a preventive war. And a desire to maintain the balance of power, or status quo, did play a part in England's motivation.

However, not *all* preventive actions are wars to maintain the balance of power. There can be numerous other motivations at work in a state's decision to initiate a preventive action. Thus, a more useful and inclusive definition is that *a preventive action is one fought to forestall a grave national security threat.* True prevention is a reponse to a serious threat that lies in the future, not an attack that is already underway.

Just as we must be careful to not be overly restrictive in our definitions, we must also be careful not to define preventive action too broadly. In a recent article, former Deputy National Security Advisor James Steinberg defined four categories of "preventive force," including: action taken against terrorists; action taken to eliminate a dangerous capability; interventions in the case of state failure; and the preventive use of force to effect regime change.[19]

However, this is an overly expansive definition, and the last two of Steinberg' categories do not qualify as true "preventive action." For instance, consider Steinberg's example of the use of "preventive force" to handle an infectious disease outbreak. In this case, the state utilizing "preventive force" is preventing something from happening (the spread of an infectious disease), but only in the sense of "stopping something from occurring." Similarly, Steinberg's example of Afghanistan does not stand up to close scrutiny. U.S. action in Afghanistan was punitive and retaliatory, not preventive.

In fact, almost any action a state (or individual) takes can be framed in terms of stopping *something* from happening. A state might grant an extension on loan payments to another state, in order to make sure they did not default on their obligations, but this does not qualify as preventive action. By construing the definition of preventive action either too broadly or too narrowly we risk distorting any potential findings that may lead to a motivational theory of preventive action.

One other particularly important motivational factor in preventive war is fear. Fear, or suspicion, of others' intentions plays an important role in preventive war decisions. The same issue that is at the heart of the "security dilemma" in traditional international relations theory is central to our discussion here. As technology has improved—nuclear weapons are almost immeasurably more powerful now than they were in 1945, as well as smaller and more easily obtainable—the consequences of making a mistake in underestimating the danger have become an even more powerful factor in leaders' decisions. Other kinds of weapons of mass destruction (WMD), such as biological or chemical, only add to the weight placed on the judgment of leaders. This poses a critical dilemma for leaders who are faced with such threats. If they overreact, their decision can lead directly to armed conflict, but on their own terms; if they underreact, they risk destruction.

THE CONCEPT OF PREVENTIVE ACTION

There is also an important distinction to be made between preventive *wars* and preventive *strikes*. It is important to frame preventive war as one type of *preventive action*. This distinction has serious implications as to whether or not to take preventive action. A preventive strike, one against an opponent's nuclear facilities, for instance, will certainly have substantial consequences. However, there is an enormous difference in scale between an air strike against a uranium-enrichment plant and the launching of a preventive war that ends in invasion and occupation.

Many years ago, Huntington drew the distinction between total and limited preventive war, but even he left out a large category of preventive action.[20] A preventive strike is not really a limited war. However, Huntington was certainly on the right track by making clear that there can be *differences of degree* in preventive actions.

Thus, we might think of these two types of actions as leaving different footprints. A preventive strike, if it does not escalate into a war, would likely be perceived as far less costly to decision-makers contemplating such an action. Conversely, a preventive war might be less likely, as it would incur more risks—such as losing the war, massive loss of life and resources, substantial international condemnation, and even the possibility of other states balancing against you.[21] This is not to say that preventive war is no longer a possibility, but rather that decision-makers would have to perceive the stakes as being extremely high to incur such large risks. Preventive strikes are limited in their scope, and are generally not intended to provoke wars, though the possibility of escalation cannot be overlooked.[22] When we speak of preventive wars, we are generally speaking of an instance where a state has launched an attack, and it is understood that a general war is likely to follow.

TYPES OF PREVENTIVE ACTION

In a broader context, we can identify three types of preventive action. The first type occurs when a state decides that a conflict is inevitable, and it is thus in the interests of that state to initiate military action while it has the advantage, and on its own terms. The advantage can be that of surprise, superior capabilities, or both. The second type of preventive war occurs when a state believes that a future development will create an unacceptable or intolerable situation for them, and they must act now to prevent that development. These two types are very closely related, and are both functions of leaders believing that "time is somehow beginning to work against [them]."[23] Similarly, in both situations, leaders calculate that the risk of war or military action is so great—or the costs of a potential development (such as the acquisition of nuclear weapons) so high—that it is worth guaranteeing war in order to have the advantage of surprise and/or superior resources. The final type of preventive action occurs when the development that a state had feared has already happened. The development, whether it is the seizing of property, or the development of new capabilities (such as the announcement that an adversary has constructed its first nuclear weapon), creates a situation that is deemed intolerable by another state. Thus, the British initiated a war against Egypt in 1956 not to maintain the status quo, but to return to it, and to prevent Egypt from using its newfound power over Britain (the ability to choke off Britain's oil supply).

One final type of preventive action must be mentioned, and that is the "humanitarian war." In this type of war, the motivation is usually preventing some greater humanitarian disaster, such as an attempt to end genocide. As an example, if the United States, acting in concert with other countries or international organizations, entered the sovereign territory of the Congo with a view to restore order and to prevent a terrible humanitarian disaster, then it would fall under the category of a humanitarian intervention. Even though the motivation is to prevent something, this does not fall under the definition of a true preventive war. In order for a war to be considered preventive, there must be an element of necessity related to a vital national security interest in the motivation.

IS PREVENTIVE ACTION AGGRESSIVE?

Aggressive wars occur when a country simply attacks or invades another state's territory, or attacks its citizens or vital interests. Aggressive wars generally occur because states believe that the possible benefits (i.e., territory, populations, resources, money) outweigh the potential risks (defeat, loss of credibility in international system, economic sanctions, etc.). Wars fought to enlarge empires, such as those initiated by Adolf Hitler and Napoleon Bonaparte, are examples of aggressive wars.

The motivations of the leader are important, therefore, in helping to classify whether a war is considered preventive or aggressive. Thus, even if Country A technically attacks first, it is still considered a pre-emptive war if leaders in Country A believe themselves to be in imminent danger. Clearly, in the case of preventive war, the danger to the country initiating the attack is much less immediate (no armies would be massing on their borders), and therefore the war is much more likely to be seen as aggressive. However, if it is a true preventive war, there is a basic motivational aspect that is defensive, and not aggressive (though an aggressive element can be present as well). Moreover, an action to forestall an attack by another nation, or a possibly catastrophic chain of events, is of a different quality than an attack that is purely motivated by a desire for gain (in territory or resources), and our terminology should reflect this important difference.

Some scholars make no such distinctions and believe that there has to be an intrinsic link between aggression and preventive war. Neta C. Crawford noted a trend to equate preventive war with aggression, and predicted that preventive action threatens a "world of bloody and exasperated war."[24] However, aggression is not necessarily a primary or defining characteristic of preventive wars. Fear of plausible consequences, based on credible information, is defensive. If the motivation for a war is based primarily on a desire for more resources, an intense animosity or enmity, or a wish to extend a country's influence or power, then it is not a true preventive war, regardless of a leader's protestations to the opposite.

However, not all scholars have associated preventive war with aggression. While Levy focuses primarily on the shifting balance of power as a source of motivation for war, by terming it the "preventive motivation" *for* war (based on a fear of a negative change in the status quo), he clearly separates aggression from the preventive motivation for war.[25]

So, in order to be considered a true preventive war, the motivation must be primarily defensive in the minds of the leaders waging the war. Outside observers, or later historians and academics, might debate whether the leader had no choice but to launch a preventive war. But what is central to such a debate is whether the decision-maker, operating within the constraints imposed by limited information and his or her own psychological framework, had a reasonable belief that the war was necessary in order to prevent a serious threat to vital national security interests.

Moral duty to help prevent humanitarian disasters simply does not fulfill this requirement. The number of humanitarian disasters that elicited indignation, but not action, evinces this. Leaders who initiate preventive action do so because they believe they have no other options available to protect a real national security interest. This may seem counterintuitive; after all, from the outsider's point of view, leaders have much more agency in issues of preventive war than in pre-emptive war, when they may be attacked at any second. And yet, the cases in this book illustrate that leaders who initiate preventive wars or strikes do so with some degree of felt necessity, even desperation in some cases, because they feel that it is the only possible action. In cases of humanitarian interventions, other states can (and often do) ignore the problem, or intervene ineffectually precisely because there are no vital national interests at stake.

It is often difficult to distinguish the various types of wars and preventive wars, because very few leaders publicly acknowledge any aggressive intent. Most wars of aggression are couched in terms of self-defense and response to a threat, further confusing the issue of what exactly pre-emption and prevention mean. It is an important task, therefore, to separate the definitional elements of these terms from their added political connotations.

PREVENTIVE ACTION AND THE LOGIC OF COERCION

In order to better understand the dynamics of preventive military action in the international system, it is necessary to have a basic understanding of its relationship with coercion. Is preventive action the result of a failure of coercion? Or is it the "ultimate" in coercion? Since coercion technically involves only the threat of force (or very limited use of actual force), a preventive war cannot by itself be an act of coercion.[26] However, a limited preventive strike might be considered an act of coercion. And because the goal of a coercer is to use "enough force to make the threat of future force credible," any action that makes future threats more credible would qualify as coercion.[27] This creates a paradoxical situation in which a failure of coercive diplomacy in the present may have the effect (intended or otherwise) of augmenting a country's coercive capability in the future.

Deterrence is a type of coercive strategy in which State A deters State B from a given action by making clear its commitment to defend its interests and/or to retaliate and punish State B.[28] The implications of deterrence theory for preventive war are numerous. Deterrence is intrinsically connected to conflict, and thus to prevention as well. If immediate deterrence is a failure of general deterrence, then preventive war reflects a failure of both.[29]

A failure of general deterrence can result in a preventive war for several reasons. First, a peacetime buildup and deployment of forces around the world holds the very real possibility of threatening other countries. Of course, this may be the goal to a certain extent, but if taken too far it can become counterproductive. If other states begin to feel sufficiently threatened by such deployments, they may to initiate preventive action. The shotgun that you bring home to defend your family does not need to be pointed at your neighbors to make them suspicious of your intentions (or worry for their own safety).[30] And the buildup of a peacetime military is more analogous to bringing home an arsenal of weapons than a single shotgun.

General deterrence can also fail for lack of credibility. Credibility requires not only the capacity to follow through on threats, but also the ability to make your opponent believe that you have the *will* to do so. This is a communication failure, in which the deterring country does not make clear enough (or the threatening country misunderstands)[31] either what its vital interests are, or its dedication to defending them. A country that is being deterred might believe that there is a relatively low cost to aggressive action, either because the deterring country does not consider something a vital interest, or because they do not have the means or will to defend it; but this is not necessarily a preventive war. However, it is also possible that the build-up of capabilities necessary to achieve a credible general deterrence might threaten another country, which, if not reassured of the deterring country's peaceful intentions, might launch a preventive war before the capabilities are further increased.

A failure of immediate deterrence can also lead to a preventive war. Consider the situation in which immediate deterrence often occurs: a crisis. Inherent in crisis situations is a significant amount of uncertainty. If deterrence has already failed on a general level, then the deterring state might believe war to be inevitable, in which case it might launch a preventive action while it still has a relative advantage (at the very least, the advantage of surprise).

Or, in another situation, a state might believe that its adversary will not be influenced by a deterrent threat, because they are not rational, or are determined to start a conflict. In fact, states often attribute such hostility and aggressive intentions to their adversaries; it only matters how much emphasis is placed on those characteristics, and whether or not they are mitigated by other considerations. If decision-makers believe those particular traits to be dominant, and not checked by other factors (i.e., international constraints, domestic constraints, etc.), then they might decide to act preventively since a conflict is inevitable.

Should a state wait until immediate deterrence has also failed before initiating what would then be a preventive action? The implication of a state launching a preventive action without attempting to specifically utilize an immediate deterrent threat (or even soon after it has used such a warning) is that it does not have faith in the coercive power of its deterrence. If a state truly believed that it had communicated its warning effectively, and that the other state knew that it had the means and the will to follow through on its threat, then war would not be inevitable; indeed, it would be almost certain to not occur.

In fact, this exact situation is illustrated in several of the case studies that follow. In some cases, the consequences of a miscalculation leading to a deterrence failure are so disastrous, so horrific, that leaders might attempt bold or risky actions to reduce their probability. However, because the probability of the "worst-case scenario" occurring can only approach zero, preventive action becomes more likely in a world where WMD have become increasingly miniaturized, more powerful, and available to those who would seek to kill. Because there is no way to completely eliminate the threat, leaders are increasingly likely to attempt to eliminate the source of the threat.

NUCLEAR DETERRENCE, TRANSITION PERIODS, AND PREVENTIVE WAR

In the recent past, deterrence has most often been discussed in relation to nuclear arsenals. This is partly because the systematic, analytical study of deterrence coincided with the beginning of the Cold War and the nuclear arms race in the 1950s. In recent years, nuclear deterrence literature has focused to a greater extent on nuclear proliferation, and its implication for both the effectiveness of deterrence and the likelihood of war. The crux of the debate is this: nuclear weapons are widely considered responsible for the "long peace" of the Cold War.[32] However, while some believe that the spread of nuclear weapons to countries other than the original members of the "nuclear club" will promote stability, others believe that nuclear proliferation, if not slowed or stopped, will drastically increase the chances of a preventive or pre-emptive war.[33]

One of the most important points to come out of the debate between proliferation optimists and pessimists is the importance of "transition periods." "Transition period" describes a moment, or a period of time, in which the strategic balance between two countries is on the verge of a major shift. For the purpose of this work, there are two important transition periods. One occurs when a country is developing—but has not yet constructed—a nuclear bomb, while the second occurs when the size of a country's nascent arsenal is extremely small, and they do not yet have a secure second-strike capability.[34]

Both of these transition periods have important implications for preventive war decisions. In both situations, there is a pronounced advantage to offensive action. Additionally, both transition periods engender the belief that a "window of opportunity" is closing. A state may still have the advantage while another country constructs a nuclear deterrent, or before they have secure second-strike capability, but that advantage is unlikely to last very long. If other factors are present, such as the belief that a rival's behavior is completely unpredictable, or that they might actually use their nuclear weapons, the temptation to initiate preventive action increases.

THE LEGALITY OF PRE-EMPTION AND PREVENTION

One strain of debate concerning preventive and pre-emptive action is the legality of such action. "Legality" here refers to compliance (or at least perceived compliance) with international law. One important source of international law governing the use of force is set out in the charter of the United Nations. The relevant section of the UN Charter, Article 2 (4), mandates that member states refrain from the threat or use of force against other states.[35]

However, there is an exception to this ban, which can be found in Article 51: "Nothing in the present Charter shall impair the inherent right of individual or collective self-defense if an armed attack occurs against a member of the United Nations."[36]

However, the UN Charter does not mention pre-emptive or preventive action by name in the charter; it only reserves for states the right to self-defense. Thus any debate concerning the legality of preventive or pre-emptive action has necessarily focused on whether the right to self-defense was invoked appropriately. There are a number of questions that this debate centers on, such as, What constitutes an attack? How can one distinguish between an attack and anticipatory self-defense?[37] And, if the right of anticipatory self-defense does exist in legal terms, how far in advance can this right be invoked?

The first question, regarding what exactly constitutes an attack, is especially important. Notice that Article 2 (4) prohibits both the use of force and the threat of force. However, Article 51 leaves out any mention of "threats" and instead says only that states have the right to self-defense if "an armed attack occurs." Note also that Article 39 of the UN Charter authorizes the Security Council to deal with any "threat to the peace, breach of the peace, or act of aggression."[38]

It is unlikely that the framers of the document simply forgot to put the language of "threats" in Article 51. Instead, as Michael Bothe points out, the reason lies in the primary objective of the UN, to constrain the unilateral use of force.[39] Thus, the Security Council, which can only act multilaterally, can use force legally even with a lower standard of aggression, including threats of force. Individual states, however, not acting under the auspices of the UN, have a higher standard, and can only invoke the right to self-defense in response to an actual armed attack.

This leads to the question of whether there is any legal support for anticipatory self-defense. The UN Charter was written in 1945, at the dawn of the atomic age. However, even before the devastating power of nuclear weapons, states made the case for self-defense before they were actually attacked.

In 1837, U.S. Secretary of State Daniel Webster, writing to condemn British action in sinking the *Caroline*, an American ship, wrote that "[the right to invade another state's territory can be justified as self-defense only in] cases in which the necessity of that self-defense is instant, overwhelming, and leaving no choice of means and no moment for deliberation."[40]

This formation of self-defense, known commonly as the principle of "necessity and immediacy" makes a good deal of sense in today's strategic environment. Consider as a hypothetical example that State A has overwhelming evidence that State B, a nuclear power, is about to launch an attack on it. Even if State A is not absolutely certain that the attack will involve nuclear weapons (let us imagine that it is a possibility), should State A wait to be attacked before responding?

The commonsense answer to such a question is that of course they should not. In an era where biological, chemical, and nuclear weapons proliferate, and even conventional weapons have a destructive power unimagined in the era of the *Caroline*, it would be foolish to expect a state to wait to be attacked before responding. This then is the basis of the concept of pre-emptive self-defense. By the strict definition of the UN Charter, it would seem to be illegal, yet State A, in such a situation, would be able to make a strong, defensible case that its actions did not violate the spirit of customary international law.

However, the right to anticipatory, or pre-emptive, self-defense is considerably less clear in the real world than it is in hypothetical examples. In the real world, intelligence is not definite, technology can be "dual-purpose," and as a result of advances in military technology, states often do not have a tremendous amount of advance warning of an impending attack. Moreover, while technology has quickened the pace of crisis decision-making, it has also raised the stakes. The threat of a WMD is potentially so devastating that it might make leaders more inclined to take great risks to prevent such an attack.

However, while it is important to have laws that reflect common sense, it is possible to "overcorrect" and swing the pendulum too far in the opposite direction. Renowned legal scholar Myres McDougal argues that Article 51 of the UN Charter should be interpreted to mean that a state may use military force when it "regards itself as intolerably threatened by the activities of another."[41] This is perhaps as dangerous an interpretation as one that requires a country to absorb a nuclear attack before responding, since it seems to validate and legitimize reactions based purely on fear and suspicion, both of which are abundant in this age of catastrophic terrorism. Clearly, the answer lies somewhere in the middle. Thomas Franck offers the following definition of "legal" pre-emption: "[action] undertaken in reasonable anticipation of an *imminent* large-scale armed attack of which there is *substantiated* evidence."[42] We must keep in mind that there is no way to completely get rid of the uncertainty inherent in these types of calculations. Substantiated evidence is a good general benchmark, but one that might not be possible in all circumstances (for instance, in closed societies).

Recently, the UN—in recognition of the changed circumstances and threats of the current global environment—issued a 130-page report on issues facing the international community, including the use of pre-emptive and preventive force. The report concluded that any instances where anticipatory self-defense is seen as necessary should be presented to the UN Security Council. As for those states that might be "impatient" with such a course of action, "the risk to global order and the norm of non-intervention on which it continues to be based is simply too great for the legality of unilateral preventive action." While acknowledging that the international community is obligated to be concerned about "nightmare scenarios" of catastrophic terrorism and rogue states with WMD, the report concludes that only the Security Council can legally take action preventively or pre-emptively.[43]

That the United Nations dealt with the issue of preventive and pre-emptive action speaks volumes about the relevance of such issues in the current global climate. However, the UN report demands the same process for both pre-emptive and preventive action: both are to be referred to the Security Council. It is highly unlikely that even if the Security Council were a highly efficient decision-making body, it would be able to act fast enough to authorize and carry out pre-emptive action. Furthermore, while the UN's "clarification" of the legality of anticipatory self-defense is a necessary and well-intentioned first step, the report does not take into account the reality of the international system. While it is true that making sure the Security Council does not vote on these issues is certainly not the optimal solution, neither is it likely that states will refer such grave threats to their security to a decision-making body that many agree is badly broken.[44]

The legality of pre-emption, and to a much greater extent prevention, would then essentially hinge on the ability of the pre-emptor (or preventer) to make a convincing case before the world community that they were in imminent danger and had acted in good faith (i.e., had not manufactured intelligence, but had responded in a proportional manner), based on reasonable intelligence.

The reason prevention is not as legally acceptable as pre-emption is that preventive action, because of its very nature, means responding to a threat in a future more distant than pre-emption. Thus, it is harder to make the case that the unilateral use of force was the only option available to the initiator.

I raise these issues here not to comment on the legality of pre-emption, or prevention for that matter, but rather to lay them out as a set of considerations that leaders must address in their strategic calculations. Such concerns are primarily relevant insofar as decision-makers believe that they are important, and the implications for action that derive from such a belief. The fact is that whether legal or illegal, both pre-emption and prevention occur and are increasingly part of leaders' strategic calculations.

RISK-TAKING AND PREVENTIVE WAR

Intrinsically tied to preventive war is the issue of risk-taking in international politics. What leads decision-makers to take risks? Is risk-taking related primarily to the personality of the decision-maker, or to the circumstances of a situation? There are two schools of thought on this issue, both of which have merit.

Prospect theory holds that risk-taking is best explained, or understood, by an examination of the context of the decision.[45] The theory holds that individuals evaluate outcomes with respect to deviations from a reference point (rather than to net assets); that they give more weight to losses than to comparable gains; and that they are more likely to incur risks if the issue is framed in terms of "losses," and conversely less likely to incur risks for comparable gains.[46]

The second school of thought on this issue, personality theory, focuses on individuals, rather than the situational context, or framing of the situation. This approach is heavily dependent upon close examination of the personality, psychology, and leadership style of the individual decision-maker. In an early study of personality traits, Kogan and Wallach found that although not *all* people fit into these categories, there were particular kinds of people who might be described as either "risk-takers" or "conservatives."[47]

In the end, it is unlikely that either of these two approaches explain risk completely, or by themselves. History is replete with examples in which one of the approaches provides more explanatory power than the other. Because of this, there has evolved a "middle ground" in which personality theory acts as a *complement* to prospect theory in explanations of decision-making under risk or uncertainty.[48]

TOWARD A THEORY OF PREVENTIVE WAR

The theory developed in this book draws on five case studies: British action in the Suez Canal Crisis; Israel's strike on the Osiraq nuclear reactor; American preventive war thinking, 1946–1954; Indian preventive war

thinking, 1982–2002; and the American preventive war against Iraq beginning in 2003. Several different variables that appear to be associated with
decisions concerning preventive war are examined: the "declining power
motivation"; an inherent bad faith relationship with an adversary; a belief
that war is inevitable; the belief that there is only a short "window" in which
to act; a situation that favors the offensive (or is believed to); and black-and-
white thinking.

While all of these factors appear to be influential in preventive war decisions in the case studies that will be analyzed, the leadership style and the
psychology of the decision-maker prove to be very important in developing
a theory of preventive war. The importance of leaders—their psychologies,
motivations, and choices—is an element that runs through all of the cases,
and helps to explain the outcomes in the five cases examined. Rather than a
factor that can be categorized as either present or not present, leadership
psychology appears to act as a catalyst that can either emphasize or diminish
the importance of the other variables. As an example, transition periods,
and alterations in the strategic balance between two rivals, occur with relative frequency; however, preventive war does not. How can we explain this?
In fact, transition periods play an important role in four of the five cases,
and yet in two out of those five, the decision-maker considered, but decided
against, preventive war. Transition periods, like the factors noted above, can
be very important, but strategic calculations must be filtered and interpreted
by individuals who decide how much importance to attach to them.

Leadership Psychology

The importance of individuals as an idea is contrary to many mainstream
theories of international relations. Many of these theories argue against the
importance of individuals in international relations. They concentrate on
"big picture" factors, such as the structure of the international system, or the
relative capabilities and balance of power. To the extent that they reference
motivation at all, it is usually in the form of imperatives like "human nature"
that leave little room for individual psychology, leadership, or choice.[49] The
case studies examined herein make clear that individuals do, in many circumstances, exercise vast influence over the course of events. One basic
reason is that individual leaders can filter similar information in different
ways. Another is that not everybody reacts the same way to similar circumstances or reaches similar judgments about them. President George W. Bush
saw Iraq as a serious threat and invaded, while Al Gore says he would not have
done so. Or to take another example of the way in which different leadership
psychologies lead to potentially different outcomes, it is not at all difficult to
believe that Shimon Peres would have acted very differently than Menachem
Begin had Peres been prime minister in 1981. Thus, central to any analysis of

preventive war decision-making is a close examination of individual motivation, perception, and ultimately, judgment.

Of course, individual decision-makers face constraints. They must deal with the realities of their circumstances, whatever their personal inclinations and views. Some options are too absurd or dangerous to even contemplate. It would be difficult to imagine Israel's Menachem Begin ordering a strike against the nuclear capabilities of the United States, or a land invasion and occupation of Iraq; Israel simply does not have the necessary capabilities, and it would be unlikely that anybody within the Israeli government would allow such foolhardy courses of action. However, most questions lie between extremes, and in the exact area where individual judgment and discretion matters most.

No theory is likely able to predict with certainty whether preventive or pre-emptive action will occur. However, there are factors that substantially increase the odds of a state initiating preventive action, as well as providing considerable explanatory power after the fact. The following elements appear to be important, in varying degrees, in the five case studies.

Declining Power in Relation to an Adversary

Leadership psychology and leaders' beliefs are instrumental in understanding decisions to initiate preventive war, but they are not the only factor leading to such decisions. Jack Levy noted in his work on the "preventive motivation" for war that preventive wars are fought not by *rising* powers seeking to *change* the status quo, but by *declining* powers seeking to *preserve* the status quo. Thus, a decline in power relative to an adversary might lead a state to initiate preventive war in order to put down the challenger. It might also lead the declining power to initiate preventive action in order to forestall the rising power from attaining a particular capability (such as the ability to produce nuclear weapons). In both cases, the declining power seeks to maintain its position relative to an adversary. It should be noted, though, that the status quo does not have any inherent value. Therefore, a change to the status quo, if it did not pose an unacceptable risk to the status quo power, might not compel preventive action. The type and degree of change of the status quo would seem to be at least as important as the *fact of the change* itself.

It is also important to define what, exactly, is meant by "declining power." Is it declining power if a country believes that the rise in power of its adversary will result in rough parity? Or does the situation have to result in a substantial and real material power imbalance? For the purposes of this work, declining power will refer to a situation in which a state believes that its power is declining relative to another country, and is fearful of the consequences of that decline—without specifying what the consequences must be for the factor to be present.[50] One reason for focusing on relative decline (as opposed to an absolute decline) is that by doing so it is possible to link material realities with the psychology of perception. It is likely that leaders' perception of the end result of the decline—parity or imbalance—will affect their behavior. This is a point that will be drawn out in the case studies.

Inherent Bad Faith Relationship with an Adversary

A relationship where both parties believe the other to be a mortal enemy is a pervasive and important factor in preventive war decisions. As long as there is the possibility that a conflict might be resolved by peaceful means, war becomes less likely. However, in conflicts that are marked by a history of mutual suspicion and hostility, confidence and trust-building measures have difficulty gaining traction, as each side fervently believes that the other side will never cooperate. This is a psychological version of the security dilemma in which even actions taken in good faith are assumed by the adversary to be a trick of some kind. This relates directly to the empirical observation that certain cognitive beliefs can become reified, even in the face of conflicting information.[51] The "inherent bad faith" model describes an image of the enemy that has become rooted in moral absolutes, and is "closed" to conflicting or dissonant information.[52]

The bad faith image contributes to the desire to initiate preventive action by making war or conflict seem inevitable, and by increasing the chances of escalation (and thus preventive or pre-emptive war) in even a relatively minor crisis.

Related to this is the image of the enemy. Are they perceived as untrustworthy, but a relatively minor threat? Or are their capabilities potentially dangerous enough that malicious intentions alone might be enough to induce preventive action? How trustworthy are they? After all, international agreements and treaties are only useful in solving disputes so long as states are trusted to keep their end of the agreement.

Arthur Gladstone outlines the basic framework of the psychological conception of the enemy: "Each side believes the other to be bent on aggression and conquest, to be capable of great brutality and evil-doing . . . to be insincere and untrustworthy. . . . Many actions which are ordinarily considered immoral become highly moral."[53]

Heikki Luostarinen writes that an enemy image is a belief held by a certain group "that its security and basic values are directly and seriously threatened by some other group."[54] The idea of an inherent bad faith image is simply the enemy image extended over time, and hardened in the mind of the decision-maker. This is a particularly important factor, as the perception of an enemy's *intentions* can be much more significant than their material capabilities.[55] Additionally, strong enemy images may also cause a greater polarization of good and evil in the mind of the decision-maker.[56] This has particular relevance for decision-makers who are already predisposed toward a black-and-white view of the world.

A Belief that War (or Serious Conflict) Is Inevitable

The belief that war or conflict is inevitable is dangerous insofar as leaders of a state believe themselves to be in a strategically advantageous position relative to an adversary. If leaders believe war is inevitable, and believe their country to have the advantage now, then it is in the state's interest to act while it is in an advantageous position. Again, individual perception is relevant. Who believes war to be inevitable is important. Is it just a single leader? Is it all, or most, of their trusted advisors? Is there a broad consensus that conflict is inevitable? Is the strategic advantage diminishing or increasing?

While the specific belief that war is inevitable is very important, the more general manifestation of this is that time is working against a country. This belief, though it can sometimes be no more than a vague notion in the minds of decision-makers, is no less powerful for its ambiguity. In fact, this belief appears to correlate closely with decisions to initiate preventive war. This vague sense of foreboding about the future permeates many of the key decision-makers' statements that appear throughout this book.

A Belief that There Is Only a Short "Window" in which to Act

It is well established that crisis situations can force decision-makers to act in a manner that is not always optimal. Similarly, the belief that there is only a short window in which to act can lead decision-makers to believe that something must be done before it is too late. This window is a limited period of time in which one state has a strategic advantage over another. This type of "window-thinking" usually prescribes some positive action to either reverse or forestall the trend toward a period of danger in the future. It might be thought of as a "slow-motion crisis."

The idea of "windows of opportunity" has been thoroughly documented, though scholars have given different accounts of its importance.[57] However, this book presents evidence that the concept of windows of opportunity can be an important factor in decisions to initiate preventive action. The case studies in this book illustrate the weight that decision-makers give to window-thinking, and its impact on preventive war decisions.

A Situation that Favors the Offensive (or Is Believed to)

A situation that is believed to favor the offensive is a contributing factor toward preventive war since it leads decision-makers to believe that the only way to win a war is to strike the first blow.[58] If the threat of war is great enough, striking the first blow (though it changes war from a possibility to a certainty) might be seen as the only option. This type of thinking is exacerbated by the highly destructive nature of nuclear weapons, which are so potentially devastating that the first blow might end up being the only blow.

Black-and-White Thinking

The last factor that is important in preventive war decision-making is the individual leader's "worldview," and its permeability or openness to change. This is a complex factor to quantify and code, and it is thus important to be as specific as possible from the outset. The idea of a "worldview," as it is used here, is taken from Nathan Leites' work on the operational code construct. Leites used the operational code concept to refer to the aspects of Bolshevik beliefs that were pertinent to the realm of political action, and therefore influenced Soviet decision-making.[59]

In 1969, Alexander George reformulated Leites' concept of an operational code into a series of questions, the answers to which formed a leader's operational code. These questions regard different aspects of the decision-maker's relevant political beliefs. For the purpose of this work, the following questions are relevant: One, what is the essential "nature" of political life? Is the political universe essentially one of harmony or conflict? What is the fundamental character of one's political opponents? Two, what is the utility and role of different means for advancing one's interests?[60]

A worldview/belief system is, in essence, a leader's assumptions about the nature of the world that operate as a cognitive filter. As George puts it, it is a set of general beliefs about the "fundamental issues of history and central questions of politics." It is slightly more expansive than James David Barber's definition of a worldview as "primary, politically relevant beliefs, particularly... [the] conception of social causality, human nature and the central moral conflicts of the time."[61] The definition used in this work is closer to George's, which includes operational codes (fundamental views about the *nature* of the world) as well as ideologies.[62]

The specific content of a leader's worldview matters, but so do its structural aspects. How open is that view to new or conflicting information? How nuanced or complex is it? Consider Glad's work on "black-and-white thinking." She describes the structure of such a worldview as one that sees the "world as divided into two camps, with all morality on one side, all evil on the other, with two possible outcomes—to win or to lose. There is no political middle ground."

Glad notes that this type of Manichean view of the world is also linked to a certitude that this is the correct view.[63] In her work, this is presented as a criticism, however it is also the case that this self-confidence allows leaders to make difficult decisions that are sure to provoke heavy criticism, such as initiating preventive action.

The black-and-white worldview also has implications for the inherent bad faith image, with which it interacts and can reinforce. Additionally, both the black-and-white worldview and the inherent bad faith image are connected to a leader's propensity to see the world in moral dichotomies: good and evil, right and wrong.

It is important, however, to distinguish between two types of black-and-white thinking. First, there is the idea of black-and-white thinking as essentially a simplistic way of processing information. In this view, people take in new information and immediately place it in one of two possible categories. This is the sense in which the term is often used, and seems to carry with it the implicit assumption that this is a poor way to process information.

The second type of black-and-white thinking is more complex. In this view, people are able to process information in a much more complex and nuanced manner before deciding which of the two categories it fits into. This is an important distinction to make, as it carries with it significant implications about the type of leader one is dealing with. In the first type, there is little room for complexity or a nuanced understanding, while in the second there is, but the end result is "boiled down" so that the decision-maker is not lost in endless shades of gray.

It is important not to assume a direct link between a leader's worldview and the output; the foreign policy action that results. There can be numerous sources of "slippage" between decisions and implementation.[64] However, to the extent that individual leaders and advisors are important to preventive war decisions, their individual worldviews are critical to the decision-making process. All of the factors mentioned above interact with the fundamental beliefs of an individual leader. A leader's worldview has important implications for what types of action they believe to be the most effective (i.e., diplomatic, military, economic), the prospects for peaceful resolution (whether conflict is inevitable), and the nature of their political opponents (how rigid their enemy image is).

The elements noted above are the foundations of a motivational theory of preventive war. They are not static, however. Different elements carry different degrees of importance, and thus power to explain preventive war decisions in different circumstances. Clearly illustrating the evidence of these elements (or factors), and examining the circumstances in which they take on more or less significance in decision-making, will move us some distance toward a fuller understanding of these critical decisions.

COMPARATIVE CASE STUDIES AND PREVENTIVE WAR THEORY

The purpose of this book is to isolate and assess the motivations that incline decision-makers toward preventive action. In order to facilitate this kind of analysis, it is important to have a variety of different and distinct cases to analyze.[65] In choosing these cases it was important to find ones that were suitably different, and yet, upon close examination, had similar issues at their core. The cases analyzed herein are not meant to be an analysis of American foreign policy, or the foreign policy of any particular country. Rather, the cases were selected from a variety of countries and time periods in order to better isolate the variables that relate to preventive military action. Choosing examples from different countries helps guard this work against being too culturally or geographically specific, thus enhancing the chances for developing a more comprehensive explanation of the motivations for preventive war. Choosing cases over a span of time allows us to see whether certain factors are evident across time periods, or are period specific. Finally, choosing cases with variability in the values of the dependent variable (whether preventive action was chosen) allows us to examine circumstances when preventive war could have been chosen but was not. This might well provide valuable insights into the circumstances that both facilitate or impede such decisions.

A conscious decision was made to concentrate on the post–World War II period. This is not because instances of preventive action are more prevalent now, but rather that World War II is a very important boundary in several ways. Previous to 1945, the United States was a significantly smaller force in international politics. And, although the current international system (post-Soviet collapse) is different from the Cold War, it is much closer in its basic structure to it than to the traditional European balance of power model, which dominated international relations up until the second half of the twentieth century.

Another important way in which World War II represents an important boundary is in terms of technology. The world pre-1945 simply cannot be compared with today's. The development of the Internet, nuclear weapons and biological weapons, missiles that go farther and faster than ever before, and "smart bombs" that can go through the window of a house have changed the basic framework of warfare. Obviously, to pick any date as a cutting off point is to some extent arbitrary; why 1945 and not 1957, when ballistic missiles were developed? However, for the purposes of this book, World War II represents the most significant shift, but is not so far in the past to make cases from around that time irrelevant.

This book will examine five different cases. Case one will be the Suez Canal Crisis of 1956, and will examine British motivations for their preventive action (in which they colluded with France and Israel) against Egypt. Case two will examine the Israeli preventive strike on the Iraqi nuclear reactor, Osiraq, in 1981. Case three will examine the arguments within the U.S. government for going to war preventively against the Soviet Union during the Truman and Eisenhower administrations, and the reasons that it decided not to do so. Case four will examine preventive (and pre-emptive) thinking in India during the years 1982–2002. The fifth and final case examines the U.S. decision to wage preventive war against Iraq in 2003.

While there are common threads in all five cases, there are also significant differences, one of which is the role of nuclear or catastrophic weapons. The U.S.-Soviet case study deals with nuclear issues, but that conflict takes place at the very beginning of the study of nuclear strategic thought and deterrence, and thus is dealt with in a very different way than later case studies. The Osiraq case deals with nuclear weapons, but primarily in the subcategory of nuclear proliferation, and the effects of proliferation on war-propensity and security. The India-Pakistan case deals with nuclear weapons and deterrence in a very recognizable way: the threat of mutually assured destruction (MAD) is always in the background, but the issue of inadvertent escalation is as well. In the final case, nuclear weapons do play an important role, but their significance is transformed (and amplified) by the events of September 11. It is only when the link was made between terrorists, rogue states, and the proliferation of WMD that nuclear weapons became the focus of the Bush administration. Only the Suez case ignores nuclear issues for the most part, though nuclear weapons were in production at the time of the crisis. Thus, though four of the cases deal with nuclear or catastrophic weapons, all do so from very different angles.

2

Preventing What?
The Suez Canal Crisis

On October 29, 1956, Israel invaded the Sinai. This action followed months of negotiations between Egypt, France, England, and the United States over Egyptian president Nasser's nationalization of the Suez Canal. It is now known that Britain secretly colluded with France and Israel to wage a preventive war against Egypt. The plan called for Israel to launch an attack on Egypt at a prescribed time, and England and France to send troops to Egypt in the guise of "peacekeepers" in order to reestablish control over the canal. However, economic pressure by the United States soon forced Britain and France out of Egypt in a rather humiliating fashion. Henry Kissinger later wrote, "by the time the smoke cleared, the Suez Crisis had destroyed the Great Power status of both Great Britain and France."[1]

This case study focuses on British decision-making during the crisis. It examines the Suez crisis from the nationalization of the canal through the ensuing months, and ends at the Sevres Conference, where Israel, Britain, and France made the final decision to use force. However, in order to analyze that decision, it is also necessary to trace the origins of the crises in the British policy from the early 1950s, through the building of the canal, and, finally, to the sequence of events that led British leaders to conclude that the use of force was the only option left to them.

This case highlights the importance of perception in decisions regarding preventive war. The British decided to take preventive action after Egypt's nationalization because of their perception of both Egypt's intentions, and their own capabilities. British decision-makers, and in particular, Anthony Eden, had locked into the idea of Nasser as an "enemy" with evil intentions, who would try to humiliate Britain and/or blackmail it through control of the transportation of oil through the canal. Simultaneously, British leaders disregarded warnings over the potential consequences of their action, believing that their influence in the world was such that they could weather the storm of criticism and condemnation that might follow. This involved a certain amount of wishful thinking in the minds of British leaders who, contrary to the severe warnings from American officials (including President Eisenhower), believed that they might get away with it.

This case also highlights the importance of specific individuals. Discussions of policy options took place, but ultimately one man made the decision. This suggests that a decisive individual leader can exercise great influence over preventive war decisions. Even in a democratic government, where individual agency might be mitigated by bureaucratic politics and interagency bargaining, the power of the individual is readily apparent.

What is particularly interesting about this case is that it presents a unique variant of Jack Levy's "declining power" motivation for preventive war.[2] Levy wrote that "the preventive motivation for war arises from the perception that one's military power and potential are declining relative to that of a rising adversary, and from the fear of the consequences of that decline."[3]

However, in this case, the decline had, for the most part, *already occurred.* This is not to say that Egypt, as the "rising adversary," had surpassed Britain in military power, but rather that Britain's decline was already well under way by 1956. However, Britain's perception of its own power and influence had not yet caught up to the realities of its current situation. If, in fact, it can be shown that there was a preventive motivation for war in the sense that Levy envisions, then this case would be an example of a country that was fighting a preventive war decades too late. In fact, Britain's relative decline had little to do with Egypt, and much to do with the destruction wrought on it by two successive world wars, and the rise of American hegemony in the Western world. Thus, this case does not fit Levy's framework very well, at least without some modification.

These observations provide a different perspective on traditional realist theories of preventive war. Thus, it is not only the *actual decline* of military power that matters to decision-makers (if this were true, Britain would have launched a preventive war decades earlier), but also their own perceptions of their nation's relative place in the world. Contrary to Levy's argument, Britain was not fighting for a return to the actual status quo, but rather to a status quo that had existed before World War I, almost fifty years previously.

Additionally, British action in this case fits into the second type of preventive war outlined in Chapter 1. British action in this case was not intended to crush a rising power, though the end goal of the military action would certainly have accomplished that. Nor was it intended to prevent Egypt from acquiring a particular capability; Egypt had already drastically altered the balance of power by seizing the canal. British action was intended to prevent the utilization of Egypt's newly acquired power. Egypt's seizure of the canal had given it the ability to exert influence over the British Empire through its control of British oil-shipping routes. The possibility of blackmail by Egypt was exacerbated by British perceptions of Nasser as a mortal enemy.

PRELUDE: THE ASWAN HIGH DAM

The Suez Canal Crisis originated with the building of another major project in Egypt, the Aswan High Dam. Nasser had proposed construction of this dam to regulate irrigation of the Nile Valley, to secure the subsistence of all of Egypt against drought, and any other natural disasters.

At this point Anthony Eden was not yet firmly opposed to Nasser. In fact, he was the prime advocate of a joint Anglo-American effort to finance the dam, with America shouldering ninety percent of the actual cost. Most scholars agree that his early attitude was partly shaped by his desire to bring Egypt into the Western sphere, and to prevent the Soviets from gaining a foothold in North Africa. The American ambassador, Winthrop Aldrich, recalled an encounter with Eden where the prime minister voiced his fear that a Russian offer to finance the dam would give the Soviets a "dangerous foothold in an area vital to the interests of Great Britain."[4]

In a top-secret letter to Harold Macmillan, Ivone Kirkpatrick (Permanent Under Secretary for Foreign Affairs) confessed, "You should know that the Prime Minister is much exercised about the Middle East and is in two minds, oscillating between fear of driving Nasser irrevocably into the Soviet Camp, and a desire to wring the necks of Egypt and Syria."[5]

On December 14, 1955, Great Britain and the United States made a formal offer to finance the Aswan Dam. Part of the impetus for this came from Eden, who became even more agitated after the Soviet Union (through the Czech government) sold Egypt a large shipment of MiG fighters, tanks, and other heavy equipment. The arms deals convinced Eden that, in the words of Foreign Secretary Selwyn Lloyd, it was "vitally necessary for the West to take over responsibility for the Aswan Dam."[6] The money would be given in two stages: limited funds during the preliminary stage (i.e., surveying) and the bulk of the money for the actual construction during the second phase. However, far from placating Nasser and drawing him closer to the West, funding for the dam seems to have spurred him to further antagonize the West without fear of reprisal.

Quickly after the British-American announcement of funding, Nasser rejected American entreaties to facilitate Arab-Israeli negotiations. Then, pro-Egyptian riots broke out in Jordan, which obliged King Hussein to dismiss Glubb Pasha, the British commander of the Arab Legion.[7] Soon after that, in May, Nasser withdrew Egypt's recognition of the government of

Chang Kai-shek and established diplomatic relations with the People's Republic of China. This move apparently was especially traumatic for John Foster Dulles, the American Secretary of State, who was deeply committed to Taiwan.[8]

Anthony Nutting, a deputy Foreign Minister, explained the American position following these events:

> The administration's foreign aid programme had recently run into serious trouble in Congress . . . in this climate it would be courting a further rebuff to ask for an appropriation for the Aswan loan. Although the government had tried hard to get back on terms with the Arab world . . . there were powerful anti-Arab, and more particularly anti-Egyptian, voices in Congress. . . . Zionist influences were [also] very strong . . . and only a month before Egypt had upset the apple-cart still further by recognizing Communist China . . . it was just not practical politics for the administration to go ahead and ask Congress to approve so large a loan to Egypt.[9]

A few days later, Dulles sent for the Egyptian ambassador to the United States and told him that the United States was backing out of the Aswan Dam loan. Eden and the British government soon followed suit. Nasser was informed of this at a meeting in Yugoslavia with Marshal Tito and Jawaharlal Nehru. It was likely a great humiliation to get this news while in the company of the two leading figures of the non-aligned world. Upon hearing the news, the French Ambassador to Washington, Maurice Couve de Murville, predicted of Egypt: "They will do something about Suez. That's the only way they can touch the Western countries."[10]

SEIZURE AND INITIAL REACTIONS

On July 26, Nasser announced the nationalization of the Suez Canal in a public speech in Alexandria.[11] Later in the speech, when Nasser spoke the name "De Lesseps," it was a signal for the Egyptian military to seize the canal. It was a daring move, which caught the world almost completely by surprise.

We can get a feeling for the initial reaction of British leaders through the minutes of the first cabinet meeting. The cabinet

> agreed that we should be on weak legal ground in basing our resistance on the narrow argument that Colonel Nasser had acted illegally. The Suez Canal Company was registered as an Egyptian company under Egyptian law; and Colonel Nasser had indicated that he intended to

compensate the shareholders at ruling market prices. Our case must be presented on wider international grounds; our argument must be that the canal was an important international asset and facility and that Egypt could not be allowed to exploit it for a purely internal purpose. . . . The cabinet agreed that for these reasons every effort must be made to restore effective international control over the Canal. It was evident that the Egyptians would not yield to economic pressures alone. They must be subjected to the maximum political pressure which could be exerted . . . and, if need be, the use of force.[12]

This excerpt from the cabinet meeting gives us a broad picture of the choices that were available to Britain at that moment. The first option, the legal argument, did not have enough power behind it, as the case was particularly complex. The force of international law was not wholly on either side (or to look at it another way, it was on both sides).

The British had condemned the act as a "high-handed act of seizure against an international company,"[13] which violated the international guarantee written in the Constantinople Convention of 1888 allowing for free navigation. However, Nasser's argument was that under the terms of the Khedive's concessions, the Suez Canal Company was an Egyptian joint-stock company, and as such could be nationalized without breaking international law.[14] Of this dilemma, Nutting wrote, "In fact, as frequently happens in international disputes, both arguments could be supported on legal grounds, which made it all the more necessary that the issue should be resolved by political and diplomatic negotiation and agreement."[15]

Thus, it seems that even at this early stage there was little chance of resolving the dispute on legal grounds. Britain did not have a watertight legal argument, and thus could not exert the moral and legal pressure necessary to compel Nasser's cooperation.[16]

In addition, British leaders recognized early that economic pressure was also not feasible. In the first cabinet meeting after the nationalization, the possibility of using economic pressure was discussed:

Egypt had £102 million in her blocked account, of which no more was due to be released until January 1957. In addition she probably had £14 millions available on current account of which some £7 million was held by the Bank of England and the remainder by commercial banks. *The blocking of the current balances would probably not seriously incommode Egypt at the present time.*[17]

Thus, only one day after the nationalization of the canal, both economic and legal pressure had been ruled out as effective means to resolve the dispute. The only options still available were: One, do nothing, and let Nasser's action stand; two, use political pressure and diplomacy; or three, use military force to take back control of the canal. On July 27, Eden wrote a telegram to President Eisenhower, which declared:

> We are all agreed that we cannot afford to allow Nasser to seize control of the canal in this way, in defiance of international agreements. If we take a firm stand over this now we shall have the support of the maritime powers. If we do not, *our influence* and yours throughout the Middle East will, we are all convinced, be finally destroyed.[18]

Eden went on to say that he was convinced that economic pressure alone would not resolve the issue, and that he was, of course, prepared to begin negotiations on the matter with the help of other governments. However, the letter ends: "My colleagues and I are convinced that we must be ready, in the last resort, to use force to bring Nasser to his senses. For our part we are prepared to do so."[19]

This letter is telling in that it shows that Eden was not prepared to let this action stand. Only one day after the initial action, his attitude toward this seems to have crystallized: Nasser's aggression could not stand. Likewise, he was already convinced that economic and legal pressure would not be able to influence Egypt. Thus, the only two options left were diplomatic negotiations and the use of force, which Eden was already prepared to use "as a last resort."

However, in the initial cabinet meetings, Eden made a remark that is revealing of his intentions: "Colonel Nasser's action had presented us with an opportunity to find a lasting settlement of this problem, and we should not hesitate to take advantage of it."[20]

The language of this remark indicates that Nasser's action had given the British an opportunity to take care of a larger problem, not just the nationalization of the canal. And what was that larger problem? It was Egypt's problematic leadership and the British loss of influence in the Middle East.

BRITISH PRESTIGE AND INFLUENCE

Before proceeding further, it is important to have an understanding of British influence and power in the second half of the twentieth century. Derek Varble wrote "Britain emerged from World War II with formidable military forces."[21] However, this statement obscures the larger trend in the second half of the twentieth century—the steady erosion of British influence in the world.[22] Britain had started the century as the pre-eminent colonial power in the world, as well as a Great Power. However, much had changed since the pre–World War I era, and Britain was no longer in the position it once had been in.

In fact, the nationalization of the canal was only the latest in a series of blows to British prestige. Between 1945 and 1951, Britain had withdrawn from India, Greece, Turkey, and Palestine.[23] In 1951, Iran's Premier Mossadeq had nationalized the oil industry and thrown out the Anglo-Iranian Oil Company.[24] In Egypt in that same year, King Farouk's ministers had denounced the 1936 Treaty with Britain that allowed for the stationing of British forces in the Suez Canal zone.[25] In fact, in 1954, in an attempt to palliate Egypt, Britain had agreed to withdraw all of its military personnel from the Suez Canal Base within two years![26]

And finally, on March 1, 1956, General Glubb was dismissed from his post in Jordan. General Glubb was the chief of the General Staff and commander of the Arab Legion, a post he had held since 1939. He was a respected officer, and his unceremonious dismissal seems to have been taken by Eden as a personal insult. Nutting writes:

> A few hours later, after the news had reached London, the Prime Minister of Great Britain declared a personal war on the man whom he held responsible for Glubb's dismissal—Gamal Abdel Nasser.... For Eden, such a blow to Britain's waning prestige as an imperial power, capable of influencing men and events in the Middle East, could not be allowed to go unpunished.[27]

Harold Macmillan, then chancellor of the Exchequer, recalls that after finding out about Glubb, Eden raged,[28] "I want Nasser destroyed, not removed, destroyed."[29]

And Evelyn Shuckburgh, Eden's private secretary, reports that on March 3, Eden had thought aloud about "reoccupation of Suez as a move to counteract the blow to our prestige which Glubb's dismissal means."[30]

Thus, we can see that this crisis came at a particularly sensitive time period for Britain. It was a period of transition. Kissinger wrote that after India, Egypt "represented the most important legacy of Great Britain's imperial past."[31] However, after granting India its independence in 1947, the Suez Canal was one of the last vestigial reminders of the great British Empire as it had been in years past. Nutting explains this curious phenomenon in the following passage: "One of the more curious features of modern British history is that, while generally prepared to accept this transformation in respect to the Indian and Colonial Empires, successive British Governments were to show an extreme reluctance to abdicate control in the Middle East."[32]

This was perhaps out of a desire on the part of British leaders to remain relevant. The fact that Egypt and the Suez Canal (and their influence in the Middle East) were the last remnants of their once great empire might have caused Britain to hang on to them even more tenaciously. Thus Harold Macmillan declared that "if Britain did not confront Nasser now, it [Britain] would become another Netherlands."[33]

Britain was in a somewhat unique position in the world. Its material power had been seriously weakened by two successive world wars, and its influence around the world had been eroded by the steady growth of nationalist movements throughout the empire. However, it still regarded itself as a Great Power, and certainly evidenced a strong desire to remain relevant in world politics. This no doubt affected its behavior in the crisis, and probably precluded simply allowing Nasser's action to stand.[34] Eden's belief that acting decisively against Nasser would restore some of Britain's international reputation is well illustrated by his comments.

Britain's declining position was clearly important, but this and the crisis were filtered through the feelings and experiences of Anthony Eden, the primary decision-maker in this case. He had grown up during the height of the British Empire. He was born during the Victorian age, in 1897, and was educated at Oxford, where he received a First degree in Oriental languages— Persian and Arabic.[35] Though he ended up as a career politician, he always saw himself as an intellectual, an Arabist, who applied his talent to the realm of foreign policy.

In a study of the formation of elite attitudes, Karl Deutsch and Richard Merritt wrote: "Even spectacular events usually do not result in massive or permanent shifts in collective beliefs . . . often it takes the replacement of one generation by another to let the impact of external changes take its full effect."[36]

This point has particular relevance for leaders whose careers span different eras. Anthony Eden, born in Victorian England, died in 1977, after Great Britain had relinquished much of its empire. The Suez crisis shows that even the decline of British power in the aftermath of the two world wars had not managed to fundamentally alter Eden's perception of Britain's "place in the world." During the crisis, the legal advisor to the Foreign Office, Sir Gerald Fitzmaurice, reminded Eden and others that, with regard to the use of force, "justification that would have been accepted without question fifty or even twenty-five years ago would by now be completely rejected."[37]

OIL

Prestige was not the only reason that the Suez Canal was important. The Suez Canal provided Western Europe with oil. Over 1.5 million barrels a day were shipped from the Middle East, through the Suez Canal, to Western Europe.[38] To ship the oil on an alternate route, around the Cape of Good Hope, would require twice the tonnage of tankers.[39]

Originally, much of the value of the canal was that it provided easy access for Britain to its empire in India. However, even as India became independent in 1947, the canal began to assume importance in a new role. The canal cut the 11,000-mile journey from the Persian Gulf to England down to 6,500 miles.[40] By 1955, petroleum accounted for two-thirds of the canal's overall traffic, and two-thirds of Europe's oil supply passed through it.[41]

Eden understood this and described the importance of the canal:

> In recent years its importance had been greatly increased by the development of the Middle Eastern oilfields and by the dependence of Western Europe on them for a large part of its oil supplies. In 1955, 14,666 ships had passed through the canal. Three quarters of them belonged to NATO countries and nearly one-third were British. The Government determined that our essential interests in this area must be safeguarded, if necessary by military action.[42]

Though Anthony Nutting, head of the British Foreign Office, did not often agree with Eden, he too recognized the unique strategic role of the canal. Nutting asserts that the canal was important for conveyance of the "lifeblood of British industry": oil.[43] Though various pipelines transferred oil from the Middle East to the Mediterranean, these overland routes were susceptible to "Middle Eastern chaos," such as Syrian instability and the problems caused by the creation of the State of Israel.[44]

The Suez Canal was thus a unique structure that straddled the boundaries of two time periods. For some, it represented the grandeur of the British Empire, but it also represented the future, in the form of the transportation of oil and of ensuring the security of that commodity. The Suez Canal was vitally important to Western Europe for a combination of reasons (prestige, precedent, Nasser), but the most critical was the security of its oil supply. Eden wrote of the canal:[45]

> We estimated that the United Kingdom had reserves of oil which would last for six weeks, and that the other countries of Western Europe owned comparatively smaller stocks. This continuing supply of fuel, which was a vital source of power to the economy of Britain, was now subject to Colonel Nasser's whim. The oilfields of the Middle East were then producing about 145 million tons a year. Nearly 70 million tons of oil had passed through the Suez Canal in 1955, almost all of it destined for Western Europe. Another 40 million tons of oil reached the ports of the Levant by pipelines running through the territories of Egypt's then allies, Syria and Saudi Arabia ... More than half of Britain's annual imports of oil came through the canal. At any time the Egyptians might decide to interfere with its passage. They might also

prompt their allies to cut the pipeline. We had to gauge the implications of bringing oil from the Persian Gulf by the long haul around the
Cape of Good Hope.[46]

Thus, once nationalization of the canal had occurred, Egypt, both directly
(through its control of the canal) and indirectly (through influence with its
allies, which had increased along with Nasser's prestige in the Arab world
after the nationalization) had the means to apply serious pressure on Western Europe. Combined with the fiery anti-Western rhetoric of Gamal Nasser,
Britain and France did seem to have cause to worry.

It should also be noted at this point that the potential worries of Britain
and France over the security of their oil was in some ways balanced out by
the actions of Nasser (as distinguished from his incendiary speeches). Nasser,
probably consciously wary of providing any justification for strong action,
refrained from offering any real provocation after the initial seizure. According to Nutting, "Nasser had offered no real provocation that would
justify the use of force. He had seized an Anglo-French company, but he had
not done any injury to British or French lives, nor had he stopped a British
or French ship passing through the Canal."[47]

Furthermore, one might wonder why Nasser would ever prevent a British
or French ship from passing through the canal. The supposed reason for the
nationalization of the canal was to provide money for the construction of the
Aswan Dam. After the *fait accompli* of nationalization, Nasser stood to finally
collect all of the profits from the canal. His interests would probably not be
served by interfering with shipping and pressing the British or French into
taking forceful action.

However unlikely it might have been that their shipping would be interfered with, for France and Britain the point was probably moot. As the
rest of this case study will illustrate, Nasser's control over the canal already
exceeded what British and French leaders were prepared to accept. In international politics, power is not just the actual use of force, but the ability to
credibly threaten force in order to influence the behavior of others. Nationalization of the canal gave Nasser power over Britain and France even if
he never interfered with a single ship. The growing importance of oil meant
that Britain and France would be "under Nasser's thumb" for the foreseeable
future if they allowed his actions to stand.

NASSER AND "APPEASEMENT"

Contributing to the developing crisis was the changing perception of
Nasser on the part of British leaders. In 1952, Selwyn Lloyd reported being
"favorably impressed" with Nasser during their first meeting.[48] And, as late

as March 1954, Shuckburgh reported that Eden had "come to the conclusion that Nasser is the man for us."[49]

However, between 1954 and the Suez crisis, the British perspective on Nasser had changed dramatically. By the time of the Glubb incident in March of 1956, Eden had already taken to comparing Nasser to Mussolini.[50] In fact, Eden compared Nasser to Hitler so often that Winston Churchill once remarked, after a conversation with Eden, that he "never knew before that Munich was situated on the Nile."[51] In March 1956, Nutting wrote a memo to Lloyd asserting that "appeasement of Nasser" would not work, and that Nasser would likely break any deal that he made. Lloyd reports that this memo confirmed his own intuition.[52]

The allusion to "appeasement" and fascist dictators by British leaders is telling in what it reveals about the historical analogies that resonated with them. Though the war itself was obviously fresh in the minds of British leaders, it was the year 1936 that was probably at the back of the minds of Eden, Lloyd, and Nutting. The year 1956 was the twentieth anniversary of the 1936 remilitarization and reoccupation of the Rhineland by Hitler. It was also the twentieth anniversary of Western Europe doing nothing to oppose Hitler, a decision that had been widely condemned in the intervening years. Macmillan had gone against the tide in advising forceful action in March 1936. Eden, however, had not; claiming that public opinion in Europe would not support action against Germany for "returning to their own backyard."[53] However, he had a falling out with Neville Chamberlain in 1938 after the Munich conference, implying that the "lesson of appeasement" had been quickly learned.[54]

Scot Macdonald wrote, "the 1930's analogy *dominated* both Eden and British decision-making."[55] There is much corroboration for this statement. Kirkpatrick, for example, drafted much of Eden's correspondence and one letter, written to Eisenhower, drew at length upon the Rhineland analogy "which was clearly in the forefront of the PM's mind."[56]

For instance, one letter from Eden to Eisenhower read:

In the nineteen-thirties Hitler established his position by a series of carefully planned movements. . . . It was argued either that Hitler had committed no act of aggression against anyone, or that he was entitled to do what he liked in his own territory, or that it was impossible to prove that he had any ulterior designs . . . Similarly, the seizure of the Suez Canal is, we are convinced, the opening gambit in a planned campaign designed by Nasser to expel all Western influence and interests from Arab countries . . . You may feel that even if we are right it would be better to wait until Nasser has unmistakably unveiled his intentions. But this was the argument which prevailed in 1936 and which we both rejected in 1938. Admittedly there are risks in the use of

force against Egypt now. It is, however, clear that military intervention
designed to reverse Nasser's revolutions in the whole continent would
be a much more costly and difficult undertaking.[57]

This letter clearly indicates the importance of this historical analogy for
Eden. This "lesson" was most likely learned by most people of his generation.
However, Eden's experience was somewhat unique. In 1936, as British for-
eign secretary, he personally had a hand in appeasing Hitler. Then, in 1938,
after learning his lesson, he was unable to exert influence over Chamberlain.
Now, in 1956, confronted again by aggression, he was in a position to *act*.

A leader's personal experiences often carry disproportionate weight in
their thinking. "Events seen and participated in leave disproportionate im-
pressions . . . the lessons drawn from firsthand experiences are overgeneral-
ized. So if people do not learn enough from what happens to others, they
learn too much from what happens to themselves."[58]

DIPLOMACY AND NEGOTIATIONS

On August 1, Dulles arrived in London to take part in meetings between
the United States, France, and Britain. It seemed at first as though the
countries were in agreement for the most part. Nutting recalls that Dulles
spoke of finding a way to make Nasser "disgorge" the canal, and also of the
possibility that force might be necessary.[59]

The French were slightly more anxious, and their foreign minister

declared that his Government was unanimous in desiring urgent and
decisive action . . . the repercussions of Nasser's action touched France
closely in another and vital sphere. From the first, Pineau emphasized
the effects that it would have in Algeria and upon the entire French
position in North Africa. If Egypt were allowed to succeed in grabbing
the canal, the Algerian nationalists would take fresh heart. They would
also look to Egypt for backing, which they would certainly receive, both
in arms and clamour. France could not permit this threat to develop.[60]

However, though there seems to have been a superficial unanimity of
approach between the three powers, it was clear to Eden even in this early
meeting that France and Britain were much closer to each other in their
positions than either was to the United States. Already, in a private note to
Eden, Dulles warned against "precipitous" military action.[61]

The next conference took place on August 16, and this time included the
eight original signatories of the 1888 Convention as well as the twenty-four
principal users of the canal. Egypt was invited to the conference, but refused

to attend. In the end, eighteen of the twenty-two nations that attended the conference voted for an international board of eight nations to manage the canal.[62] The board would include Egypt, but would be overwhelmingly dominated by Western powers. However, in a public speech before the conference, Eden made public his comparison of Nasser to fascist dictators:

> Why not trust him? The answer is simple. Look at his record . . . Instead of meeting us with friendship Colonel Nasser conducted a vicious propaganda campaign against this country. He has shown that he is not a man who can be trusted to keep an agreement . . . The pattern is familiar to many of us . . . We all know this is how fascist governments behave, as we all remember, only too well, what the cost can be in giving in to Fascism.[63]

The conference appointed Sir Robert Menzies, prime minister of Australia, to travel to Egypt with a proposal.[64] Menzies arrived in Cairo on September 3 in an attempt to negotiate a settlement with Nasser. However, Nasser countered that it was Britain and France that had created this predicament, and that nothing would induce him to accept a solution that derogated from "Egypt's absolute right to run the canal as an Egyptian national undertaking."[65] By September 9, Menzies was forced to return to London with the mission a complete failure.

Eden wrote of this time period:

> Her Majesty's government accepted that every diplomatic method must be employed and exhausted, and shown to be exhausted, before resorting to military action . . . There was always the danger that the passage of time and the multiplication of talk would weaken the resolve of the eighteen powers. The risk of letting Nasser keep his prize might in the end be greater than the risk of using force.[66]

This excerpt illustrates very clearly the perception on the part of Eden that time was working against the British. This is an important component of preventive war thinking, and has serious implications for action. If decision-makers believe that time is working against them, they are much less likely to give diplomacy a serious chance. Part of the reason that the United States and Britain had such starkly different reactions to the crisis was that each had very different interpretations of *time*. For the Americans, there was "no rush to act," because time was working against Nasser.[67] Eden's belief was the direct opposite of this, as he believed that Britain's position worsened, and Nasser's improved, with every minute that passed.

On September 13, Dulles came up with another proposal to negotiate a settlement. Under this proposal, the Suez Canal User's Association would collect dues on either end of the canal, just outside of Egypt's territorial waters.[68] Nasser was invited to join the association, and abdicate control to an international body, but the plan would go ahead without him if he abstained. However, once again, Dulles publicly disavowed the use of force, thereby undercutting the effectiveness of any political pressure that might have induced Nasser to compromise.[69]

COLLUSION

By early October, France had already been involved in negotiations with Israel on a possible military option. In a meeting in early September, Pineau declared that "after Nasser's nationalization of the canal, it had become clear to France that force would have to be used against Egypt . . . France would try to convince the British that Anglo-French military measures were the only course, but . . . was doubtful that she would succeed."[70]

Israel, for its part, agreed that military action was necessary, but was worried that Britain might decide to join Jordan in the campaign against Israel (if Jordan attacked Israel).[71] It also became clear over the course of these meetings that France had no suitable bomber aircraft, without which Egypt's airfields would remain intact and the battle might drag on. It was at this point that the substantive meetings ended, as no further planning could take place without the participation of Great Britain.[72]

On Sunday, October 14, Nutting and Eden met with French representatives. Albert Gazier, the French Minister of Labour, cautiously asked Eden what Britain's response would be if Israel were to attack Egypt. Eden replied that Britain "had no obligation . . . to stop the Israelis attacking the Egyptians."[73] Eden then asked his secretary to stop recording the minutes of the meeting and asked General Challe, a French representative, to speak openly. Nutting recalls that

> the plan, as he put it to us, was that Israel should be invited to attack Egypt across the Sinai Peninsula and that France and Britain, having given the Israeli forces enough time to seize all or most of Sinai, should then order "both sides" to withdraw their forces from the Suez Canal in order to permit an Anglo-French force to intervene and occupy the Canal on the pretext of saving it from damage by fighting. Thus the two powers would be able to claim to be "separating the combatants" and "extinguishing a dangerous fire," while actually seizing control of the entire waterway and of its terminal ports, Port Said and Suez. This would . . . restore the running of the Canal to Anglo-French management.[74]

While Nutting attempted to stall for time, Eden would brook no delay. He asked Nutting to prepare a meeting of ministers for the upcoming Tuesday. When Nutting suggested that they invite Sir Gerald Fitzmaurice, the Foreign Office legal advisor, Eden replied: "Fitz is the last person I want consulted.... The lawyers are always against our doing anything. For God's sake, keep them out of it. This is a political affair."[75]

Nutting describes his perception of the risks of Challe's plan:

> Apart from the immorality of the collusion with Israel, the French proposals meant that we should be acting flatly contrary to the Tripartite Declaration by attacking the victim of aggression instead of the aggressor. We should also be in breach of the U.N. charter, plus the 1954 agreement with Egypt, which allowed us to send troops in to the Canal Zone only at the request of the Egyptian Government. And even if we were prepared to ignore every moral issue, our chances of "getting away with it" were minimal. We should have the Americans against us... The UN would denounce us... The Commonwealth would be divided... The Arab world would, of course, be united against us... there would be a widespread sabotage of oil installations and probably a total stop on oil deliveries to Britain and France... we might never regain our reputation in the Middle East... Finally, we should confirm the deep-seated suspicion of many Arabs that we had created Israel... to serve as a launching platform for a Western reentry into the Arab world.[76]

On October 21, Eden decided that Selwyn Lloyd should travel incognito to Paris the next day to meet French and Israeli leaders.[77] The meeting itself was to take place at Sevres, France. The house at which the conference was held was rife with symbolic meaning. It was held at the villa of a family that had supported de Gaulle against the Vichy regime, and had been used as a Resistance base during the war.[78] This was most likely not lost on French politicians still haunted by the specter of Munich. Abel Thomas, director-general of the French Ministry of Defense, conveyed his thought to the Israeli leaders at the beginning of the conference: "One day the Sevres Conference will no doubt be publicized... It therefore depends on us whether it is remembered as the Yalta conference or as the Munich conference of the Middle East."[79]

The talks revolved around essentially the same plan discussed before by the British and the French. Israel, however, felt as though it was being asked to solve Britain and France's problems by accepting the opprobrium of aggression followed by the indignity of a British ultimatum.[80] Lloyd did not agree on anything that night, but instead flew back to London to consult with Eden. One thing that stands out about this meeting is the detailed strategic and tactical discussions[81] that the participants had, contrary to Eden's later declarations that there was no collusion or conspiracy.

At meetings the next day at Sevres, the French negotiating team worked with Israel to determine which areas were close enough to the canal, where, if Israel attacked, Britain would be "forced" to send troops. Donald Logan, private secretary to Lloyd, recalls:

> The Israelis did not conceal that their main objective would be Sharm el-Sheikh on the Straits of Tiran to enable them to maintain passage for their ships to the port of Aqaba. We emphasized that a move in that direction would not pose a threat to the Canal. Eventually, sketch maps were made and we were assured that there would be military activity in the region of the Mitla Pass. More than that we could not get, but the Mitla Pass being reasonably close to the Canal we concluded that the Israelis sufficiently understood the British position.[82]

Finally, upon Israeli urging, a document was signed, of which there were three copies, which later became known as the Sevres Protocol. The protocol declared that the Israeli Defense Forces would launch an attack on the evening of October 29 in the vicinity of the canal. Upon being "informed" of the attacks, Britain and France would simultaneously make appeals to the Israeli and Egyptian governments to halt the fighting. Additionally, the British and French government would demand that Egypt temporarily accept the occupation of the canal by British and French soldiers (and that they would do so regardless of Egypt's response).[83]

At 5:00 PM on October 29, Israeli paratroopers were dropped on the Mitla Pass, and the Suez War began. On Wednesday, October 31, after the British delegation to the UN vetoed an American proposal for a cease-fire, Chairman of the Senate Foreign Relations Committee Walter George commented: "They are more or less conniving in an attack against Egypt and are using that as a prearranged pretext. . . . It is almost certain that Britain and France are working in collusion with the Israelis."[84]

On that same day, Anglo-French forces began air attack on Egyptian airfields. British paratroopers landed and occupied the canal on November 5.[85] On November 6, Macmillan, then chairman of the Exchequer, informed the British cabinet that a run on the pound had been orchestrated by Washington, causing the pound to lose one-eighth of its value. Macmillan was then informed by the Eisenhower administration that the United States would support an IMF loan to prop up the pound if a cease-fire was signed by midnight.[86] The cease-fire was signed, the conflict ended, and the Anglo-French forces withdrew from the canal area. However, even later, Eden publicly claimed that "there was not foreknowledge that Israel would attack Egypt."[87]

SELF-IMAGE

Lord Bolingbroke, an eighteenth-century scholar, wrote:

The precise point at which the scales of power turn ... is imperceptible to common observation: and, in one case as in the other, some progress must be made in the new direction, before the change is perceived ... they who are in the sinking scale do not easily come off from the habitual prejudices of superior wealth, or power, or skill, or courage, nor from the confidences that the prejudices inspire. They who are in the rising scale do not immediately feel their strength, nor assume that confidence in it which successful experience gives them afterwards. They who are the most concerned to watch the variations of this balance, misjudge often in the same manner, and from the same prejudices. They continue to dread a power no longer able to hurt them, or they continue to have no apprehension of a power that grows daily more formidable.[88]

Along the same lines, John Stoessinger wrote that "most national leaders will not examine their prejudices and stereotypes until they are shaken and shattered into doing so. People, in short, learn and grow largely through suffering."[89]

Much has been written about how accurately leaders are able to perceive the actual balance of power. However, though much has been written of the formation of our perception of *others*, there has been too little attention paid to the formation of a state's *self-image*. However, it is precisely this issue that is at the heart of this case. Hans Morgenthau, in his work on realism, relies on a calculative model. The essence of this model is that "national power" can be calculated by adding together such factors as geography, population, armed forces, and some slightly more ambiguous variables, such as national character.[90]

However, though these factors are undoubtedly important components of national power, is there any real way to make such a calculation? This case illustrates that these power calculations are not made as easily as Morgenthau assumes. If, for instance, Eden had calculated ahead of time the influence that the United States had on Britain (and the true wishes of the U.S.), he might have been more willing to seek a diplomatic solution. These factors of national power, all easy enough to calculate on their own, are almost impossible to add together. Indeed, Morgenthau concedes that a true evaluation of power is "an ideal task, and hence, incapable of achievement."[91]

CONCLUSION

British initiation of a preventive war, in this case, is based on two central issues. First, the psychological perceptions of British leaders caused them to see in Nasser an enemy similar to Hitler or Mussolini. The analogies that British leaders used to categorize Nasser also prescribed a specific solution: aggression must be met with force. The effect of the Munich analogy, so often invoked by other leaders, must have had particular resonance for Eden, who had been so intimately involved in the decision to appease Hitler. In fact, Eden declared himself to be "haunted" by the mistakes committed in dealing with Hitler.[92] The second cause of British action was their belief that their position in the world allowed them to act unilaterally. British leaders believed that Britain was powerful enough to act in defiance of international law (and American wishes).

However, these factors were necessary, but not sufficient. They set the stage for the decision to launch a preventive war, but it was the individual leadership of Eden, and his unique psychology, that drove the decision. Eden embodied the slow transition of Britain into the post–World War II era; an era in which they were no longer the dominant force in world politics. As an Oxford-trained Arabist, educated during the height of British imperialism, he embodied a Britain that by 1956 no longer existed. Yet, as often noted, individuals can be slow to change, and even slower to change their fundamental worldviews. This stand against Nasser was, according to Eden, a chance for him to correct the mistakes made by Britain (and himself) in the past.

This case is an interesting synthesis of older, previous theories of preventive war alongside a cognitive explanation. Declining power and capabilities are a factor, but not in the sense described by Levy. Likewise, historical analogies are important in this case, but have not previously been used in preventive war theories. Declining power, hostile image of the enemy, and other factors might be present, but they are not the driving force in preventive war decision-making. It is how leaders *interpret and perceive* these factors that is critical in any explanation of preventive war. It is thus critical to examine the beliefs and perceptions of the individual decision-maker alongside material factors.

3

Israel's Preventive Strike against Iraq

At 5:30 PM on June 7, 1981, six Israeli F-15 and eight F-16 fighter jets dropped their payload of 2,000-pound bombs on the Osiraq[1] reactor in Tuwaitha, outside Baghdad.[2] In order to reach Iraq, they flew more than 1,000 miles undetected over the hostile airspace of Jordan and Saudi Arabia. They dropped the bombs in a single pass lasting just over two minutes and flew back to Israeli airspace without incident.

The implications of Israel's preventive strike on Iraq's nuclear facility were immediately clear to the world community. Many condemned the strike, some supported it (if only tacitly), but none doubted its ramifications. Israel had carried out the first preventive strike on a nuclear facility in history, and it had done so successfully, effectively destroying the Iraqi reactor without suffering a single casualty. This case study will examine the events that led up to Israel's decision to bomb the reactor and its implications for the theory of preventive war.

This case is important in that it shows the importance of individual decision-makers in the context of preventive war. The theories of preventive war put forward up to this point have, for the most part, focused on relative power and capabilities. However, Iraq's nuclear ambition did not affect Israel only because it decreased their *relative* power (although it undoubtedly did, especially within the Middle East). In fact, considerations of the balance of power do not seem to have played an important part in Israeli considerations. Rather, it was the effect on their sense of security that was important. By 1981, Israeli decision-makers believed that the situation had progressed to a point where it was, or was about to become, intolerable. Thus, a key factor in this case is the image of the adversary held by key Israeli decision-makers, who saw Iraqi nuclear ambitions as dangerous because of the combination of their intentions and capabilities. This case cannot be explained without reference to the perception of Iraqi intentions, as a capability-driven explanation does not explain why Israel did not attack nascent nuclear programs in other states. Thus, it was the combination of the Israeli image of Iraq and the perception of their dangerous intentions (coupled with disturbing advances in their capabilities) that drove the decision-making of a determined, strong leader. The leadership of Menachem Begin provides an example of a leader who is self-assured in the face of criticism, and has the courage of his convictions. No explanation of the Osiraq strike can be complete without dealing with these varied factors.

In addition to the specific importance of leaders, this case very clearly exhibits three of the factors mentioned in Chapter 1. First, there was an "inherent bad faith relationship" between Israel and Iraq. Second, there was a belief that conflict was inevitable between the two states. In fact, this case is an illustration of a sub-category of this factor in which many decision-makers believe a state of war to exist. Third, the timing of this strike was driven by the belief that there was only a short window in which to act. This was true not only because of the nature of the threat (a soon-to-be active nuclear facility), but also because of domestic political considerations (upcoming elections).

IRAQ AND ISRAEL

It is important to begin this case study with a sense of the historical relationship between Israel and Iraq. An understanding of the tumultuous relationship between the two countries is necessary to comprehend the general frame in which Israeli decision-makers analyzed (on both a conscious and unconscious level) the actions of Iraq.

On May 14, 1948, the day Israel came into existence, an Iraqi brigade was already in the midst of attacking Israeli forces. By the time the fighting had ended, Iraq had 16,000 soldiers stationed in Palestine.[3] And, while Egypt, Lebanon, Jordan, and Syria entered into armistice agreements with Israel, Iraq refused, preferring to hand over its military gains to the Jordanian Arab Legion.[4] Though they returned home in 1948, Iraqi forces reappeared on Israel's borders in 1967 during the Six Day War and again in 1973 in the Yom Kippur War.

Perlmutter, Handel, and Bar-Joseph wrote:

Unlike any other Arab state directly at war with Israel, Iraq consistently and stubbornly refused to even consider the conclusion of a ceasefire or armistice agreement with Israel; at the end of each of their conflicts the Iraqis simply withdrew their forces far back into the homeland and reappeared on the scene whenever a new war broke out. Iraq is, therefore, from both the practical and the legal point of view the only Arab state in a permanent state of war with Israel.[5]

It is thus generally agreed that Israel considers Iraq "amongst their most implacable and aggressive enemies."[6] This had important implications for the preventive strike on Osiraq in 1981. This "enemy image" would most likely have precluded any significant rapprochement even if Iraq had been conciliatory. However, such behavior on the part of Iraq was not forthcoming, and the potential threat of the Iraqi nuclear program was likely magnified by the image of them already held by Israel.

A question arises here as to whether Iraqi behavior solidified Israeli views so that no change was possible. This has been argued in other circumstances. Jerel A. Rosati (and other scholars) have argued that John Foster Dulles rejected new information that was inconsistent with his "inherent bad faith" image of Soviet leaders, by engaging in a number of psychological heuristics.[7] Thus, he was unable to recognize any genuine attempts at conciliatory behavior. In the case of Israel and Iraq, the bad faith image existed, and was likely stronger than Dulles' image during the Cold War. The Soviet Union never directly attacked the United States (in a direct military battle), yet Iraq, by 1981, had already fought Israel in three major wars. Iraq's rhetoric was inflammatory (so was the Soviet Union's to Dulles), but its actions for the most part were much worse.

Much of the literature on bad faith images has focused on the opportunities (for conciliation or trust-building measures) missed because of cognitive rigidity.[8] Leaders are said to disregard "good" behavior by an adversary, or believe that such behavior was "forced," and not genuine. However, in these circumstances, Israel's image of Iraq over the years was reinforced not by misinterpreted signals, but by aggressive and militant behavior. This might fit into the school of "you're not paranoid if they really are out to get you."

Yet, in spite of their unwavering image of Iraq as an enemy, Israeli self-images appear to have been relatively stable. Michael Oren wrote of Israeli psychology that there existed

> an ambivalence within the Israelis: an overblown confidence in their invincibility alongside an equally inflated sense of doom. To the West, Israelis portrayed themselves as inadequately armed Davids struggling against Philistine giants, and to the Arabs, as Goliaths of incalculable strength. . . . Moshe Dayan told Pentagon officials that Israel faced mortal danger, and, in the same breath, that it could smash the combined Arab armies in weeks.[9]

This is an interesting observation, and perhaps true in general, but in this particular crisis, I do not believe that it applies (at least as Oren describes it). The nature of the threat posed by Iraq magnified only the first half of Oren's equation, the "sense of doom." Perhaps another type of crisis would have triggered another reaction, but the catastrophic nature of nuclear weapons, combined with the existing perception of Iraqi intentions, led this particular threat to be seen as one to Israel's very existence (at least by Begin). This explains Begin's frequent use of Holocaust analogies, as both are situations in which the stakes are as high as they can get: the existence of the Jewish people.

IRAQ'S NUCLEAR PROGRAM—THE EARLY YEARS

The Iraqi nuclear program can be traced back to 1959, when an agreement was signed between Iraq and the Soviet Union. The leader of Iraq, Colonel Abdel Karim Kassem, allied himself with the Iraqi Communists in his struggle for power in that same year, which naturally led him toward closer relations with the Soviet Union.[10]

The Soviet Union agreed to construct a small nuclear research reactor in Iraq. Construction began on the reactor, an IRT-2000, in 1963.[11] The reactor was rated with a 2 MW capacity.[12] The Soviets also built a small radioisotope laboratory. Because of the low capacity of the reactor (and the fact that it used uranium enriched to only 10 percent) it did not seem to arouse alarm in any other countries.[13] There has been speculation in recent years that the Iraqis approached Moscow for an additional reactor and were refused, but this information has yet to be confirmed.[14]

In any case, Moscow's historical caution with regard to the proliferation of nuclear technology likely assuaged the potential fears of Israel and the West. Snyder wrote that "Moscow has historically been quite cautious and strict in its nuclear assistance efforts, always insisting that nuclear client states follow the letter of the law in operating Soviet-sponsored facilities. They are, in fact, much more cautious with such investments than are Western governments."[15]

Snyder's characterization of Soviet discretion with nuclear technology seems to have been shared by Israeli intelligence analysts. The Director of Israeli Military Intelligence in 1974, Shlomo Gazit, recalled: "We were not worried about the Russian reactor operating in Iraq. We knew that the Soviet Union would not permit its exploitation for the production of nuclear arms."[16]

Iraqi leaders soon began to realize this. The Soviet Union delayed any new improvements for years, and continued to supervise the facility very closely. However, the relationship with the Soviet Union had one benefit for the

Iraqis: it had provided Iraqi scientists with the technical training necessary to realize that they would never fulfill their goal of a large nuclear program (and certainly never the construction of nuclear weapons) through the Soviet Union.

THE RISE OF SADDAM HUSSEIN

The rise of Saddam Hussein was concurrent with the building up of the Iraqi nuclear program. It was Saddam's ambition that drove the expansion of the Iraqi nuclear program and his character that worried the Israelis. However, a short examination of Hussein's rise is instructive for another reason. The story of his rise to power, and his ruthlessness once in power, would have been known by all Israeli leaders, and would have been a factor in their considerations.

Hussein was born in 1937 in the area of Tikrit to a relatively poor family.[17] He joined the Ba'ath Socialist Party in 1955 as a student. Four years later he was assigned, along with several comrades, to assassinate the country's leader, Colonel Kassem.[18] The attempt on Kassem's life failed, and Hussein was shot in the leg during the confusion.[19] He escaped and quickly fled the country to Syria, and then finally to Cairo. He was handed down a death sentence in absentia by a military court in Iraq.[20]

Hussein spent the next few years as a political exile in Egypt. During this time, he was arrested for threatening to kill another Iraqi expatriate, but was released by the Egyptian President, Colonel Nasser.[21] However, Hussein was welcomed back to Iraq in 1963, by which time the Ba'ath Party had managed to kill Kassem and establish control over Iraq. Peter Beaumont wrote that

> by the late 1960's . . . a new version of Saddam had emerged. Although still a violent thug, he commanded respect, and had transformed himself from being a dim student from Tikrit into an autodidact who read widely and whose greatest understanding was of the use of violence and intimidation in the pursuit of political power.[22]

The Ba'ath Socialist Party firmly established itself as the ruling party in Iraq after a two-stage coup in 1968. Thus began a process by which power was centered around the town of Tikrit, and in the hands of the minority Sunni population. As a first cousin of General Ahmed Hassan al-Bakr, Saddam was well placed to prosper in the new regime. Al-Bakr made Hussein deputy secretary general of the Iraqi Ba'ath Party and deputy chairman of the Revolutionary Command Council (RCC), and conferred upon him the rank of General.[23]

In September 1970, al-Bakr announced his resignation to Saddam. However, realizing that his reign would not last long because he was a thirty-three-year-old with no military experience, Hussein forced al-Bakr to withdraw his resignation until the time was right. He had by then come to be referred to as "the strongman of Baghdad" and recognized as the real power behind al-Bakr.[24] He spent the next nine years before he was actually named president consolidating power and purging Iraqi society of anybody involved in (or suspected of being involved in) "subversive activities." He also began providing funding to terrorist organizations such as the IRA and PLO.[25]

IRAQI NUCLEAR PROGRAM—OIL AND THE WEST

Under Saddam's leadership, Iraq embarked on an ambitious modernization program. The key to this program, and and to Saddam's nuclear ambitions, was Iraqi oil. In the 1970s, Iraq had the sixth largest oil reserves in the world, estimated then at 41 billion barrels.[26] Revenues from oil exports raised the Iraqi GNP from $2.5 billion in 1967 to $16 billion in 1976.[27]

Perlmutter, Handel, and Bar-Joseph wrote that Iraqi leaders counted on their status as one of the West's biggest oil suppliers to give them leverage in acquiring nuclear technology and information in Western Europe. From Iraq's point of view, France and Italy were the most likely candidates, as both seemed willing to sell nuclear technology to Iraq and were especially proficient in the field of uranium and plutonium enrichment.[28]

In December 1974, newly-elected French Premier Jacques Chirac traveled to Iraq. During his visit, Chirac was hosted by Hussein, whom he referred to as "a personal friend."[29] The trip produced a string of contracts for French companies worth as much as 15 billion francs. More ominously, France signed a general "nuclear cooperation agreement" with Iraq.[30] Yves Girard, who accompanied Chirac on the trip, recalled: "It was a time of great confusion. . . . Everything that there was to be sold could be sold. And we wanted to do the selling. We were determined to keep an inside track on the contracts."[31]

During the 1970s, French dependence on Iraq was on the rise. In 1973, France's imports of Iraqi oil came to 357,000 tons, and 15 percent of all French oil. By 1979, that number had risen to 489,000 tons and 21 percent of all French oil.[32] Simultaneously, Israeli concerns had begun to mount. Angus Deming reported that "Israel's intelligence experts began to worry seriously about Iraq's nuclear intentions in 1976, when the budget for Iraq's Atomic Energy Commission jumped from $5 million to $70 million a year."[33]

But it was not just Iraqi expenditures that had unnerved Israeli leaders. The rhetoric of Iraqi leaders had become increasingly belligerent. In 1973, Iraq Oil Minister al-Baqi al-Haditi told a Greek journalist, "Israel must be eliminated ... by armed struggle and threats against the imperialist powers that protect Israel."[34]

On the eve of a trip to France in 1975, Saddam Hussein announced that Iraq's search for "technology with military potential" was a response to Israel's military dominance. Hussein also asserted that the Franco-Iraqi agreement was the "first actual step in the production of an Arab atomic weapon."[35]

THE REACTOR

Iraq's first choice for a reactor was a 500 MW electricity-powered gas-graphite reactor.[36] This reactor had been used by the French primarily as a source of plutonium for the Force de Frappe, the French nuclear arsenal.[37] The request must have been a warning sign for France given the nature of the reactor. As Shai Feldman wrote, "If the Iraqis were seriously interested in power generation or civilian research, the gas-graphite reactor was inappropriate. If, however, Hussein coveted a source of plutonium for a nuclear weapons program, the graphite reactor was a good choice."[38]

There is some confusion about the French response to this request. Weissman and Krosney reported that Chirac originally agreed to the Iraqi request.[39] However, whether or not Chirac assented, the reactor had not been made since 1972, and the French were forced to refuse (regardless of their inclination to sell the reactor). Instead, Chirac offered Hussein the advanced "Osiris" reactor.[40]

While the French and the Iraqis continued to negotiate the terms of the deal, the Israeli foreign minister, Yigal Alon, paid a visit to France in April 1975. The director of Israeli Military Intelligence, Shlomo Gazit, recalled: "We issued a comprehensive survey which analyzed the significance of Franco-Iraqi contacts and the threats posed thereby to Israel. This survey was disseminated to all echelons required to know thereof, military and political."[41]

The purpose of the visit was to convey Israel's concern over "the possibility of Iraq's misuse of the nuclear technology and fuels whose purchase it was negotiating with France."[42] However, French president Yves Giscard unconvincingly declared that France, though not a signatory to the Nuclear Non-Proliferation Treaty, would adhere to the spirit of the Treaty, and not transfer either nuclear weapons or technology for their production to Iraq.[43]

The deal that was eventually signed between France and Iraq included a 70 MW Osiris-type reactor and a smaller 800 kW Isis-type reactor. The Osiris reactor is a Materials Testing Reactor (MTR) whose primary function is to test how various materials used in the construction of nuclear power plants wear when bombarded by a high neutron flux. The fuel for both reactors was to be uranium enriched to over 92 percent. France had agreed to sell Iraq over 70 kg of such fuel.[44]

Interestingly, France decided to limit the shipment of the fuel to many small deliveries that would contain only enough fuel to run the reactor for a certain time.[45] This seems to suggest that even France was worried that Iraq might attempt to divert the uranium for other purposes.

Israel's concern also rested on the suitability of Osiraq to produce plutonium. "Blankets" of natural or depleted uranium can be placed at thirty-one sites around the reactor core and bombarded by the high neutron flux to produce quantities of plutonium.[46] The Israel Atomic Energy Commission predicted that Osiraq would produce 7–10 kg of plutonium a year. A group of French physicists, using very restrictive calculations, assessed that Osiraq would produce about 6 kg every fourteen months.[47]

Thus, the reactor was worrisome on multiple accounts. It required enriched uranium, which might be diverted by the Iraqis; the reactors had the capability to produce significant amounts of plutonium as a side reaction; and finally, its size seemed to indicate that Iraq's intentions might not be only in the realm of peaceful nuclear energy. Snyder writes that the Osiris reactor was designed for nations engaged in the production of nuclear power reactors. It was not an electricity-generating reactor, but rather a research reactor. Additionally, although Iraq had claimed to be interested in a civilian power-generating program, the natural choice for such a program would be a very different reactor. However, these reactors are not useful for the production of excess plutonium, nor do they use enriched uranium. The Iraqis chose a reactor that was completely unsuited to their stated needs, but well suited to a clandestine nuclear weapons program.[48]

However, the problem (though serious), was not yet urgent. The *Washington Post* reported in 1977 that General Mordecai Gur, the Israeli Chief of Staff, said he believed "Iraq might be able to develop a nuclear capability within five to seven years."[49]

1977–1979: ISRAELI CONCERNS MOUNT

In 1978, Naim Hadad, a senior member of the RCC, declared: "If Israel owns the bomb, then the Arabs must get an atom bomb. The Arab countries should possess whatever is necessary to defend themselves."[50] Even French officials seem to have become concerned at this point, and in interviews, they "nervously conceded that they have heard rumors that Iraq is interested in nuclear weapons."[51] Yigal Alon paid another visit to France, where he warned, "Providing a nuclear capability to irresponsible Mideastern states is a perilous act."[52]

However, Hussein was not content with his newly purchased reactor. He also wanted a reprocessing plant. Spent fuel from a typical light water reactor (such as Osiris) contains around 0.8 percent plutonium. Thus, 1.2 metric tons of spent fuel must be reprocessed to obtain 10 kg of plutonium, a very inefficient process. Snyder reports that there "is no commercial incentive to utilize plutonium."[53]

Italy seemed to be an ideal choice. Like France, it relied heavily on imported oil, particularly from Iraq. In 1979, Italy was importing one-fifth of its oil from Iraq.[54] In 1979, Italy sold Iraq a small "hot-lab" capable of separating plutonium from uranium and other fissile materials. This lab could only produce very small quantities of plutonium (several grams per year).[55]

Italy also sold Iraq a large-scale plutonium separation facility capable of producing large amounts of plutonium. However, Italy described the facility as a "demonstration model," and had modified it so that it had no biological shielding. The Israeli report released after the bombing indicates that Israeli decision-makers were convinced that the facility could be easily modified to produce large amounts of plutonium.[56]

Disturbingly, Israel also noticed that Iraq had purchased over 250 tons of uranium from Brazil, Portugal, and Niger between 1977 and 1979. As Iraq's reactor was not powered by natural uranium (nor had it contracted for such a reactor), the purchases were suspicious. Feldman notes that natural uranium might be used to conduct blanket irradiation to produce plutonium.[57]

"CARAMEL" FUEL

It was during this same time period that France succeeded in developing a new type of nuclear fuel. Dubbed "Caramel," it was designed especially for use in research reactors such as Osiris. Its U^{235} content was only 6–10 percent, in contrast to the 93 percent enriched uranium typically used in such reactors. It thus solved two problems at once: it eliminated the need for large amounts of costly U^{235} while also reducing the risk of weapons-grade uranium being diverted for other purposes.[58]

However, efforts of almost three years to persuade Iraq to accept the new fuel failed in the end. Hussein demanded 93 percent enriched uranium, contending that the new fuel "was not yet in industrial production."[59] In a *Washington Post* article of 1980, Milton Benjamin reported that the French announced their decision to abandon efforts to substitute "caramel" fuel for enriched uranium in their shipments to Iraq. Benjamin commented that this was a "major blow" to the nuclear nonproliferation policy of President Valery Giscard d'Estaing, and quoted U.S. nonproliferation officials who called the decision "distressing." Those same U.S. officials also predicted that

Iraq was the Arab state most likely to develop atomic weapons capability in the 1980s.[60]

The article went on to declare that:

Iraq's secrecy regarding peaceful nuclear research is unusual. Virtually all of the 22 developing countries with nuclear research reactors take considerable pride in discussing the projects. Iraqi officials attending the end of the conference of the International Nuclear Fuel Cycle Evaluation here [in Vienna], however, flatly refused to discuss any aspect of their interests.[61]

Israel's response to Iraq's refusal was immediate. Prime Minister Menachem Begin called Iraq's deal with France "a very grave development."[62] Cody reports that Deputy Defense Minister Mordechai Tsipori suggested in a public speech that Israel's response might include more direct actions than a diplomatic protest. Tsipori asserted that if diplomatic entreaties to the United States and France failed, Israel would be forced to "consider its next step."[63]

By 1979, Israeli concerns over the Iraqi nuclear program had increased significantly. The director-general of Begin's office, Matityahu Shumuelevitch, added that "Israel cannot sit and wait for an Iraqi bomb to fall on its head."[64]

MENACHEM BEGIN

All of these factors played a significant role in the Israeli decision to launch a preventive strike. But the linchpin of this decision was the psychology of Menachem Begin, and his determination to act on his instincts and beliefs. The May 1977 elections in Israel brought the Likud party to power after twenty-nine years of Labour Party domination.[65] These elections also brought Menachem Begin to power. The following is an incomplete survey of Begin's formative years. It is not possible in a work of this length to trace the development of a man to whom entire books are devoted.[66] However, it is important to have some understanding of Begin's general worldview and psychology, so that we might better understand the framework through which he filtered events.

Menachem Begin was born in August 1913, in Brest Litovsk, Poland.[67] In the years following World War I, Poland was one of the hotbeds of nascent Zionism. Begin's childhood seems to have been troubled from the very beginning. He recalls being harassed for being Jewish, as well as being forced to take examinations on the Sabbath, against his wishes.[68] In his teens, he joined Hashomer Hatzair, a Zionist youth movement, and later,

Betar, a paramilitary youth movement.[69] In 1930, Begin heard Ze'ev Jabotinsky, the leader of Betar, speak. He later spoke of Jabotinsky as "the greatest influence in my life."[70] It is telling that Begin's idol, Jabotinsky, was an outspoken advocate of justice through force. In a famous quote, he declared that the answer to Arab resistance was "an iron wall of Jewish bayonets."[71]

In 1939, while serving as the leader of Betar in Poland, Begin married Aliza Arnold.[72] He spent the next two years in Vilna, undergoing military training, and biding his time until he could travel to British-mandate Palestine.[73] After being arrested for a short period, Begin was allowed to enlist in a Free Polish Army under General Anders, which left in 1942 for Palestine.[74] In 1943, Begin became the head of the clandestine Irgun Tzvai Leumi (National Military Organization), the anti-British paramilitary group.[75]

As head of Irgun, Begin led his followers by writing and speaking. His rhetoric was powerful and uncompromising, referring to the British as "Hitlerites" and to moderate Jews as "cowards" and "synagogue clerks."[76] In July 1946, Begin masterminded the blowing up of the King David Hotel in Jerusalem. Ninety-one people were killed in the blast, for which Irgun took responsibility. Though Begin declared that he did regret the death of the seventeen Jews in the blast, "he did not mourn the British dead, since Britain had not mourned the six million Jews who died in the Nazi Holocaust."[77]

Begin's view of Arabs is similar to his early portrayal of the British as "Hitlerites." Amos Perlmutter wrote that

> Begin has always remained insular. For a man who can speak eloquently about Jewish suffering, and appear to feel it in his heart and soul, he is curiously indifferent to the sufferings of others, especially when the victims are Arabs. . . . Begin remains profoundly ignorant about Arab customs, culture and aspirations. He sees only one thing: the dire threat they represent to Israel. The PLO are Nazis. Arafat is Hitler.[78]

The analogy of the Holocaust was particularly important to Begin, who had lost much of his family in the death camps. Sofer wrote of Begin:

> The decisive lesson Begin learned from the Holocaust was expressed in the conception of revolt, of the rise of a generation that would wreak vengeance and fight back. He regarded hatred of Jews as a universal phenomenon. . . . As opposed to the Jew who goes passively to his death, Begin spoke of the "fighting Jew" who had "arisen and will never again disappear."[79]

Indeed, Silver writes that

the immersion of Menachem Begin himself in Holocaust imagery was often so deep that his allusions were misunderstood by those who did not share his perspective and his psychological outlook...in approaching foreign policy matters, Begin and his associates have constantly referred to the Holocaust experience as if such reference were a ritualistic obligation.[80]

Of his inclinations as a leader, Sasson Sofer wrote of Begin:

Begin had a heroic view of leadership. The heroic leader acts primarily in the domain of statecraft and in military affairs. He leads the nation to grandeur...he is a gallant ruler—forceful, authoritarian...His [Begin's] penchant for historical parallels took him to Jefferson, Lincoln, and Garibaldi in the nineteenth century, Churchill and de Gaulle in his own time.[81]

1979–1981: DECISION

Thus, by 1980, it seems clear that Israeli leaders had zeroed in on the Iraqi nuclear program as one of the top threats to Israeli security. At this stage, before the decision to initiate preventive action was made, we can take stock of the options available to Israel. First, they could continue to pursue diplomatic routes to compel France to stop their aid to the Iraqi program; second, rely on international law and safeguards to keep the Iraqi program producing only nuclear *energy*; third, use military force in some manner; or fourth, do nothing.

By 1980, it was clear that diplomatic pressure on France was not having the desired effect. By itself, Israel possessed virtually no leverage with which to compel French behavior at that time. Moreover, even the United States was not able to make much difference. In 1977, the United States, having discovered that the French were going to send Iraq enriched uranium that had been bought from the United States, threatened to place an embargo on shipments of uranium to France. However, France got around the problem by supplying Iraq with enriched uranium from its own military stockpiles.[82] Additionally, by 1980, France had already begun to make shipments to Iraq, making any change of heart far less likely.[83]

Would international law or nonproliferation safeguards have provided sufficient reassurance for Israel? The Nuclear Non-Proliferation Treaty, which Iraq was party to, took effect in 1970. It prevents the five "weapons states" (United States, USSR, Britain, France, and China)[84] from exporting

nuclear weapons or the technology to make them to any other country. However, for those signatory countries that were not weapons states, such as Iraq,
the treaty allowed them relatively free access to nuclear technology so long as
they remained open to inspections.[85] The question then remains, to what
extent were these inspections and safeguards adequate?

The inspection agency responsible for monitoring nuclear programs is
the International Atomic Energy Agency (IAEA). Whenever IAEA inspectors
discover dangerous activities, they are reported to the Agency's Board of
Governors, and then to the United Nations Security Council and General
Assembly. However, beyond referring the matter to the UN, the IAEA has no
recourse except to withdraw a state's rights and privileges as an IAEA
member.[86] This system is supposed to act as a deterrent, because any illegal
activities would (hopefully) be discovered early enough for effective action to
be taken. In an interview, IAEA spokesman Georges Delcoigne summarized
his agency's role: "We are not a police agency. We are an accounting system.
We work with the authorities."[87]

Presumably, the authorities involved would be the members of the UN
Security Council. And thus, the enforcement of the nonproliferation regime
in Iraq would depend to a large extent on the will of the UN to enforce it.
Israel had good reason to not place their faith in such measures, as France,
the country responsible for Iraq's nuclear program, possessed a veto in the
UN Security Council.[88] In addition, past experience dictated that violations
of IAEA rules went almost unnoticed by the international community. In
1979, Iran's Revolutionary Council banned IAEA inspectors from the country
with absolutely no repercussions, a fact that would surely have been noticed
by Israeli leaders.[89]

Thus, by 1980, the decision was really between doing nothing at all, or
some kind of military action (there was a broad spectrum of possibilities in
the early debates). In the summer of 1980, the Israeli General Staff Senior
Officer Forum met to discuss the growing threat of Iraq's nuclear program.
We have evidence that the forum was evenly divided in their opinions. Those
who opposed the attack on Osiraq did so on the grounds that it would not
destroy the 12 kg of enriched uranium the French had already supplied Iraq,
nor any other small stockpile they had acquired from other sources. Thus,
those who opposed the raid did so because even if it was successful, the Iraqis
might still be able to produce a nuclear bomb, and would probably have an
increased incentive to do so.[90]

Those who supported the raid conceded that the amount of enriched
uranium that Iraq had was not enough to construct even one bomb. However, they argued, if Iraq was able to activate the reactor, it would continue
to acquire enriched uranium indefinitely (up to 37 kg a year), and eventually produce enough plutonium to construct two to three bombs per
year. They also argued that a strike now might induce Italy and France to

reconsider their assistance to the Iraqi regime, and perhaps add stricter controls.[91]

Those in favor of the raid, including Chief of Staff Raphael Eitan narrowly edged out those against it.[92] Around this time, Israeli Foreign Minister Yitzhak Shamir summoned the French charge d'affaires to his office to officially express Israel's "profound concern" over French assistance to the Iraqi nuclear program. He was told that France saw no reason why Iraq should be denied the use of peaceful nuclear energy.[93] A few months later, Iraq announced that it was halting regular visits by IAEA inspectors at the reactor, because the safety of the inspectors could not be assured (as a result of Iraq's war with Iran).[94]

Even at this stage, however, there were doubts expressed by those in the Israeli government. For instance, General Yhoshua Saguy feared that the bombing would cause a "deep rift and severe crisis between Israel and the United States," and that "it would take the Iraqis at least five years to build a bomb, thus giving Israel sufficient time to try non-military methods."[95]

Ian Black and Benny Morris report that Saguy's opinion was supported by Deputy Prime Minister Yigael Yaidin, Interior Minister Yosef Burg, and the IDF's head of planning, Major-General Avraham Tamir.[96] Likewise, Labour Party leader Shimon Peres expressed his concerns to Begin in a top secret note in May 1981. Peres was convinced that the "election" of French President Mitterand, a socialist and a personal friend, would provide a solution to the Iraq problem.[97] He declared in his note to Begin that should Israel continue on this course of action, it would be "like a tree in the desert" in the international community.[98]

Begin seems to have been aware of the potential consequences of the raid.[99] In an article published after the attack, William Claiborne wrote:

> According to informed Israeli sources, Begin and his senior advisers talked at length on numerous occasions about the likely world reaction to the bombing mission, particularly the reaction from the United States. Begin, it is understood, was warned that the air strike could result in a suspension of U.S. arms shipments to Israel and that it might tip the balance against Israel on the proposed sale of U.S. radar sentry planes to Saudi Arabia, over whose territory the Israelis would have to fly.[100]

In response to the idea that Mitterand's election might solve the problem, Begin declared in a cabinet meeting that such an event would only delay Israeli action, not change the actual situation. "It was not a French reactor," he said, "but an Iraqi reactor. The problem was not France, but the existence of the state of Israel."[101]

Premier Begin then transferred the decision on the timing of the raid to a subcommittee of three—himself, Agricultural Minister Ariel Sharon, and Foreign Minister Yitzhak Shamir.[102] Perlmutter wrote of Begin:

Begin was receiving more cautionary advice from other directions, but on this issue he was adamant. He was determined to destroy Iraq's nuclear reactor installation. There were others in the government and cabinet who were more reluctant to confront the issue in military terms . . . But Begin would have none of it. He was not about to listen to expert advice, intelligence or military, not when, as he saw it, the very existence of the state of Israel was at stake. For Begin, it was an ideological decision, a question of averting another Holocaust while weighing the issues of American and Soviet responses.[103]

TIMING OF THE RAID

Since the raid had been agreed upon in principle in October of 1980, the question of timing centered on two issues: when exactly the reactor would become "hot," and the upcoming Israeli elections.

Silver reported that "a majority of the Government's expert advisers thought that the reactor would not go critical for three years, but a minority believed that it might do so in July 1981. The weight of opinion in the intelligence community in Washington was that it was about a year away."[104] This was confirmed by a *New York Times* report immediately after the attack on the reactor quoting U.S. State Department and intelligence officials as saying that they believed Iraq had acquired enough enriched uranium and "sensitive technology" to make one nuclear weapon by the end of 1981.[105]

Much of the timing issue seems to have been driven by Begin's belief that to bomb the reactor after it had gone "critical" would cause thousands of radiation casualties in Baghdad.[106] Though experts disagree on whether or not this would actually have happened, it seems clear that Begin was not prepared to accept responsibility for such a catastrophe. Silver's judgment of Begin's motivations seems to be confirmed by Begin's explanation at a news conference after the raid: "We faced a terrible dilemma. Should we now be passive, and then lose the last opportunity, without those horrible casualties amongst the Baghdad population, to destroy the hotbed of death?"[107]

The second issue was the forthcoming Israeli elections, to be held on June 30. On May 13, in a cabinet meeting, Begin declared:

Perhaps, this room will soon belong to Shimon Peres. The substance of his letter is known. Can we deduce from it that when he officiates as

Prime Minister he will order the reactor attack? Can we [members of the present Cabinet] afford to leave the stage and bequeath to our children this dreadful danger, of a gravity unprecedented since the extinction of the ovens at the extermination camps?[108]

Following the bombing, a Begin aide was quoted as saying "he [Begin] believed that Peres would never have the guts to order the raid. And Begin could not bear the thought of Israel living in terror of an Iraqi bomb."[109]

AFTERMATH

The strike against the reactor was finally carried out on June 7, 1981, at around 5:30 PM. The official report released by the Israeli government listed three major reasons for the decision to bomb the reactor:

1. Imminent realization by Iraq of its plans to acquire military nuclear capability.

2. Iraq's declared maintenance of a state of war with Israel and its persistent denial of Israel's right to exist.

3. The failure of Israel's diplomatic efforts to prevent the extension of foreign assistance to Iraq in the implementation of its nuclear program.[110]

The official statement released by the Israeli government on June 8 expands upon those reasons by adding the line: "On no account shall we permit an enemy to develop weapons of mass destruction against the people of Israel."[111]

In the days following, Prime Minister Begin was active in defending the bombing, using much more emotional terms than the official statement. In an interview with David Shipler on June 10, Begin declared: "Six hundred thousand casualties we would suffer ... which would mean, in terms of the United States, 44 million casualties, in terms of Egypt, over 8 million casualties. Where is the country that would tolerate such a danger knocking at its door?"[112]

Begin then ridiculed assertions by France that the $275 million reactor, first ordered in 1975, was merely for research and the generation of electricity, noting that Iraq had purchased enriched uranium of the type used in the bomb dropped by the United States on Hiroshima at the end of World War II.[113]

In a June 10 article, William Claiborne quoted Begin as saying: "If the nuclear reactor had not been destroyed ... another holocaust would happen in the history of the Jewish people. There will never be another holocaust in the history of the Jewish people. Never again, never again!" and reported "Invoking memories of the Nazi holocaust, Israeli Prime minister Menachem Begin warned tonight that if Iraq rebuilds a nuclear reactor capable of producing atomic weapons, Israel 'will use all the facilities at our disposal to destroy that reactor.' "[114]

Following the bombing, Israel was largely condemned by the international community. On June 12, the IAEA passed a resolution condemning the bombing, and promised to consider a suspension of Israel's privileges in the nonproliferation regime. On June 13, the UN Security Council passed a resolution that declared that the Israeli action had been in violation of the UN Charter, as well as "the norms of international conduct."[115] Begin won the next election, defeating Labour leader Shimon Peres, who had opposed the bombing.

In the end, Iraq's nuclear program was set back by many years, and France took the opportunity to reconsider its previous commitments and cancel future shipments of uranium to Iraq.[116]

CONCLUSION

This case illustrates many of the same factors that were present in the Suez case. There was an "inherent bad faith" image of the adversary, a belief that conflict with Iraq was inevitable, and a short "window of opportunity" in which to act. Perhaps most importantly, there was a strong leader at the center.

This case is a clear illustration of the importance of the individual in preventive war decisions. This is a fact that Begin seems to have been aware of, as he timed the raid specifically because he did not believe that Shimon Peres would act. Would Israel have attacked Iraq if there was no Saddam Hussein? Would Israel have chosen to attack the reactor if Shimon Peres had been in power instead of Menachem Begin? There are no simple or clear answers to these questions, but they are important to keep in mind while reading this case. Israel is a democracy, and yet the beliefs and action of individuals seem to be able to exert a dramatic influence on the international system. This is certainly a blow to traditional realist theories that stress capabilities and material power. In this case, one might argue that it was the spectre of Nazi Germany that drove Menachem Begin to order the attack, almost as much as any potential Iraqi capability.

We might add one more factor that was present in this case, which is the use of a strong historical analogy to explain or justify an action. In this case, Begin used the analogy of the Holocaust to justify the preventive strike. In Chapter 1, Arthur Gladstone was quoted as saying that the "enemy image" can be so extreme that highly immoral actions become moral, because they are in opposition to such evil.[117] The framing of an Iraqi nuclear weapon as tantamount to a potential Holocaust gives license for action that might otherwise be considered immoral. If the situation is framed as a potential holocaust, then the implication is that one should do everything possible to avert it; normal standards of morality do not apply.

However, this factor is not a primary one, and it would be difficult to argue that the use of strong historical analogies is a *cause* of preventive war decisions. Rather, it is likely that the presence of such analogies in a crisis shows that a decision to use force has already been made, or at least gives us insight into the leader's thought process. One would not compare another leader to Hitler and then not do anything to oppose him. Thus, the prevalence of strong analogies gives us a clue as to whether preventive action will or will not be taken. In this case, the primary decision-maker, Begin, used the analogy of the Holocaust fairly often. We will see if this pattern holds true in other cases.

4

How Real Was "Dr. Strangelove?"
American Preventive War Thinking Post–WWII

In a 1955 article, Henry Kissinger wrote about American preventive war planning that there had always been an air of "unreality about a program so contrary to the sense of the country and the constitutional limits with which American foreign policy must be conducted."[1] However, this case will show the very opposite; preventive war thinking within the presidential administrations, the government, and the public sphere, was very real indeed. Though such a course was not chosen in the end, top U.S. decision-makers wrestled with the complex moral and practical problems associated with preventive war in a serious manner. This case will not only examine the reasons why such a war never occurred, but also examine the reasons for which the idea appealed to so many U.S. leaders.

There is an obvious emphasis in this case on the shifting balance of power between the United States and the Soviet Union. However, this material reality was seen and filtered through the understandings and beliefs of decision-makers, whose perception of the nature of the conflict, and the intentions of their adversary, colored the implications they drew from "objective" estimates of relative strength. If only a shifting balance of power/capabilities caused states to go to war preventively, then this case would have had a different ending. Instead, the moral sensibilities of U.S. leaders played as strong a part in repelling them from the notion of preventive war as their perception of the Soviet danger did in attracting them to it. Similarly, views of the conflict as a "cold" or a "hot" war had very different implications, particularly for President Eisenhower.

This case is also an illustration of an instance in which decision-makers did not make the distinction between a preventive war and a preventive strike. In a 1957 article, Samuel Huntington argued: "Americans undoubtedly have an instinctive dislike of preventive war.... Perhaps this dislike is rooted in an overly narrow conception of preventive war."[2] All discussions of preventive action took for granted that such action would inevitably lead to a total war. This did not stop many from continuing to advocate preventive action, but perhaps contributed to the ultimate decision not to act preventively.

Huntington goes on in that same article to differentiate between a *total* preventive war and a *limited* preventive war. This is a distinction that has already been made in this book, and is particularly relevant for this case. Because American decision-makers assumed that any preventive action against the Soviet Union would trigger either a nuclear response or an attempted occupation of Western Europe, the risks of a preventive war were too great. Even if the United States managed to destroy the atomic capability of the Soviet Union, the Soviets' conventional superiority would allow them to overrun Western Europe. Thus, even if the situation (of living under the threat of atomic attack) was considered intolerable by some decision-makers, the alternative of preventive war was not any better. Ultimately, it was this threat (of conventional retaliation), combined with a moral aversion (to the notion of America initiating a preventive war) by both presidents, which dictated U.S. foreign policy during the years 1946 to 1954. Thus, though relations between the two countries deteriorated progressively, there was not a point at which a preventive war would have solved the United States' problems without creating larger ones.

"WINDOW" THINKING

One important strain of thought that runs throughout this case is "window" thinking. This refers to the idea that the United States had a strategic advantage over the Soviet Union, first in the form of an atomic monopoly, and then (after the Soviet development of an atomic bomb) in a numerical and technical advantage in atomic weaponry. But the concept applied here refers specifically to the idea that the United States would only have such an advantage, or "window of opportunity," for a short while, and thus, there would only be a short time in which to act.

This type of thinking was extremely prevalent during the Truman and Eisenhower administrations from roughly 1945 to 1954, and formed the backbone of most arguments for preventive war. Its proponents argued that if conflict with the Soviet Union was inevitable (as many believed it to be), then the United States must act immediately, while it still had a strategic advantage.

This concept was put into words as early as 1945, when Assistant Secretary of War Robert A. Lovett sent a memo to Gen. George C. Marshall declaring that U.S. preeminence in the atomic field was a "wasting asset," but by wise maneuvering during the next five years, the United States might be able to forestall the danger that would confront it once another nation achieved atomic capability.[3]

A 1951 report to the National Security Council by the chairman of the National Security Resources Board, W. Stuart Symington, asserted: "As things are now going, by 1953, if not 1952, the Soviet aggressors will assume complete command of the world situation, because by then no nation, regardless of the size of its atomic stockpile, could defend, or fully retaliate, against a sudden surprise atomic attack.[4]

At various times, it was declared that the "window was closing," or even that it already had.[5] However, the concept and the reality that gave rise to it were always present in the minds of decision-makers. For some, it led to containment, while for others, America's "wasting asset" prescribed the more aggressive strategy of preventive war.

IMAGE OF THE ENEMY

The other important concept that is present in this case is the intensely negative perception of the Soviet Union by U.S. decision-makers. These perceptions are particularly important given the concept of window thinking; the implications of diminishing superiority are dependent on what kind of adversary you believe yourself to be facing. Are they rational and calm, or are they unpredictable? Are they militant and aggressive, or status-quo oriented? Can they be trusted to uphold agreements? Are they likely to become more aggressive in the future or less aggressive?

The term "Cold War" in some ways obfuscates the issues faced by U.S. decision-makers in the years immediately following World War II. It was not yet a Cold War then. In fact, there was much uncertainty about what form the struggle with the Soviet Union might take. In the years immediately following World War II, it was not taken for granted that there would not be a "hot" war between the United States and Russia. For instance, George Kennan, then ambassador to the Soviet Union (and one of the architects of U.S. foreign policy in the postwar years), wrote the following dispatch in September 1945:

It would be highly dangerous to our security if the Russians were to develop the use of atomic energy...There is nothing—I repeat nothing—in the history of the Soviet regime which would justify us in assuming that the men who are now in power in Russia...would hesitate for a moment to apply this power against us if by doing so they thought they would materially improve their own power position in the world...To assume that Soviet leaders would be restrained by scruples of gratitude or humanitarianism would be to fly in the face of overwhelming contrary evidence on a matter vital to the future of our country.[6]

Similarly, a 1950 memo by the director of the Policy Planning Staff at the State Department, Paul H. Nitze, conjures up a disturbing image of Soviet behavior: "In the aggregate, recent Soviet moves reflect not only a mounting militancy but suggest a boldness that is essentially new—and borders on recklessness."[7]

As Marc Trachtenberg points out, it was a serious concern for American leaders that if the Soviets were so hostile and aggressive in the early years when America had a nuclear monopoly, what would they be expected to be like once that monopoly had been broken?[8] Certainly, the descriptions by U.S. decision-makers do not lead one to believe that the United States had much faith in Soviet behavior. On the contrary, the prevailing opinion seems to have been that it was actually *likely* that the Soviet Union might initiate a major war with the United States. The added risk was that the end of America's atomic monopoly might spur the Soviet Union to even more aggressive behavior. Deborah Larson points out that the failure of the London Foreign Ministers' Conference in 1947, at which Molotov "was intractable as ever," proved that a U.S. monopoly on atomic weapons would not make the Soviets more manageable. Larson adds that "privately, Truman feared even atomic weapons would not deter Soviet aggression."[9]

The essence of these two related strains of thought is contained in the following passage from a memo by Stuart Symington:

The estimated Soviet atomic bombing capability is growing at a rate which, some time in 1952, will find the Communists strong enough to destroy much of our capability of immediate retaliation, and seriously cripple the United States itself. And who doubts any longer that the Soviets will attack when ready?[10]

It is this combined view—that time is running out, and the United States cannot trust the Soviets to be responsible with atomic weapons—that spurred preventive war thinking during this era.

THE TRUMAN ADMINISTRATION

President Harry Truman's administration ran through a unique period in American history. Truman was a wartime president, but he also occupied the presidency during the postwar period, when the Cold War began. It is during Truman's administration that we can see the nascence of strategic thought, as well as of the perceptions of the Soviet Union that shaped the framing of the entire conflict, and spurred much of the preventive war thinking during this era.

The first few years after World War II were dedicated primarily to building up the American nuclear stockpile, not to the development of strategy. Until 1947, Truman was not even aware of the size of the U.S. atomic stockpile, and was then shocked to find out that it was only a small fraction of what he imagined it to be.[11] By 1948, the stockpile of nuclear weapons in the United States had reached a level of quantity (if not quality) that freed decision-makers to start reevaluating U.S. atomic and military strategy. In early 1949, Truman ordered his secretary of defense, as well as the AEC, to conduct intensive studies on the capabilities of the U.S. nuclear arsenal and the implications of atomic weapons for foreign policy.[12]

On September 3, 1949, the Air Force's Long Range Detection System informed Truman that the Soviet Union had tested an atomic bomb. The American monopoly on nuclear weapons had been broken much earlier than expected. Even Truman conceded that his intelligence experts had assumed that the Soviet Union would not have atomic capability until at least 1952.[13] It was the loss of the atomic monopoly that led to a major rethinking of U.S. strategy, culminating in the writing of NSC-68.

It is likely that the Soviet test also led to an increase in window thinking within the U.S. government. If the United States was wrong in its estimation of Soviet atomic capabilities already, then how much time did they have before the Soviets "caught up" with U.S. capabilities? Though window thinking was present before 1949, the Soviet atomic test probably intensified such beliefs, as the window appeared to be closing more quickly than expected.

Before moving on to a close examination of NSC-68, however, it is important to understand some of Truman's personal views on preventive war. Unlike many of the decision-makers who will be discussed in this case, there is little evidence that Truman even toyed with the idea of preventive war. In his memoirs he wrote: "I have always been opposed to the thought of such a war. There is nothing more foolish than to think that war can be stopped by war. You don't 'prevent' anything by war except peace."[14]

However, like many other U.S. leaders, he was struck by the vulnerability of the United States to Soviet attack.[15] After a 1952 briefing in which he was told that 75 percent of a Soviet armed attack would make it through U.S. defenses, the minutes of a meeting reported: "The President stated that he had been startled by the briefing on this very problem which he had been given that morning in the Cabinet room. *As far as he could see*, said the President, *there wasn't very much of a defense in prospect except a vigorous offense.*"[16]

However, this comment must be taken in context, and was likely not an allusion to a preventive war, but a pre-emptive attack that would stop Soviet planes before they could reach American borders. However, it does show that Truman was grappling with the same basic problems that confronted all U.S. decision-makers during this period: a monopoly, and later just a great superiority, of atomic weapons *had not guaranteed American security.* The United States was still vulnerable to aggressive attack.

Though he himself might not have advocated a preventive war, he was certainly aware of those around him who did. In his memoirs he discusses those in his administration who, in 1950, advocated a preventive war against Russia and China.[17] He even acknowledges that many high-ranking navy officers were in favor of such a war.[18]

NSC-68 (1950)

In 1950, a joint State-Defense Department group was formed to examine the current state of national security, taking into consideration President Truman's decision to pursue a hydrogen bomb.[19] Secretaries Acheson (State) and Johnson (Defense) had joint responsibility and produced a report for the president.

At first glance, this document also seems to repudiate the idea of a preventive war against the Soviet Union. Its writers declared:

> Some Americans favor a deliberate decision to go to war against the Soviet Union in the near future. It goes without saying that the idea of "preventive" war—in the sense of a military attack not provoked by a military attack upon us or our allies—is generally unacceptable to Americans. Its supporters argue that since the Soviet Union is in fact at war with the free world now and that since the failure of the Soviet Union to use all-out military force is explainable on grounds of expediency, we are at war and should conduct ourselves accordingly . . . This is a powerful argument in the light of history, but the considerations against war are so compelling that the free world must demonstrate that this argument is wrong.[20]

The document goes on to declare that a preventive war, in the current state of military balance, would not induce the Soviet Union to give up its struggle, or prevent it from overrunning and occupying Western Europe.[21] It also reiterated that an American preventive attack, "despite the provocativeness of recent Soviet behavior," would be "repugnant" to many Americans.[22] Thus, the document makes the argument that preventive war is not acceptable on two separate levels: it is morally repugnant, and would, in practice, not accomplish U.S. goals.

However, the document is much more complex. After listing the moral considerations of waging a preventive war, the document goes on:

These considerations are no less weighty because they are imponderable, and they rule out an attack unless it is demonstrably in the nature of a counter-attack to a blow which is on its way *or about to be delivered. (The military advantages of landing the first blow become increasingly important with modern weapons, and this is a fact which requires us to be on the alert in order to strike with our full weight as soon as we are attacked, and, if possible, before the Soviet blow is actually delivered.)*[23]

Thus, while preventive war was ostensibly ruled out as a viable option, the architects of NSC-68 had, in fact, made pre-emption a full-blown policy. But before moving on to that issue, let us take a look at some of the basic assumptions of the strategy enunciated in NSC-68.

Two key points underlie the arguments in NSC-68. The first of these is that it was taken for granted that the United States was not dealing with an "ordinary adversary," but an implacable enemy. In a 1950 memo, Secretary Acheson wrote:

The Soviets are intent on world domination and have extended their sphere of influence materially in the past several years. They have no intention of stopping and are determined to bring about a situation where we will be confronted by having the rest of the world under their domination.[24]

NSC-68 even declared:

The fundamental design of those who control the Soviet Union and the international communist movement is to retain and solidify their absolute power, first in the Soviet Union and second in the areas now under their control. In the minds of the Soviet leaders . . . achievement of this design requires the dynamic extension of their authority and the ultimate elimination of any effective opposition to their authority . . . The United States, as the principal center of power in the non-Soviet world and the bulwark of opposition to Soviet expansion, is the principal enemy whose integrity and vitality must be subverted or destroyed by one means or another if the Kremlin is to achieve its fundamental design.[25]

These are strongly worded statements and have important policy implications. NSC-68, a document of official U.S. grand strategy, had declared that the fundamental design of the Soviet Union required it to subvert or destroy the "integrity and vitality" of the United States. This is a characterization that might be used by more modern administrations to describe the aims of terrorist organizations. The implication is this: there can be no compromises. Subverting or destroying the United States is not a peripheral goal of the Soviet Union; it is the *basis of their foreign policy*, and necessary for the achievement of their stated goals and long-range plans.

The second assumption made in the document is that the United States is moving into a period of extreme danger. This is a combination of window thinking (the United States has military superiority, but only for a short time) and the concern over growing Soviet capabilities, which in a few years might eclipse those of the United States.

In his memoirs, Paul Nitze writes that intelligence reports indicated that if the United States did nothing to stop the trend, 1954 would be the year of "maximum danger" for it. It would be in that year that the Soviet Union would have sufficient atomic stockpiles to threaten unacceptable damage to the United States.[26]

In NSC-68, it is declared:

> It is estimated that, within the next four years, the U.S.S.R. will attain the capability of seriously damaging vital centers of the United States, provided it strikes a surprise blow and provided further that the blow is opposed by no more effective opposition than we now have programmed. Such a blow could so seriously damage the United States as to greatly reduce its superiority in economic potential ... In time the atomic capability of the U.S.S.R. can be expected to grow to a point where, given surprise and no more effective opposition than we now have programmed, *the possibility of a decisive initial attack cannot be excluded.*[27]

It is almost an understatement to say that the United States believed itself to be entering an extremely dangerous period. The combination of Soviet intentions (as U.S. leaders perceived them), combined with the military capabilities described above was seen as quite horrifying. After all, nuclear first strikes are not particularly likely as long as there is a relative balance in capabilities (so that it is believed that the enemy would have the potential to retaliate). If, as the architects of NSC-68 believed, the Soviets would soon be able to destroy the U.S. capability to retaliate (in a "decisive initial attack"), then there is an advantage to a surprise attack. In a system with adversaries as hostile and untrusting of one another as existed in 1950, this would have been a powder keg waiting to explode.

Marc Trachtenberg wrote of the document: "One has the sense ... that the architects of NSC-68 could scarcely bring themselves to accept the conclusions that followed from their own arguments. It seems instead that they settled, as a kind of psychological compromise, for the lesser strategy of 'rollback.'"[28]

Trachtenberg is correct in his initial argument. The arguments of NSC-68 (implacable enemy, shift in military balance which would leave the United States vulnerable in only a few years) were the exact same arguments made by those who favored a preventive war. NSC-68 makes those same arguments, but seems to shrink away from the implications that should follow from them. Instead, they settled for a policy of pre-emption.

There is evidence that the idea of preventive war was discussed in the policy meetings leading up to NSC-68. General Nathan F. Twining of the U.S. Air Force (and later, chairman of the Joint Chiefs of Staff, 1957–1960) was one of those involved in the policy planning sessions for the document. He writes in his memoirs that the idea of preventive war "was argued with much more vigor" than either isolationism or a status quo approach.[29] Twining never came out openly in favor of preventive war, but he does mention in its defense that it was "defended by some very dedicated Americans."[30]

Twining writes in his memoirs that he advocated a policy called "containment plus," which is essentially containment plus initiative. He wrote that:

> The United States does not intend to initiate military conflict, but it will have [to] begin it if the U.S.S.R. and Communist China persist in their attempts to enslave more of the free world. The United States will be ready to fight. . . . The nation must refuse to be bound to the dogmatic principles of statesmanship while its enemy lives by the law of the jungle. The stakes to humanity are too high.[31]

Although he does not come out and say it, this would seem to imply that the United States should do anything it can to attain victory over the Soviet Union, even if it means striking the first blow. Certainly, Twining's statement gives one the impression that he would not shy away from a preventive attack on moral grounds.

PUBLIC DEBATE

In 1973, George Quester wrote that preventive war had "hardly ever broken into public discussion."[32] He also wrote of the American failure to discuss, or even consider the option of preventive war.[33] However, evidence contained in the public record appears to show just the opposite: preventive war was on the minds of many people, not just those within the U.S. government.

This is relevant because it shows that the debate over preventive war was just that: a debate. The idea of preventive war was certainly not part of mainstream discussion within society, but neither was it consigned to the fringe. It might not have emerged as official U.S. policy, but neither was it solely the realm of fanatics and hawks. The very fact that it was debated in the public sphere suggests that there were a significant number of people who considered it a viable option.

Winston Churchill stands out as one of the most notable figures to have openly advocated preventive action against the Soviet Union. In 1948, Churchill declared during a parliamentary debate:

> I believe it is right to say today that the best chance of preventing a war is, in accord with the other Western democracies to bring matters to a head with the Soviet Government, and, by formal diplomatic processes, with all their privacy and gravity, to arrive at a lasting settlement.... Even this method, I must say, however, would not guarantee that war would not come. *But I believe it would give the best chance of coming out of it alive.*[34]

However, what was only implied in that particular speech was spelled out in other conversations. When asked how Britain, with its small size and densely concentrated population, might take part in an atomic war, Churchill replied (in 1946): "We ought not to wait until Russia is ready. I believe it will be eight years before she has these bombs. America knows that fifty-two percent of Russia's motor industry is in Moscow and would be wiped out by a single bomb."[35]

Note that in this quote, the practical problem that eventually deterred the United States from a preventive war does not appear. Churchill seems convinced that (morality aside) a preventive nuclear first strike would work; in that it could destroy Moscow's ability to retaliate. Interestingly, what held U.S. decision-makers back to a great extent was the fear that the Soviet Union might overwhelm Western Europe in response, a fear that Churchill seems not to have had.

In 1954, at a political conference in Bermuda, Churchill was asked what might happen to Germany if there was war between Russia and the United States. He replied: "Poor lambs, they would be over-run and our neutrality would not save us. I wanted America to have a showdown with the Soviet Republic before Russia had the bomb."[36]

In this quote, Churchill does acknowledge the threat of the Soviet army. However, he seems to imply that this was only a threat because the Soviet Union had developed the A-bomb. In fact, even without atomic weapons, Soviet conventional superiority would likely have allowed them to occupy large portions of Western Europe.

Winston Churchill was not the only notable public figure to advocate a preventive war against the Soviets. Lord Bertrand Russell, the British philosopher, did as well. A 1948 *New York Times* article quoted Russell as saying: "The Western democracies must either fight Russia before she develops an atomic bomb or lie down and let the Soviet govern them...Simply fearing the horror of a future war is no way to prevent its occurrence...Anything is better than submission."[37]

William L. Laurence, one of the leading writers on atomic energy and weapons and the science correspondent for the *New York Times*, declared that there was only one alternative to a preventive war against Russia: international control of atomic energy.[38] He advocated the following:

We must...announce to the world a new doctrine....It should stipulate that any nation refusing to give up its sovereign "right" to manufacture atomic bombs declares itself, by that very refusal, to be an aggressor nation, subject to the proper sanctions under the United Nations charter. The charter also grants individual nations the right to defend themselves against any threats to their security.[39]

Laurence then went on to say that the espousal of his new doctrine would have the effect of saying to the Kremlin:

Much as we would dislike to do so, we would find ourselves compelled, from sheer necessity, to destroy your atomic plants before they are ready to operate. If that means war, it will be a war you will force on us by your insistence on *an atomic armament race which must inevitably lead to war anyway*. Under the circumstances, it would be to our advantage to have it while we are still the sole possessors of the atomic bomb.[40]

Public debate over preventive war illustrates the moral complexities involved in such propositions. A 1954 Gallup Poll recorded that 13 percent of those polled favored a war with Russia "while we still have the advantage."[41] This is not an enormous segment of the population, but neither is it a small segment. Though the question was not asked then, one might imagine that the number would have been higher in the months before the Soviets exploded their first A-Bomb (and we had a monopoly on atomic weapons, thus lowering the risks involved). Related to this issue is the use of atomic weapons in general. Though it is taken for granted that there are certain normative constraints on the use of nuclear weapons, they might not have been as strong then as they eventually came to be. Sixty-six percent of those polled believed that the United States should use the atomic bomb *first* in a conflict with Russia (70 percent believed "the U.S. should not wait until another nation has used it on us before we use it").[42]

The importance of this section was to illustrate the extent to which preventive war was debated in the public sphere. Such evidence suggests that the idea of a preventive war against a nuclear power was discussed among decision-makers and some segments of the informed public as a real possibility.

The traditional rational-actor model in international relations would predict that such an option would not be seriously discussed, as the potential losses would be too great. However, the prevalence of preventive war discussions in the public sphere shows that cognitive biases, the image of the enemy in particular, can exert a strong influence on calculations based on "pure rationality" and cost-benefit analysis. In addition, a rational-actor model does not take into account the morality of preventive war. The claim of morality is present here as the "moral self-image," which caused leaders to believe that the American public would not approve of a preventive war because of the way in which they envisioned their country.

PREVENTIVE WAR THINKING WITHIN THE GOVERNMENT

While it is important to showcase the public side of the preventive war debate, it is doubly so to show the thinking of those who were in positions to influence U.S. policy. This section will focus on the opinions of those within the government and the armed forces: those who had the ear of the president.

In a meeting of under secretaries of state in 1949 (months before the Soviet A-bomb test), Secretary Charles E. Bohlen argued that the United States was not then in the "military phase" of its relations with the Russians. But, Bohlen cautioned, the United States must "look ahead."

> He [Bohlen] cited hypothetically that if in 1953 we should find that the Russian war wounds are healed, her industry re-established, her military on a firm footing and in possession of the atom bomb, we might be in a position to say: "What should we have done in 1949?" Will it be a question of too little and too late?[43]

Thus, the presumption was that Russia acquiring atomic capability was a threshold that, once crossed, greatly increased American strategic vulnerability. This is clear when Bohlen implies that once Russia gets atomic bombs, any U.S. action will be "too little and too late," and the United States would no longer have the strategic advantage in a potential war. The obvious implication of this argument is that *the window of opportunity was closing, and the United States must not let Russia acquire atomic capability.* This is not an argument for preventive war per se, but possibly just a preventive strike against Russian atomic research centers. However, as already mentioned, the Soviet Union surprised U.S. officials by detonating an atomic bomb in late August 1949.

Preventive war thinking seems to have been prevalent among those who were thinking seriously about the implications of the new atomic weapons. Thus, Senator Brian McMahon, chairman of the Atomic Energy Commission, and later chairman of the Joint Committee on Atomic Energy, wrote a letter to President Truman in November 1949, declaring:

> The contention is made that a war involving the supers would leave behind such chaos and vengefulness as to create a worse situation, with a darker outlook for lasting peace, than the one existing at present . . . Yet our first duty consists in doing what is necessary to win . . . because of manpower limitations and the oceans that separate us from Eurasia, we could not use surface forces to invade and occupy Russia. The only choice left open is heavy reliance upon strategic air power, despite our own immense vulnerability to nuclear weapons . . . Without American victory—which supers alone might render feasible—there would be no post-war existence for our country, must less post-war problems. I might add that, to my mind, almost nothing could be worse than the current atomic armaments race and that victory in a future war, whatever its sequel in other respects, would at least assure effective international control over weapons of mass destruction.[44]

This passage has all of the trademarks of preventive war thinking. McMahon asserts that, first, victory is necessary, and, second, the United States must do anything it can do to win. The idea that "nothing could be worse than the current atomic armaments race" implies that a preventive war against Russia, though not ideal (and possibly even morally reprehensible), might be the only course open to the United States, as there would be nothing worse than the continuation of the arms race. We might call this the "lesser evil" argument. Essentially, this acknowledges that a preventive war might not accord with notions of morality and justice, but that the alternative might be far worse. This argument simultaneously acknowledges the moral complexities of preventive war, while at the same time demanding that they be set aside for the moment.

Taking notes in a 1950 policy-planning meeting, Secretary of State for Near Eastern Affairs Dean Rusk recalled the comments of Gen. Hoyt Vandenberg:

> If we now believe that the Soviet Union plans to initiate an early war, he [Vandenberg] thought the point of greatest danger would be August 1951, which he related to the completion of the European harvest. He

said if that is correct, between now and August 1951 would not work in our favor since we would not improve our ground potential significantly but would in that period have given the Soviets a chance to produce additional atomic bombs. [Rusk comments:] *He did not say so specifically, but the implication was that it would be better for us to precipitate hostilities at an early date in order to prevent further USSR atomic buildup.*[45]

This passage refers clearly to a preventive war. Vandenberg's belief that the Soviet Union "plans to initiate an early war" and that the United States should thus initiate one first does not qualify as pre-emption. The threat is *looming*, not *imminent*, an important distinction. In order for Vandenberg's plan to qualify as pre-emption, the United States would have to wait until the Soviet Union was literally about to launch its attack, something that Vandenberg does not seem to advocate.

At this time, Vandenberg was an extremely influential person in the U.S. military. In 1950, he was chief of staff for the Air Force, after having been director of Central Intelligence. He was a highly decorated war hero who helped plan the Normandy invasion, and served at the request of President Truman until he died in 1954. He does not appear to have been regarded as an extremist or "hawk," and his opinion must therefore have carried some weight within the government. However, such thinking was not confined to the upper reaches of the national security planning staff.

A 1950 *Newsweek* article reported that members of Congress had begun to speculate "on what had formerly been an almost forbidden subject—preventive war."[46] According to the report, Representative Henry Jackson (D., WA) asserted on the floor of the House:

The atomic bomb has succeeded in preventing the outbreak of a hot war, but it has left the world living in armed camps. If the camps should come to possess hydrogen bombs, even this condition of an armed truce might well become intolerable. What should be our course of action if a part of the world should fail to accept participation in the scheme of international control of hydrogen energy? That may well be the No. 1 question confronting our scientists and statesmen in the hydrogen age.[47]

Though it does not explicitly say so, there are key words in this speech that evoke the idea of preventive war. The idea that should both sides eventually possess hydrogen bombs (which, even by 1950 seemed almost certain) the situation might become "intolerable" is code for "we have to do something." In fact, though it was two years later, Jackson seemed to echo many of William Laurence's points from 1948—the United States should seek international control of energy, but if that does not work, it might have to pursue more "aggressive" tactics to prevent the Soviets from continuing to develop nuclear weapons. Once again, this comes from a respected figure; Jackson was later to become a member of the Senate Select Committee on Intelligence as well as chairman of the Democratic National Committee.

In another 1950 article, Senator John J. McClellan (D., AR) spoke out publicly in favor of a preventive war. The *New York Times* quoted him as saying: "If Russia refuses to enter into the spirit of international cooperation for peace then, we would have our final answer, and could be governed accordingly. Under such conditions, I would favor firing the first shot in a war that would then be inevitable."[48]

He was apparently not the only congressman to have advocated such a policy. In a memo written after a meeting with several senators, Assistant Secretary of State Jack McFall reported:

> One Senator stated it as his opinion that the time had now come when we could no longer subject ourselves to the hazard of the possibility of Russia having the hydrogen bomb and that because of its devastating effect, beyond all comprehension, that we must not gamble any longer with time... Still another Senator expressed the view that his constituents were constantly after him with statements like "why don't we get into this thing now and get it over with before the time is too late?" This Senator stated that that attitude was growing by leaps and bounds in his state and that he was compelled to take note of it.[49]

A few months later, Secretary of the Navy Francis P. Matthews was quoted as saying that the United States should be willing to pay any price for peace, "even the price of instituting a war to compel cooperation for peace."[50] He added that the United States should become the world's first "aggressors for peace." In response, the U.S. State Department disavowed his remarks, declaring that Matthews' views did not represent U.S. policy.[51] However, note that Matthews advocates preventive war because he believes that the outcome of such a war would be peace. For him, there is no practical or moral dilemma to hold him back. He believes that it would work, and since peace is the ultimate goal, it has some moral legitimacy.

Less than a week after the Matthews incident, Maj. Gen. Orvil A. Anderson, the commandant of the Air War College, was suspended for a short time for remarks that he made concerning preventive war. Anderson was quoted as saying: "Give me the order to do it and I can break up Russia's five A-Bomb nests in a week. And when I went up to Christ—I think I could explain to him that I had saved civilization.[52] The article goes on to mention that Anderson was well known at the Air War College for giving students detailed expositions on the idea of preventive war, often lasting three or four hours.[53]

It is useful to examine the administration's response to these two incidents more closely. Imagine a situation where the U.S. government let it be known publicly that they were considering the idea of a preventive strike. Even the very mention of the idea would serve to make the Soviet Union believe that they must strike pre-emptively before the United States could initiate a preventive attack. The United States would then be forced to attack pre-emptively against Russia's attack, and so on. This is the very situation described by Schelling in his section on the reciprocal fear of surprise attack.[54]

In addition, had the government decided to initiate a preventive strike, it would have only been effective as a surprise attack, to take place before the Soviet Union could move or hide its atomic stockpiles. Remember, a preventive strike would only have had value if the United States was confident that it would prevent Soviet retaliation by destroying their capability to retaliate effectively. Similarly, there seems to be ample evidence that even if it was not an official government policy, it was discussed, often at the very highest levels of government. Therefore, we might take the official statements with a grain of salt, and instead focus on the very weak punishments meted out to Matthews and Anderson.

In a 1954 briefing to representatives of the various branches of the armed services, Gen. Curtis LeMay, then head of Strategic Air Command (SAC), was asked the question, "How do SAC's plans fit in with the stated national policy that the United States will never strike the first blow?" His response was:

I have heard this thought stated many times and it sounds very fine. However, it is not in keeping with the United States history. Just look back and note who started the Revolutionary War, the War of 1812, the Indian Wars, and the Spanish-American War. I want to make clear that I am not advocating a preventive war; however, I believe that if the U.S. is pushed in the corner far enough we would not hesitate to strike first.[55]

In the end, the question was, how far would the United States have to be pushed before a preventive war would be acceptable? Would the United States have to be under attack, or in imminent danger of attack? Or could a combination of (perceived) harmful intentions plus mounting capabilities be enough to push the United States to strike first?

The Joint Chiefs of Staff

In 1945, less than two weeks after the bombing of Hiroshima, Gen. George C. Marshall ordered a study of the military implications of atomic weapons. The Joint Strategic Survey Committee (JSSC) presented its conclusions on

October 30, 1945:

> Concerning the possible changes in techniques of warfare, the JSSC saw
> the atomic bomb primarily as a strategic weapon....However, its
> advent accentuated the value of surprise, and so emphasized the need
> "not only of readiness for immediate defense, but also for striking first,
> if necessary..." Later in its analysis the JSSC repeated this thought,
> holding that an effective action against the source of an atomic attack
> on the United States might require "us to strike first."[56]

General Eisenhower, however, did not approve of the analysis, as it did
not discuss the "present US strategic superiority stemming from atomic
monopoly nor its transitory nature," or in other words, America's closing
window of strategic advantage. He thus ordered the JSSC to revise its draft in
light of his comments. The newest draft concluded:

> The United States must have either a hard-boiled and enforceable world
> agreement against the use of atomic weapons or, with its allies, exclusive
> supremacy in the field. The United States was now in the best position
> to obtain and enforce a world agreement—five years hence would be
> too late...certain features of the atomic bomb should be kept in mind.
> *Defense against it would always be inadequate, but top priority should be
> given to effective means of stopping the carrying vehicles.*[57]

In effect, this is an early argument for pre-emption, and possibly prevention. The implication of this study is that should a "hard-boiled and enforceable agreement" not come to pass, then the United States must prevent
its enemies from *acquiring nuclear capability*—utilizing a preventive strike.
And should its adversaries come into possession of atomic weapons, "top
priority should be given to effective means of stopping the carrying vehicles,"
which is to say a pre-emptive strike on their bombers (in a similar scenario to
Israel's pre-emptive attack in 1967 against Egyptian planes). This strategy
might be considered to be defensive, and not pre-emptive. However, the first
part of the passage suggests that the United States should, along with its
allies, maintain "exclusive supremacy" in atomic weapons. If the Soviet Union
would not agree to international control of atomic weapons, then it is unlikely that anything short of a preventive strike against their nuclear facilities
would achieve U.S. supremacy.

Similarly, in 1946, Gen. Leslie Groves, director of the Manhattan Project,
wrote:

> If we were truly realistic...we would not permit any foreign power with
> which we are not firmly allied, and in which we do not have absolute

confidence to make or possess atomic weapons. If such a country started to make atomic weapons we would destroy its capacity to make them before it had progressed far enough to threaten us. If there was only some way to make America sense now its true peril some 15 to 20 years hence in a world of unrestricted atomic bombs, the nation would rise up and demand one of the two alternatives essential to its very existence. Either we must have a hard-boiled, realistic, enforceable, world agreement ensuring the outlawing of atomic weapons or we and our dependable allies must have an exclusive supremacy in the field, which means that no other nation can be permitted to have atomic weapons.[58]

This is an interesting passage, because Groves has touched on the problem of timing very well. He recognized that a threshold existed between a nuclear program, and the capability to actually make weapons. Once that threshold is crossed, it is difficult to control the spread of nuclear weapons. The best option, as Groves points out, is to strike *before* an adversary state constructs a nuclear weapon.

Groves also makes an important distinction here, and one that is not often made by other decision-makers. He mentions that the United States should consider destroying an adversary's *capabilities* in a preventive strike. Unlike other U.S. leaders, Groves did not take an "all or nothing" approach to preventive action. Instead, he saw the shades of gray within that category and recognized that a total preventive war was not necessary, and should not be assumed. Groves' comment is an example of exactly the type of limited preventive strike that Israel employed over thirty years later. There is little evidence that other officials in the military made such distinctions, which contributed to the final decision not to initiate preventive action of any kind.

In 1947, a JCS evaluation board presented a report to the assembled leadership of the U.S. armed forces. The report recommended that Congress should redefine "aggressive acts" so as to prepare "for the possibility that a pre-emptive strike by the United States might be necessary to defend against a nuclear armed enemy.[59] Although most of the report's recommendations were implemented by Congress, this particular request was dropped from consideration.[60]

PRESIDENT EISENHOWER AND THE "NEW LOOK" NATIONAL SECURITY STRATEGY

President Eisenhower's perception of American interests, and the threats the country faced, was ultimately responsible for the decision not to pursue a strategy of preventive action against the Soviet Union. Though there might have been doubts during Truman's administration, Eisenhower became convinced during his presidential tenure that the United States was involved in a "cold" war, unlike any other war it had fought. Lecturing the press in 1955, Eisenhower declared that the United States was "now conducting a cold war," and that the objective of such a war had to be more than merely "victory."[61] Thus, the National Security Council spoke of the basic objective of U.S. national security policy as "maintaining the security of the United States *and* the vitality of its fundamental values and institutions."[62] In order to do so, Eisenhower believed that defense spending must be reduced to a sustainable level, inflation controlled, and a security strategy created which would provide security over time. Eisenhower perceived the threat to the United States as twofold: the *external* threat of the Soviet Union and an imperialistic brand of Communism, and the *internal* threat of defending the United States by measures that would either bankrupt it or produce a "garrison state."

Thus, Eisenhower and his administration abandoned the "peak danger" strategy of the past. It was precisely this type of planning, for the year of "peak danger," which had resulted in exorbitant and unsustainable defense spending in the first place. Instead, Eisenhower focused on the notion of an "era of danger," which would require both fiscal responsibility and sound strategic planning. This was a major change in the framing of the problem, from window thinking to planning for the "long haul." In a public statement on April 30, 1953, Eisenhower rejected the "danger year" planning outright, saying that it was unrealistic to think that anybody could predict when another government would initiate a war.[63] Eisenhower asserted that national security "should be planned on a steady, sustained basis rather than keyed to particular years of threat."[64]

In order to justify this new strategy, Eisenhower and Dulles focused on what they perceived of Soviet intentions. Dulles argued that Communist doctrine had never really taught "primary reliance" on the notion of open war against the West.[65] Instead, as Eisenhower pointed out, the Soviet intention was to force upon the United States, through the threat of military force, an "unbearable security burden leading to economic disaster."[66] Thus, to increase military spending further (or even continue at the then current levels) in order to prepare for the "danger year" would be to play into Moscow's hands.

Notice that Eisenhower's bad faith image of the Soviets was not significantly different from his predecessors and colleagues who advocated preventive war. He did not believe that the Soviet Union was less hostile, but simply believed them to be long-term strategic planners, and less risk-prone than previously thought.[67] He did not believe their *goal* to be different—the worldwide domination of Communism and the fall of the United States—but did not believe that they would risk general war when they believed *time to be on their side.*[68]

There is an interesting point to be made here about the morality of preventive war. In her article on the formation of a "nuclear taboo" in the United States, Nina Tannenwald argues that the normative basis for nuclear nonuse can help to explain instances where the United States chose not to use nuclear weapons.[69] However, as she points out, the moral prohibition had little effect on Eisenhower, who actively sought ways to destroy the taboo. In 1953, he agreed with Dulles that "somehow or other the taboo which surrounds the use of atomic weapons would have to be destroyed."[70] Referring to the use of atomic weapons to possibly negotiate a better settlement in Korea, Eisenhower asserted that he "would not be limited by any world-wide gentleman's agreement."[71]

Thus, Eisenhower's perception of the immorality of preventive war (in addition to its other problems) did constrain his behavior, while the emerging nuclear taboo did not. Tannenwald concludes that the nuclear taboo played a part only in deterring Eisenhower from "casual" nuclear use, and his own comments suggest that he did not feel himself particularly constrained by any normative prohibition on nuclear weapons.[72] Again, this highlights the importance of individual perceptions. For Eisenhower, one moral norm was important (aggression does not fit in with U.S. values), while another (the nuclear taboo) was significantly less so. Another individual in similar circumstances could have easily placed different weight on the two normative values, thereby changing the direction of U.S. policy.

PRESIDENT EISENHOWER AND PREVENTIVE WAR

President Eisenhower's thinking on the topic of preventive war was complex and nuanced. He became president at a crucial transition time. The Soviet Union was no longer viewed as an ally, and indeed was seen by many as an implacable enemy; yet, they had attained nuclear capability. Eisenhower's thinking is important because he was an incisive thinker with substantial military experience. He was paradoxically both supportive and opposed to preventive war, and, in analyzing his views, we gain further insight into the dilemmas facing American military and civilian national security planners.

In his memoirs, Eisenhower writes that he "had long been convinced that the composition and structure of our military establishment should be based on the assumption that the United States would never start a major war."[73] This would seem to be a fairly concrete statement, and one that would rule out the possibility of a preventive strike or war. However, there is evidence that he did entertain the idea of preventive war at points, even if he ultimately decided against it.

In a memo to Secretary of State John Foster Dulles, Eisenhower comments on what he should do to "educate our people":

We should patiently point out that any group of people, such as the men in the Kremlin, who are aware of the great destructiveness of these weapons ... must be fairly assumed to be contemplating their aggressive use. It would follow that our own preparation could no longer be geared to a policy that attempts only to avert disaster during the early "surprise" stages of a war, and so gain time for full mobilization. Rather, we would have to be ready, on an instantaneous basis, to inflict greater loss upon the enemy than he could reasonably hope to inflict upon us. This would be a deterrent—but if the contest to maintain this relative position should have to continue indefinitely, the cost would either drive us to war—or into some form of dictatorial government. In such circumstances, we would be forced to consider whether or not our duty to future generations did not require us to *initiate* war at the most propitious moment that we could designate.[74]

This passage suggests that, at the very least, Eisenhower contemplated the idea of a preventive war against the Soviet Union. It also shows the effect of enemy images on such decisions. Eisenhower wrote that "any group of people, such as the men in the Kremlin, who are aware of the great destructiveness of these weapons ... must be fairly assumed to be contemplating their aggressive use." Eisenhower's image of the Soviet Union as an aggressive enemy seriously impacted his thinking. In this passage, Eisenhower equates capabilities with intent as if the two naturally go together. However, they are separate issues, and we can take from this quote that Eisenhower had already decided that the Soviet Union's intentions were malicious. Thus, the acquisition of new capabilities was especially dangerous, as it would be coupled with malevolent intentions.

In their analysis of this comment, Bowie and Immerman declare that Eisenhower was only testing the logic of Dulles' ideas by carrying them to their absolute (and absurd) ends.[75] Certainly, his comments reflect his belief that the United States could not continue its defense spending indefinitely. However, there is nothing in Eisenhower's memo that would seem to suggest that he was anything but serious. In fact, the opening paragraph asserts that he is in "general agreement" with Dulles' analysis, with only a few small comments (which are mostly in regard to U.S. military presence in foreign countries).[76] Eisenhower was not advocating preventive war, but rather noting that the then current level of military spending would produce a situation that might eventually compel U.S. leaders to seriously consider it as an option. It was this desire to develop a new strategy—one maintainable over the long term—that led to the Solarium project (discussed later), and ultimately his "New Look" policy.

In 1956, Eisenhower commissioned the air force to study the effects of a Soviet nuclear attack on the United States, given two scenarios. In the first scenario, the United States would have no warning at all, while in the second scenario it would have one month of strategic warning (of a general nature). Regarding the second scenario, Eisenhower recorded in his diary:

> The only possible way of reducing these losses would be for us to take the initiative sometime during the assumed month in which we had the warning of an attack and launch a surprise attack against the Soviets. This would be not only against our traditions, but it would appear to be impossible unless Congress would meet in a highly secret session and vote a declaration of war which would be implemented before the session was terminated. It would appear to be impossible that any such thing would occur.[77]

What is unique about Eisenhower's choice of words here is that a very similar phrasing appears a few years later in a very different context. In 1959, Eisenhower wrote a memo hinting that the United States might have to strike pre-emptively if the Berlin Crisis got out of hand. He wrote to the National Security Council (NSC) asking them how he could "be sure of the necessary support from Congress even though we might suddenly face a critical emergency and would be under compulsion to act quickly so as to avoid any unnecessary damage to ourselves."[78] Clearly, the practical problem of "*could* he do it" had been solved. What still remained for Eisenhower was the problem of reconciling preventive action with his perception of his own moral values, and those of the American public.

Solarium (1953)

After taking office in 1953, President Eisenhower ordered a basic re-appraisal of U.S. strategy in light of recent developments in atomic weaponry. The United States was on the verge of exploding a thermonuclear device, and given its underestimation of Soviet capabilities in 1949, had to assume that Russia was close on its heels. But more importantly, Eisenhower had a very specific notion of the threat that faced America. He foresaw the conflict with the Soviet Union as one of long duration, and believed that U.S. defense spending was then at an unsustainable level.[79] Solarium was an attempt to create a new national security strategy that would "achieve adequate military strength in the limits of endurable strain on our economy."[80] To this end, three task forces were set up, each with a specific position or strategy to defend. Alternative A called for "rollback," or a "strategic offensive" against the Soviet Union.[81] Alternative B called for the United States to draw a "line in the sand" around its sphere of influence and threaten massive retaliation should the Soviets cross the line.[82] This alternative was essentially a means of carrying out the policy of containment.

Alternative C was the most extreme of the three positions. Its group proclaimed that "the U.S. cannot continue to live with the Soviet threat. So long as the Soviet Union exists, it will not fall apart, but must and can be shaken apart."[83] This challenged the prevailing view that the Soviet system was destined to fall apart on its own if given time. As opposed to the conventional "window thinking" in which a country believes itself to have an advantage for a limited amount of time, this group posited that time, in fact, had been working *against* the United States. The group asserted that "the Task Force concludes from a study of the Soviet threat that time has been working against us. This trend will continue unless it is arrested, and reversed by *positive action*."[84]

Though the group stopped short of recommending a preventive war, it declared that they should be willing to undertake actions that might incur a significant risk of war.[85] In addition, the statement that "positive action" was needed to reverse the current trend of relative power was in fact the basis for many of the arguments for preventive war. When combined with the statement by the group that the time would soon come when the situation would be "unbearable" for the United States,[86] it is fairly clear what course of action might be undertaken to prevent those circumstances.

In the end, very little of alternative C ended up in NSC 162/2, the statement of national security policy adopted in October 1953. However, there is evidence that Eisenhower wanted a policy comprised of *elements from all three task forces*. He specifically requested that the groups work together to combine the alternatives into one unified policy.[87] However, he was told that alternatives A and C were too much opposed to one another, and could not be made to fit together in any coherent policy.[88] Upon being told that this was the case, the president was "very put out," and left it to his Special Assistant for National Security Affairs Robert Cutler to decide what to do. However, Eisenhower did later wonder aloud whether there should be a permanent Solarium project set up (with all three alternatives) that would continuously provide ideas for policy. However, nothing seems to have come from his suggestion.[89]

EISENHOWER AND PRE-EMPTION

While there is ample evidence to illustrate Eisenhower's ambivalence on the subject of preventive war, there was no such uncertainty about pre-emption; it was policy. In fact, this fits into his perception of the threat as long-term. The policy of pre-emption was a hedge against the possibility that the Soviets *might* attack. But because Eisenhower did not truly believe that the Soviets would do so—it was not their strategy to *directly* attack the United States—the United States must have another, sustainable strategy. Preventive war fits into a short-term strategy, not a long-term strategy.

Eisenhower had a strong grasp of the catastrophic potential of nuclear weapons and declared in his memoirs:

> My intention was firm: to launch the Strategic Air Command immediately *upon trustworthy evidence* of a general attack against the West. So I repeated that first priority must be given to the task of meeting the atomic threat, the only kind of attack that could, without notice, endanger our very existence.[90]

Similarly, in a meeting with the military leadership in 1954, Eisenhower indicated his "firm intention to launch a strategic air force immediately in case of *alert of actual attack*."[91]

Eisenhower's desire to keep the option of pre-emption open seems to have been carried out. In a 1954 memo to the president, Secretary of Defense Charles Wilson wrote:

> Dear Mr. President: The Joint Chiefs of Staff have recommended and I have approved, as essential to an improved position of military readiness, the deployment of additional numbers of atomic weapons to our overseas bases and the dispersal of atomic weapons to certain operational bases in the Untied States . . . The purpose of on-base storage in the United States is to permit our combat forces to react instantly to *attack or warning of attack*.[92]

Thus, Eisenhower's contention that the United States would never start a major war does not appear to have applied to pre-emption. Of course, true pre-emption is defensive, but what are the risks of launching atomic weapons upon "evidence of an attack" or an "alert?" Clearly, there are tremendous risks of miscalculation and accidental escalation. On one hand, Eisenhower would have had the desire to wait and be as sure as possible before actually launching an attack (as opposed to simply putting the planes in the air). On the other hand, he would have to have been decisive (and risk starting a nuclear war), as he would likely have had only between thirty minutes and four hours of warning.[93]

THE DANGER OF PRE-EMPTION

However, though pre-emption was primarily a defensive strategy, it created considerable risks, especially during the time period discussed in this case. We must remember that deterrence was not taken for granted in the early 1950s. Even as late as 1959, Albert Wohlstetter wrote that deterrence was in fact, more difficult than previously assumed.[94] He argued that not only did the Soviets already have the ability to launch a surprise attack using thermonuclear weapons, but that their ability to do so would *increase* over the years.[95] And, in a system in which there is still an advantage in striking first, deterrence is neither easily attainable nor inherently stable.

Thomas Schelling took up this logic in his 1960 book, *The Strategy of Conflict*. He wrote of surprise attacks:

> That is the problem of a surprise attack. If surprise carries an advantage, it is worthwhile to avert it by striking first. Fear that the other may be about to strike in the mistaken belief that we are about to strike give us a motive for striking, and so justifies the other's motive. But, if the gains from even successful surprise are less desired than no war at all, there is no "fundamental" basis for an attack by either side. Nevertheless, it looks as though a modest temptation on each side to sneak in a first blow—a temptation too small by itself to motivate an attack— might become compounded through a process of interacting expectations, with additional motive for attack being produced by successive cycles of "He thinks we think he thinks we think . . . he thinks we think he'll attack; so he thinks we shall; so he will; so we must."[96]

But it was not just professional strategic thinkers and academics who noticed this phenomenon. In his memoirs, Paul Nitze paraphrased exactly the situation that Schelling writes about describing the U.S.-Soviet balance in 1957.[97] A policy of pre-emption, especially if the Soviets knew about it, carried dangerous consequences. If the Soviet Union knew that the United States was prepared to launch an attack upon *warning of an attack*, even if the Kremlin knew that it was a false warning (and they were not actually attacking), they would be forced to attack in reality because of the United States doctrine of pre-emption. Thus, a minor crisis, if cooler heads did not prevail, might easily escalate to the nuclear level. Remember that the concept of Mutually Assured Destruction (MAD) was not in full effect in the late 1940s and early 1950s when atomic weapons were still relatively primitive, and a nuclear war was still considered by many to be "winnable."[98]

CONTRADICTIONS, CONFUSION, AND AMBIVALENCE

What is remarkable about this case is the extent to which key figures contradicted themselves on the subject of preventive war. For instance, in a private letter to Joseph Alsop (in 1954), Paul Nitze savagely criticized the notion of a preventive war. He attacked it on the grounds that (1) it would not work; (2) even the mention of such an idea "hurts the country"; (3) it would be unconstitutional; (4) the notion is "repugnant" in the moral sense; and (5) U.S. democracy would not survive the aftermath.[99]

Yet, Nitze, in his memoirs, recalls a meeting with Eisenhower during a particularly tense moment in the Berlin Crisis:

> I suggested that since demonstrative or tactical use of nuclear weapons would greatly increase the temptation to the Soviets to initiate a strategic strike, it would be best for us, in moving toward the use of nuclear weapons, to consider most seriously the option of an initial strategic strike of our own. This, I believed, could assure us victory in at least a military sense in a series of nuclear exchanges, while we might well lose if we allowed the Soviets to strike first.[100]

Nitze then goes on to explain how he, Secretary of Defense Robert McNamara, and Gen. Jerry Page discussed, in detail, a plan to take out Soviet airfields and forward bases in a preventive attack.[101]

This ambivalence of decision-makers is very important. Many U.S. leaders hated the idea of preventive war (Eisenhower, Nitze, and Kennan, among others), but were forced to address the views that were the basis for such thinking, such as dwindling U.S. superiority, a bad faith image of the Soviet Union, and the strategic implications of new atomic weapons. Again, the rational-actor model fails in this case, as it does not allow room for mixed feelings, confusion, and ambivalence. These leaders were not engaging in cool, cost-benefit analyses, but rather were trying to piece together a coherent policy position that would reconcile their moral beliefs and their "realist" strategic considerations.

CONCLUSION

By the late 1950s, the idea of preventive war seemed to have faded quite a bit. This might be due to the technological advances made by both the United States and the Soviet Union in the 1950s. By 1957, the Soviet Union had deployed long-range bombers carrying thermonuclear weapons and had ICBM capability.[102] Additionally, preventive war, as U.S. leaders saw it, had little chance of success. The supposed goal of such a preventive war would be to destroy Soviet atomic capability, and possibly change the regime (since it was the ideology of the regime that posed the long-term threat). However, U.S. leaders were not willing to give up substantial portions of Europe to achieve this goal. In the end, U.S. leaders were never confident that a preventive attack would stop the Soviet Union from overrunning Western Europe with conventional forces. The Soviet Union was too big for the United States to occupy it, and its large conventional army could withstand air attack.

Another contributory reason that the idea of preventive war had no chance of success (in the minds of U.S. leaders) was because they made the mistake of supposing *total* war to achieve *limited* objectives. The basic refrain from all the leaders throughout this case was: the United States cannot trust the Soviet Union with atomic weapons. After they tested an atomic bomb in 1949, the refrain changed to: the United States cannot live under the constant threat of nuclear attack from the Soviet Union (the threat being particularly urgent because of U.S. leaders' negative image of the Soviet Union). Thus, the crux of the issue was Soviet atomic capability. However, the solution that preventive war proponents advocated to achieve the limited goal (destroy Soviet atomic capability) was invariably phrased in terms of total war, especially by Truman and Eisenhower. There were exceptions to this; Gen. Orvil Anderson, for instance, spoke of "wiping out Russia's five A-bomb nests," in a preventive strike. But he still envisioned such an act as the beginning of a total war.[103]

However, the most important single factor was Eisenhower himself. Eisenhower came to the White House in 1953 with a very specific vision of the threat that the United States faced. Like his predecessors, he saw the Soviet Union as the major threat to the national security of the United States. However, this threat was mitigated by Eisenhower's different perception of the precise nature of the threat. Like Kennan, he believed the conflict with the Soviet Union to be of long duration. Eisenhower thus abandoned the previous strategy of planning for "danger years," the strategy embodied in NSC-68, and focused on a long-term strategy for facing Communism without bankrupting the United States.

In this case, declining power was a prominent factor, and was referred to often by those who favored preventive war, and even by those who did not. Indeed, it seemed to be the most prominent factor that was present in the case. And yet, the United States did not initiate preventive action. This is not surprising, especially if preventive war advocates center their arguments on changing capabilities and declining relative power. Though it is possible that there might be a scenario in which a leader might feel that the changing capabilities *alone* justify preventive action, it does not seem likely. This becomes clear when we think about all of the instances in which declining relative power (on a global scale) *did not* lead to preventive action. The United States did not consider preventive action against South Africa when that country became a nuclear power, or against Israel as they built their undeclared nuclear arsenal. The reason is simple: capabilities alone are not enough to explain preventive war decision-making. Relationships, images (of oneself and others), and history all play an important role in the implications that leaders draw from material calculations.

Additionally, the consequences of the relative decline in American power was not an unequal power relationship between the two states, but rather a rough parity (parity being relatively easy to achieve with nuclear weapons: a hundred nukes is as good as a thousand). Perhaps if the situation had been different, and American leaders had feared that the relative decline would result in a dangerously *unequal* power dynamic, the urge to initiate preventive action might have prevailed. However, the fear of the consequences was never sharp enough for either Truman or Eisenhower to overrule their objections to prevention.

However, though preventive war was not initiated by the United States, this case offers disturbing implications for other cases. Preventive war was not chosen by the United States because neither Truman nor Eisenhower believed it to be a viable option. A pivotal factor in this case was the instinct and beliefs of two chief executives. However, some of the most outspoken proponents of preventive action were in the military. In a country whose politics are dominated by the military (such as Pakistan), preventive war advocates might exert more influence, leading to very different decisions. In addition, comforting as it might be that Truman and Eisenhower ultimately decided against preventive war, one only has to look at the National Security Strategy of 2002 to be reminded that different presidents might have radically different perspectives and reactions to security threats.

5

To the Brink...
India and Pakistan's
Nuclear Standoff

The conflict between India and Pakistan has erupted into major wars three times in the half century since both countries attained their independence.[1] Many of the factors associated with preventive war—bad faith image, shifting capabilities, windows of opportunity, and vulnerable nuclear programs—are present in this case. However, from the standpoint of preventive war theory, the conflict between India and Pakistan has become the proverbial "dog that didn't bark" since the last major war in 1971. The question here is: Why?

The factors discussed in this case are important, and certainly did lead to discussions of preventive action. However, they did not lead to preventive action. Just as no single factor can explain the decision to initiate preventive action, neither is there a parsimonious explanation for decisions not to act preventively.

This case study will examine pre-emptive and preventive war thinking in the Indian government and military during the past three decades. My purpose in doing so is to understand why such action was *not* taken, and determine the lessons to be drawn from this case.

Many of the theoretical conditions that previous research has linked to both preventive and pre-emptive war are present in this case.

THE BEGINNINGS: 1982–1984

In 1982, Pakistan had not yet acquired the potential to produce nuclear weapons. However, it was an open secret that Pakistan had already embarked on a program to achieve such a capability. By 1981, Pakistan had purchased, through dummy corporations, a small centrifuge uranium enrichment facility at Kahuta.[2] It also possessed a hot-cell laboratory, as well as the blueprints for a reprocessing plant.[3] One journalist even reported that A. Q. Khan, the man in charge of Pakistani atomic research, was (in 1981) at work on a trigger mechanism for a nuclear explosive.[4]

Somewhat presciently, Onkar Marwah noted that "if an accident were to damage the existing plants, the equipment, presumably, could not be replaced as easily as it was bought on the first occasion."[5] He attributes this to the clandestine nature in which the project was managed, buying parts from different countries instead of the whole plant. Marwah describes it as an "erector-set" approach to acquiring the bomb. Whether or not Indian authorities were given the idea by Marwah, it is fair to assume that India was watching these developments closely. The relative vulnerability of the Pakistani nuclear facility (its location was well known, and it would have been difficult to rebuild if destroyed) must have made it a tempting target for Indian decision-makers.

On December 20, 1982, a report appeared in the *Washington Post* that cited "U.S. intelligence sources" as saying that India's military leaders had prepared a contingency plan for a "pre-emptive attack against Pakistani nuclear facilities and proposed such an attack to Prime Minister Indira Gandhi earlier this year."[6] According to the sources, Gandhi decided against the strike when she heard the proposal, but "did not foreclose the option of striking if Pakistan appeared on the verge of acquiring nuclear weapons capability."[7]

In reality, what is being discussed here was not really a "pre-emptive" strike at all, even if Gandhi did wait until Pakistan appeared on the verge of acquiring the ability to produce nuclear weapons. It would only have been a pre-emptive attack if Gandhi had said that India would wait to attack until Pakistan was about to use those same weapons. What they were really discussing here was a preventive strike. Such a strike against an opponent's nuclear facilities would have been reminiscent of Israel's attack on the Osiraq reactor that had occurred less than two years previously. Indian leaders had no doubt considered the success of Israel in destroying its enemy's capabilities. And yet, Gandhi decided not to initiate the attack.

As one might expect, the Indian government quickly denied the reports, calling them "a figment of the imagination" (India's U.S. ambassador) and "absolute rubbish" (Indian Foreign Ministry).[8] However, their denials were often strangely worded. H. Y. Prasad, Prime Minister Gandhi's spokesman, declared that there "was no proof" of such a plan.[9] When asked if such a contingency plan existed (for a preventive strike against Pakistani nuclear plants), the spokesman for the Indian Foreign Ministry cryptically replied that India had "many contingency plans."[10]

At that point, the International Atomic Energy Agency (IAEA) had been unable for twenty-one months to keep track of the amount of plutonium produced at the Pakistani plant. U.S. sources projected that, operating the plant at a reduced power level, the Pakistanis could have produced between

10 and 20 kilograms of weapons grade plutonium, enough for one to three Hiroshima-sized fission bombs.[11] The U.S. intelligence source said that a major factor in Gandhi's decision to put off the preventive strike was a concern that India's nuclear facilities might be vulnerable to a retaliatory strike by Pakistan.[12] Unlike Iraq, which was distracted by the outbreak of war with Iran, Pakistan's attention was focused intensely on India's behavior. Gandhi's decision reflected her understanding that Pakistan would be likely to retaliate, and possibly destroy Indian nuclear facilities. Even if it did not escalate into another major war, perhaps the potential cost of losing India's nuclear program was simply too high.

Pakistan declared, "We have not developed, are not capable of developing and have no intention of developing an atomic bomb." However, this denial was widely disregarded, and Benjamin noted that President Reagan had continuously and personally implored world leaders not to sell sensitive nuclear technology to Pakistan.[13] The U.S. intelligence report of a possible Indian attack came at a particularly bad time, as Pakistan and India were in the middle of bilateral negotiations, and the Pakistani foreign minister was visiting Delhi.[14] Thus, if it is to be expected that India would deny such a plan at any time, it is even more understandable that they would deny it with extra fervor at a time when it might damage important negotiations. That there were bilateral negotiations occurring might also have provided a balance to the image of Pakistan as a hostile adversary. Negotiations do not necessarily preclude preventive action, but they might signal a diminished intensity in a state's enemy image, and might make leaders less likely to believe that a conflict is inevitable, or that the other country has *only* hostile intentions.

The story of an Indian preventive strike on Pakistani nuclear plants went away for a while, but reappeared within two years. A *New York Times* article from September 15, 1984 cited a Reagan administration source as saying that Indira Gandhi had received "recommendations from some senior advisors that India conduct an air raid against a Pakistani atomic installation to prevent the development of nuclear weapons by Pakistan."[15] The article went on to note that this information came at a time when India-Pakistani relations had taken a precipitous downturn. Following the optimism engendered by the 1982 meetings, India accused Pakistan in January of threatening its security with a major arms buildup. The Pakistani press then printed a report accusing India of deploying twenty-nine army divisions on the Pakistani border. The increased tensions led to the cancellation of Non-Aggression talks that were to be held in 1983.

The report in the *New York Times* prompted Pakistan's Foreign Minister Sahabzada Yaqub-Khan to announce that Pakistan had taken "appropriate defensive measures."[16] Meanwhile, the U.S. State Department described the report as "alarmist," while conceding that intelligence information about a possible Indian attack had been received.[17] Prime Minister Gandhi also announced in a radio address that "Pakistan's nuclear program has brought about a *qualitative change in our security environment.*"[18]

A Western diplomat commented that India's fears are that "even the mere possibility that Pakistan might have a bomb exerts an equalizing influence."[19] In 1985, the prime ministers of India and Pakistan, Rajiv Gandhi and Zia ul-Haq, agreed in principle to a plan by which both countries would refrain from attacking each others' nuclear installations or facilities.[20] The agreement mandated that India and Pakistan would exchange lists of nuclear facilities at the beginning of each new year. However, the success of the agreement depended to a large extent on how complete the lists of nuclear facilities were, and whether or not the lists were believed to be legitimate. To that point, a Pakistani official who believed that India's list was not complete warned, "The agreement does not protect the facilities not mentioned on the list."[21]

We can thus see that India-Pakistan relations are prone to highs and lows. That there might be more lows than highs is significant. However, the presence of at least some upturns in relations, even if they are minor, might also have a significant effect. In terms of capabilities, India seems to have been in a similar situation to Israel's in 1981. However, Indian leaders did not appear to have the same perception of Pakistan as Israel did of Saddam Hussein. Perhaps there is something to the notion that, aside from the past thirty years, Indians and Pakistanis had lived in the same area for hundreds of years, and shared much in the way of sociocultural attitudes. Indira Gandhi was the leader of the Indian Congress Party, whose direct legacy was the belief that Hindus and Muslims could, and should, live together peacefully. The three wars fought before 1982 showed that such a proposition was not easy, but a preventive attack would have indicated a complete lack of hope, which seems to have survived, even if it is sometimes below the surface.

THE 1990 INDO-PAKISTANI CRISIS

By 1990, both India and Pakistan had the ability to quickly produce nuclear weapons (if they did not already have a small stockpile). Though neither side pre-emptively attacked, or initiated a preventive strike, this crisis highlights the decision-making of Indian leaders in a crisis situation where prevention (or pre-emption) was a real possibility.

The immediate cause of the crisis in 1990 was tension over Kashmir. On January 20, large crowds in Srinagar gathered to protest the arrest of militants, ignoring a government-imposed curfew. The police opened fire on the crowd, killing thirty-two people.[22] Three days later, Indian politicians accused Pakistan of aiding Kashmiri militants. In the background of these events, India's new prime minister, V. P. Singh, appointed nuclear scientist Raja Rammanna as the country's new minister of state for defense. Rammanna is regarded as the father of India's atomic bomb, and his appointment was widely interpreted as evidence of India's decision to give a higher priority to nuclear weapons and missile-development programs.[23]

The rhetoric quickly escalated as Pakistani prime minister Benazir Bhutto visited the Pakistani-held area of Kashmir and promised a "thousand-year war" in support of Kashmiri separatists.[24] She also contended that Kashmir was a disputed territory, a comment that seemed to renege on the 1972 Simla Accords reached by Indira Gandhi and Zulfikar Ali Bhutto (Benazir's father).[25] Benazir's comments prompted India to reinforce defenses on the Pakistani border in Kashmir. Mass demonstrations in Srinagar continued, drawing up to 100,000 people. The violence continued, as Indian police shot forty protestors within four days, bringing the total to 230 dead in the two months since the unrest began.[26] An April 2 article reported that Pakistani officials were fearful of an Indian pre-emptive strike in the early summer.[27] The same article also reported that the Indian government was being "held hostage by right-wing Hindu parties who openly advocate a policy of 'giving Pakistan a bloody nose,'" a reference to the Bharatiya Janata Party (BJP).[28]

An April 9 article quoted the BJP spokesman as calling on the government to "knock out the training camps and the transit routes of the terrorists." The statements also declared that "Pakistan's many provocations amount to so many acts of war" and that "hot pursuit is a recognized defensive measure."[29] This is a clear example of the belief that certain actions are justified because a state of war exists. That which might not be legitimate during peacetime, such as a strike against Pakistani territory, becomes so when there is a state of war.

The BJP's belligerent tone was matched by the opposition Congress Party. Rajiv Gandhi, Congress leader and former prime minister, declared that it was time the government took "some very strong steps" on Kashmir, and asserted: "I know what steps are possible. I also know what is in the pipeline and what the capabilities are. The question is, does this government have the guts to take strong steps?"[30]

The allusion to "capabilities" is likely a reference to India's potential to produce nuclear weapons. And though the BJP statement mentions "hot pursuit," what the statement in fact recommends is a preventive strike on terrorist training camps in Pakistan. The mention of hot pursuit is an attempt to frame the issue in terms of retaliation. However, there is no realistic way for India to retaliate against each individual act of terrorism, especially when it is difficult to distinguish between militants aided and trained by Pakistan (or actual Pakistani soldiers), and Kashmiris fighting for their independence. Instead, the strike would likely target all known training camps and transit routes of terrorists in Pakistan and Kashmir, in an attempt to prevent future acts. Thus, the motivation is a combination of retaliation (for past acts) and prevention (against future acts). Also, note the reference to "guts," or will. Will to carry through on one's threats is a key aspect of deterrence.

It should be noted that though the tone of the BJP statement was belligerent, its facts were sound. Robert Oakley, then U.S. ambassador to Pakistan, recalled that starting in 1989, the Pakistani Army began to play a "much more active role" in supporting the Kashmiri separatists, as well as groups like Jamaat-i-Islami. Oakley recalled that training camps within Pakistan multiplied, and material flowed in increasing amounts across the border from Pakistan to Kashmir.[31]

Oakley also recalled that, contrary to the fiery rhetoric of the politicians, the Pakistani military was actually quite calm. However, he also remembered that they were "unrealistically confident."[32] This is a dangerous feeling for a military to have. As the Gates mission made clear soon after this, there really was not a scenario in which Pakistan could gain from a war with India. One might wonder then what the Pakistani generals were so confident about. Since we can probably assume that Pakistani generals had some basic conception of the imbalance in conventional forces, the only reason that they might have for overconfidence was the belief that India would back down. However, India, with its larger conventional forces, would probably also be reasonably sure that Pakistan would want to avoid war. This raises the risk of both sides intentionally escalating as a bluff, perhaps to the point where it might be too late to step down.

The crisis escalated on April 10 as members of the Jammu and Kashmir Liberation Front (JKLF) publicly killed a hostage in Srinagar. In a statement on April 11, Prime Minister Singh told the Indian parliament that India should be "psychologically prepared for war."[33] Singh declared "Our message to Pakistan is that you cannot get away with taking Kashmir without a war. They will have to pay a very heavy price and we have the capability to inflict heavy losses."[34]

Singh, who was also the minister of defense, alleged that Pakistan had moved its radar systems to the border and made its airfields on the Indian border operational.[35] Speaking to reporters the next day, Singh claimed that Pakistan was preparing to launch an attack across India's western border and that Pakistan's army was on "red alert."[36] In a reply to the earlier remark by Bhutto, Singh also declared, "I warn them that those who talk about 1,000 years of war should examine whether they will last 1,000 hours of war."[37]

Rhetoric on the Indian side continued to grow more belligerent in the following days. On April 15, the *Washington Post* reported that that some "influential Indian leaders appear now to favor an offensive military strike against Pakistan."[38] The article quoted India's home minister Mufti Mohammed Sayeed as saying that war with Pakistan "would be fully justified if the objective of freeing Kashmir from the stranglehold of the secessionists was achieved." Coll reports that Sayeed mentioned privately that while such a war would be costly in terms of lives and property, it would be "the only option left to India" if Pakistan continued to support Kashmiri separatists.[39]

The article also stated:

> Aggressive support for an Indian offensive strike against Pakistan comes from Hindu conservatives who prop up Singh's minority government in Parliament. Leaders of the rightist Bharatiya Janata Party (BJP) argue that because of arms and training allegedly provided by Pakistan to separatist militants in Kashmir, *India and Pakistan are in effect already at war, and what remains is for India to take the war into Pakistani territory.*[40]

The article also notes, somewhat offhandedly, that previously "leaders in India and Pakistan had emphasized that they would fight only if the other side attacked first."[41] If this is true, then there is a clear and unmistakable change in tone from a policy of retaliation, to calls for preventive and pre-emptive strikes against Pakistan. Again, the BJP has reasserted that a state of war already exists. The power of such an argument is its claim to be "realistic." The claim of such an argument is that it is not cynical or hawkish, but only "telling it like it is." Similar to those in the United States and Israel who also made this argument, the BJP argument is simply that it is naïve to hold back from acting in the belief that Pakistan will change its behavior of its own volition: India is already at war, and should act accordingly. Though India did not carry out such strikes, a trend in recent years has been the increasing popularity of the BJP (though the BJP did suffer a loss in the 2004 elections), whose beliefs have not changed substantially in the intervening years.

It seems as though the Indian government was certainly thinking about preventive strikes. An *Economist* article from April 21 reported that India had published a list of forty-seven training camps for militants in Pakistan.[42]

In a news article from April 21, South Asian specialist Stephen Cohen, a scholar then at the University of Illinois who had recently returned from both India and Pakistan, said that politicians on both sides "think the other side is weak."[43] Cohen also quoted U.S. State Department sources as saying that this crisis was "qualitatively different" from previous crises, since it involved not just political differences, but a tangible dispute over Kashmir.[44]

As the crisis continued to deepen, the White House sent Deputy National Security Advisor Robert Gates to the region in an attempt to diffuse the situation. The purpose of the Gates Mission was to send a message from the

U.S. president to the leaders of India and Pakistan. Gates told the Pakistani decision-makers and military officers that the United States had war-gamed the situation from every possible angle, and there was no way that the Pakistanis would be victorious. Gates gave the same message to India with the addition that any war would be potentially devastating.[45] Most of the parties involved in the crisis agree that the Gates Mission was successful in that it allowed both India and Pakistan to back down gracefully from their public positions.[46] Both countries waited a few weeks, but by early June had withdrawn all of their military forces from the border area and the crisis was over.[47]

In March of 1993, Seymour Hersh published an article in the *New Yorker* alleging that India and Pakistan had been on the brink of nuclear war. The piece later became controversial, but it is worthwhile to mention some of his claims. The tone for the article is set by a quote by Richard J. Kerr, a deputy director at the CIA: "It was the most dangerous nuclear situation we have ever faced since I've been in the U.S. Government. It may be as close as we've come to a nuclear exchange. It was far more frightening than the Cuban missile crisis."[48]

Hersh then quotes Robert Gates as saying: "The analogy that we kept making was to the summer of 1914. Pakistan and India seemed to be caught in a cycle that they couldn't break out of. I was convinced that if a war started, it would be nuclear."[49]

Much of the controversy stems from Hersh's allegation that Pakistan had "openly deployed its main armored tank units along the Indian border and, in secret, placed its nuclear-weapons arsenal on alert."[50] Devin Hagerty correctly points out that much of Hersh's information on the nuclear aspect came from an unnamed U.S. intelligence analyst.[51] And, indeed, many of those present during the crisis reject Hersh's characterization.[52] However, Hersh's account seems to have become conventional wisdom, and in their book, William Burrows and Robert Windrem assert that Pakistani and Indian nuclear forces were on alert without bothering to cite a source.[53]

However, it is unlikely that we will have the full story of Indian and Pakistani intentions and actions until both countries release all of the internal documents pertaining to the crisis. Whether or not Hersh's allegations are correct, the basic framework of the crisis is generally agreed upon. Gary Milhollin, director of the Wisconsin Project on Nuclear Arms Control, summed up the situation: "South Asia seems to be the highest-temperature nuclear flashpoint in the world at this time. You have all the ingredients—a border dispute, historic rivalry, mutual suspicion and no nuclear doctrine in either country."[54]

We might add to these "ingredients" that both are "opaque proliferants" with admittedly small or nonexistent arsenals, making stable deterrence very difficult to achieve.

1999: KARGIL

In the 1990s, a debate began about the implication of horizontal nuclear proliferation (proliferation to new countries). A major part of this debate was over whether nuclear proliferation (which would bring along with it periods of transition, and shifting balances of power) would increase or decrease the likelihood of pre-emptive and preventive war.

In the background of this academic argument was the question of evidence. Proliferation pessimists posited that deterrence was not stable even under the best of circumstances, and especially not in emerging nuclear nations. Yet, they had few pieces of evidence to go on, or little inclination to study dyadic relationships other than that of United States and the Soviet Union. In 1981, Marwah wrote that scholarship offered "scant analysis of what happens when actual nuclearization takes place, especially in a region where states have a history of violent antagonism towards each other."[55]

The Kargil War in 1999 provided an excellent example for the arguments of proliferation pessimists.[56] The conflict began on May 6, 1999, when the Indian Army detected intruders in Kargil, a region 120 miles from Srinagar, and on the Indian side of the Line of Control (LoC) in Kashmir. A group of militants soon destroyed a large supply of artillery rounds at an Indian ammunition dump. By May 26, the Indian Army had initiated air strikes to flush out the insurgents.[57] The Indian government charged that Pakistan had backed the militants, and may have even fought alongside them.[58]

The conflict lasted over two months, and took the lives of over 1,000 Indian and Pakistani soldiers.[59] It did not end until Pakistani prime minister Nawaz Sharif flew to Washington, D.C., in July and pledged to withdraw his forces to the Pakistani side of the LoC.

In his book *The Consequences of Nuclear Proliferation*, Devin T. Hagerty wrote, "There is no more ironclad law in international relations theory than this: nuclear states do not fight wars with each other."[60] Hagerty had the misfortune to publish this only one year before the Kargil conflict. However, one event does not necessarily invalidate a rule, and Kargil might be considered an anomaly. However, there are other aspects of this conflict that make it potentially even more disturbing than the fact that two nuclear states did go to war with each other.

First, it must be noted that both sides did exercise a degree of restraint in not escalating the use of conventional forces to a higher level. However, one would not want Indian or Pakistani leaders to become comfortable with conventional conflicts under the protection of the "nuclear umbrella": the risk of inadvertent or unstoppable escalation is too great. Sagan writes that Pakistani leaders (particularly in the military) believe that the conflict was lost because Sharif lost courage and backed down too soon, and that India was exercising restraint by not crossing the border into Pakistan territory.

Likewise, he claims that India's interpretation was that Indian threats of escalation (for example, a counterattack across the Pakistani border) forced Pakistan to retreat.[61]

One might contend that the Kargil War was entered into by an elected government in Pakistan, thereby showing that democracies can be just as aggressive and reckless as dictatorships. However, the humiliating loss of the Kargil War led quickly to a return of military rule, when Gen. Pervez Musharraf took power in yet another coup. Yet, military dictatorships have initiated two of the three wars fought by Pakistan against India. Kotera Bhimaya writes: "The 1965 war was conceived, planned, and executed by the military under the leadership of President Ayub Khan, who was also a field marshal in the Pakistan Army. *What was intended as a limited action to 'liberate' Kashmir developed into a major war with India.*"[62]

This is worrisome inasmuch as it shows the dangers of inadvertent escalation. One might note as well that Pakistan's basic objectives have not changed in the slightest in the intervening years; the "liberation" of Kashmir is still a fundamental goal, and one that in fact led to war in 1999. Though the 1999 Kargil conflict was of relatively low intensity (in that it did not erupt into a full-scale war), that does not preclude such escalation in the future. It might also reinforce for Indian and Pakistani leaders the perception that war is inevitable. The hope of proliferation optimists is that the development of nuclear weapons will break the cycle of hostility and mistrust that characterize certain relationships because the destructive nature of nuclear weapons imposes restraint and caution on its owners. However, the renewed outbreak of war in 1999 demonstrates that the cycle might not be broken so easily. In addition, the conflict must have hardened Indian perceptions of Pakistani leaders as irresponsible and hostile, contributing to the bad faith image.

THE IMPACT OF SEPTEMBER 11: 2001 AND BEYOND

On October 1, 2001, the then Indian minister for external affairs, Omar Abdullah, was quoted in an Indian newspaper as advocating pre-emptive strikes against terrorists. Abdullah asserted that India had a "credible case that will stand the scrutiny" of international opinion. What he was actually advocating was preventive strikes against terrorist training camps in Pakistan-occupied Kashmir (PoK).[63] Abdullah added that he believed India should be able to claim the same right of self-defense against terrorism that America had recently used in forming its coalition in the war on terrorism. However, his wording is significant in that he advocated preventive strikes against "terrorists" (presumably those in Pakistani territory), but not against Pakistan. This is obviously an attempt to separate the issue of *limited preventive strikes* against terrorists from the larger issue of Indo-Pakistani conflict. Whether such distinction would be understood by Pakistan is dubious.

Shortly after that quote appeared, an article in the *Sunday Times* (London) asserted that Pakistan's military was shaken by reports of a possible preemptive attack against their nuclear sites. The article claims that Pakistani officers had information that either America, Israel, or India was planning attacks against nuclear facilities in Pakistan to prevent weapons from falling into the hands of Islamic fundamentalists.[64] Mills cites a Pakistani source as saying that the "[Pakistani] Generals are panic-stricken." Zia Mian, a Pakistani physicist involved in atomic research, declared, "Every paranoid fear they have had over the past 20 years about people coming to get our missiles is suddenly coming to the fore."[65]

Though this situation was resolved without any immediate violence, the example of the United States continued to be cited by India as potential justification for preventive attacks.

A wire report from India on April 11, 2003, quoted Indian foreign minister Yashwant Sinha as asserting India's right to take "limited military action" against Pakistan to prevent the harboring and training of terrorists.[66] Minister for Civil Aviation Shahnawaz Hussain was quoted similarly in April 2003.[67] Sinha even declared that Pakistan's nuclear capability and support of the Kashmir separatists made it a "fitter case" for preventive action than Iraq.[68] This can be characterized as preventive action because its fundamental purpose is not retaliation for any specific incident, but the prevention of a future terrorism.

Not surprisingly, Sinha's comments raised alarm bells in Washington, and it was soon reported that a string of U.S. officials would travel to India and Pakistan in an effort to cool down the rhetoric and apply more pressure on Pakistan to curb support for militants. U.S. secretary of state Colin Powell also declared that he saw no parallels between U.S. action in the case of Iraq, and Pakistan's threat to India.[69] One might add that the parallel is only suspect because Pakistan is arguably *more* of a direct threat to India than Iraq was to the United States.

The Institute of Peace & Conflict Studies, a think tank based in Delhi, published an article in the same month deriding Sinha for using the term preemption. However, though the author, Firdaus Ahmed, pointed out that India should be careful while drawing lessons from American conduct, his main position was something different. The heart of the article was the argument that any action against Pakistan would not be pre-emption, but rather retaliation. Ahmed argued that since Pakistan's support of terrorism had passed the threshold of an "armed attack," any Indian action would be justified under the U.N. Charter, under self-defense.[70]

Obviously, this raises the question of the motives of Indian officials in their belligerent rhetoric. Is it possible that public talk of preventive action against Pakistan (and/or terrorist groups in Pakistan) is just a ploy to compel the United States to apply more pressure on Pakistan? Of course, such a scenario is possible, even likely. But even a cursory knowledge of India's security concerns shows that preventive strikes were most likely considered.

The United States declared in its National Security Strategy of 2002 that deterrence is no longer feasible against terrorist threats.[71] India too has similar concerns. And while the United States has had a somewhat difficult time determining which states aid terrorists (and to what extent), India has no such problem. The state that is their main adversary, that trains terrorists who walk across the border and straight into the Indian parliament, is right next door, openly proclaiming support for militants. Kamal Matinuddin writes that Pakistan (by itself) has not really posed a substantive security threat to India since 1971. Instead, Matinuddin explains that the major threat to India (at least, in their own perception) lies in Pakistani support of militants and insurgents in Kashmir. He wrote:

> The perceived threat from Pakistan is mainly due to the disputed territory of Kashmir. India believes that the Pakistan military establishment is determined to use force, whenever it is in a position to do so, in order to absorb Kashmir with its own borders. It is also under the impression that the Pakistan armed forces are determined to take revenge for their defeat in East Pakistan.[72]

Matinuddin is perhaps too quick to discount the perception of a real threat from Pakistan, especially after their development of nuclear weapons. However, he is correct in pointing out that India does perceive its *most immediate* threat (though not the most *dire* threat, which would be the spectre of nuclear war) to be the Kashmiri militants, funded and aided by Pakistan. In many ways, India would have an easier time implementing a policy of "preventive strikes against terrorists." Unlike the United States' broadly conceived "war on terrorism," the terrorism against India is supported by a single state, which has buildings, camps, and supplies that can be found and destroyed.

The attack on India's parliament in December of 2001 made it unmistakably clear that there is much at stake for India. It is not just Indian interests that are in danger, as was the case for America before September 11, or simply a border region (though Kashmir obviously holds tremendous importance for India). But that particular terrorist attack struck at the heart of Indian democracy, in the middle of India's capital city.

The attack occurred on December 13, 2001, when five armed men attempted to shoot their way into the Indian parliament. They were killed, along with eight Indian citizens. The attack was backed by two Pakistan-based militant groups, Lashkar e-Taiba and Jaish e-Mohammed.[73] That India did not immediately retaliate or order preventive strikes against training camps in Pakistan can best be explained by General Musharraf's behavior. Musharraf immediately cut off funding for the two groups and arrested their leaders.[74] Although diplomatic relations were unusually strained for a while (road and rail links were cut for a time), Prime Minister Vajpayee eventually felt satisfied that Musharraf had made a good-faith effort to control terrorism. Musharraf also ended government support of all Islamic militant groups that had ties to the more general Islamic holy war movement, as opposed to indigenous Kashmiri resistance groups.[75] A year later, Indian courts sentenced three organizers of the attack to death under strict new antiterror laws, passed after the parliament attack.[76]

FACTORS CONTRIBUTING TO AN UNSTABLE CLIMATE IN SOUTH ASIA

A Hostile Image of the Adversary Linked to a History of Conflict

India and Pakistan have already fought three major wars in their relatively short history, with violence flaring up almost constantly in between. The wars have not been confined to one time period, but run from the first year of existence for both states (1948) right up to the Kargil War in 1999. In ongoing hostile relationships between states, a belief can develop that war is inevitable. We saw that this belief was particularly strong in American officials in the 1940s and 1950s with regard to the Soviet Union, though the United States had never fought a direct war against the Soviets. In this case, India and Pakistan have fought numerous wars, each one further justifying each state's view of the other as irreconcilably hostile.

Navnita Chadha wrote:

> The most fundamental aspect of Pakistan's enemy image of India is that New Delhi is unreconciled to Pakistan's independent existence. In the early years after Independence, the refusal of the Indian Congress Party leadership to concede legitimacy of the two-nation theory and its public statements about the non-viability of the Pakistani state convinced many Pakistanis that India posed an ideological as well as a military threat . . . Most Pakistanis find Indian threat perceptions of a military attack from Pakistan to be unwarranted, if not absurd . . . in their minds, India's quest for military power lies in its hegemonic designs in South Asia.[77]

Conversely, Chadha writes that India sees Pakistan as a "recalcitrant neighbor" that has consistently refused to accept the realities of the regional balance of power. Many Indians are also convinced that Pakistan is willing to use force and risk war (and indeed has already done so) to gain control of Kashmir. The continual funding and logistical support of terrorists by Pakistan is not only confined to Kashmiri militants, but also to separatists in Punjab, another important Indian state.[78]

Given these circumstances, an "inherent bad faith" model is applicable between India and Pakistan. We might also look for the belief that not only is war inevitable, but since war has occurred so often, a de facto *state of war* also exists between the two countries. Each passing year has only brought with it more suspicion. India remains convinced that Pakistan gives substantial support to Kashmiri separatists, and a political solution is unlikely in the near future. There has always been talk of Indian preventive strikes against terrorist training camps in Pakistan (as well as against nuclear facilities). It is also possible that given the new information about Pakistani sales of nuclear technology, India might feel its fears justified and once again strongly consider preventive action.

Nuclear Capability

The U.S. Department of Defense believes India to have a small stockpile of nuclear weapons components that they could deploy within a few days to a week.[79] Both countries have very small nuclear stockpiles, and therefore only first strike capability. These small stockpiles might easily be wiped out in a pre-emptive strike. The temptation arises therefore in times of conflict to "use it or lose it."

Both countries now have relatively sophisticated delivery capability. Aided by North Korea, in 1999, Pakistan acquired the Ghauri missile, the most advanced of which is the Ghauri III/Abdali, a nuclear-capable missile with a range of 3,000 km, which is the distance from the most westerly points in Pakistan (near the border with Iran and Afghanistan) to the most southerly point in India.[80] India possesses the most advanced missiles outside of the original five nuclear states, which includes the Surya II (with a range of 12,000 km) as well as a submarine-launcheable cruise missile.[81]

Adding to the uncertainty is the fact that both Indian and Pakistani missiles are based on mobile and road/rail Transport Erector Launchers (TELs).[82] That they are easily dispersible arguably strengthens deterrence because neither side can be sure of where the other side's nuclear launchers are (and they are thus unlikely to conduct pre-emptive or preventive strikes). However, the mobility of these launchers also leaves both sides unaware of where the other side's missiles are, making it more difficult to detect activity indicating a launch. Both India's and Pakistan's increasing reliance on ballistic missiles as instruments of deterrence gives decision-makers only minutes to decide upon a course of action in a crisis (as opposed to aircraft-based nuclear weapons, which would take a little bit longer and are more easily detectable).

A RAND study from 2001 concluded that India did not possess the ability (yet) to conduct a "splendid" first strike with nuclear forces.[83] Thus, Tellis concludes, an Indian pre-emptive or preventive strike would be unlikely since it would not preclude Pakistani retaliation.[84] This, of course, refers only to a planned preventive strike, not a crisis situation. In a section on crisis situations, Tellis writes that "policymakers in New Delhi argue that prudence and moral sensibility would demand responses that decelerate the pace of escalation, not speed it up...."[85] This is a sensible argument, but Indian and Pakistani leaders have not always, in the past, conducted themselves during crises in such a manner as to "decelerate" escalation.

Complicating all of this is Pakistan's adamant refusal to follow India's lead in adopting a "no first-use" policy.[86] For Pakistan, (potential) nuclear ability is meant to "even the playing field," and reduce the conventional superiority of its neighbor. In practice of course, this makes a great deal of sense. Pakistan is clearly counting on the element of uncertainty (however slight) to serve as a deterrent against potential Indian aggression. In a sense, it is just making the best of the cards it has been dealt. However, this stance carries its own risks. Pakistan must hope that it can tread the fine line between creating just enough uncertainty to deter an Indian attack, and creating so much uncertainty that it actually *incites* an attack.

Unstable Domestic Political Institutions

In Pakistan's case, no elected Pakistani government has succeeded another in fifty-six years. Pakistan has a violent political history. Many of its leaders have been killed, including Liaquat Ali Khan (Mohammed Ali Jinnah's successor), Zulfiqar Ali Bhutto (who was hung by the military), or have died in mysterious circumstances like the mysterious plane crash that killed Zia ul-Haq in 1988, as well as the numerous recent attempts on Pervez Musharraf's life.[87] Though Cohen concedes that military rule (for instance that of Pervez Musharraf's) can sometimes be more liberal and humane than Pakistan's elected governments, he admits that "the army's vision of Pakistan" has come to define the state.[88] This has the effect of placing Pakistan's nuclear capabilities in the hands of the military (arguably more prone to pre-emption or prevention[89]) and thus helping to fulfill India's worst fears about a confrontational, militaristic Pakistan.

In India, the popularity of the moderate Congress Party of India has been challenged by the right-wing BJP. When calls for war against Pakistan have been made in recent years, it is invariably the BJP politicians who made them. Though Atal Bihari Vajpayee (India's last Prime Minister) might have been said to moderate his party's hawkish tendencies, BJP rhetoric has always been bellicose, and whether or not India actually takes aggressive action, such rhetoric likely only inflames Pakistani fears about Indian intentions.[90] Thus, the relationship between India and Pakistan has all of the elements of Schelling's "reciprocal fear of surprise attack," which might cause war without a "fundamental" cause.

Shifting Balance of Capabilities and Power

There have been numerous shifts in the balance of power in the region between India and Pakistan over the years. Although the "actual power" of a country is notoriously difficult to determine, India has usually been considered to hold an advantage in conventional capabilities. However, how do nuclear weapons figure into the equation? During the Cold War, the United States developed its nuclear weapons program so quickly in part because it was thought by U.S. decision-makers that nuclear weapons would balance Soviet conventional superiority. Pakistan is said to have had very similar motivations in developing atomic weapons. However, is this correct? Or are nuclear weapons so unusable that they effectively cancel each other out, leaving the imbalance in conventional forces? The implication of the conventional imbalance is that there might be an incentive for Pakistan to strike first using nuclear weapons in a conflict, since any long-term conventional warfare would favor India. In fact, Pakistan, unlike India, has consistently refused to enunciate a "no first-strike" nuclear policy. Though such a threat might deter India to a certain extent, it also has the effect of making crisis situations particularly unstable.

There are also numerous thresholds to keep in mind throughout the case. India exploded a "peaceful nuclear device" in 1974. However, that does not necessarily mean that it had the capability to build a usable military nuclear weapon. The thresholds discussed in Chapter 1 of this book are: first, a nuclear program; second, the capability to build a nuclear weapon; third, a small stockpile of nuclear weapons; and fourth, a relatively large stockpile of weapons with a efficient and safe Command and Control apparatus and a survivable second-strike capability. Both countries are now in the third phase of nuclearization, but there have been numerous transition periods. The important thing to note is that there is still a transition period lurking in the future. Thus, this case has particular importance, as the conflict between India and Pakistan is ongoing, not a relic of the past. The perceptions and behavior of Indian leaders in the past have important implications for future crises between the two countries.

While these strategic preconditions are important, the differences between the two countries are not just philosophical; both claim and have fought over the disputed territory of Kashmir. Kashmir is an overwhelmingly Muslim state, but its Hindu ruler opted in 1948 to join the newly formed state of

India, not Pakistan. Since achieving independence from Britain, Kashmir has been a source of extreme tension between India and Pakistan.[91] Much of the problem stems from the nature of the Indian and Pakistani states. India sees itself as a secular state whose success rests on its ability to safeguard the rights of all minorities, including Muslims.[92] A Pakistani-controlled Kashmir would be an insult to a secular India. Pakistan's "two-nations theory" holds that Hindus and Muslims are not just different religious and cultural groups, but indeed different nations altogether.[93] Thus, the political rights of the Muslim nation can be safeguarded only through the formation of a separate nation-state; a Muslim-majority state within India's border is a rejection of the idea upon which Pakistan is based.[94]

In addition, there continues to be conflict over Pakistani sponsorship of militants and terrorism in Kashmir. Though Pakistan has made half-hearted denials of their complicity in aiding Kashmiri militants, they have also made telling comments such as "We don't accept this point that what is happening in Kashmir is terrorism."[95] India, however, sees the sponsorship of terrorism by Pakistan as an attempt to blackmail India. Thus the Indian prime minister recently announced (as others have in the past): "When the cross-border terrorism stops, or when we eradicate it, we can have a dialogue with Pakistan.... We totally refuse to let terrorism become a tool of blackmail. Just as the world did not negotiate with al-Qaeda or the Taliban, we shall not negotiate with terrorism."[96]

Thus, though there are political differences between India and Pakistan, as well as a history of violence dating from the first days of independence, there are also problems that are rooted very much in the present, and they are not at all abstract. [97]

CONCLUSIONS

To date, neither India nor Pakistan has initiated a preventive strike or war, defying the expectations of many academics. But *why* has India not initiated a preventive strike or war? There is an inherent bad faith relationship between the two countries, a nuclear arms race, periods of transition (and thus "windows of opportunity"), a philosophical, political, and territorial conflict, and domestic political institutions that seem to reward bellicose leaders. In addition, the past decade has brought with it an immense upsurge in terrorism on Indian territory, much of it sponsored by Pakistan. In fact there is no single factor that can explain the absence of preventive action between the two states. The three different cases within this case study are representative of very different time periods, each with important (but different) attributes.

The first period discussed, 1982–1984, seems like it should have been a perfect (strategic) time for India to have launched a preventive strike against

Pakistan's nuclear facility. Israel had just initiated a similar strike against Iraq's capabilities, and though it was criticized, it did not suffer any real negative consequences from the action. India certainly had the capability at the time to accomplish the strike against the facility. The only explanation that fits in this case is that relations between India and Pakistan had not yet deteriorated to the point where such a strike would have made sense. Remember that Israeli leaders ordered the strike because of the feeling that if Iraq obtained nuclear weapons, they would not hesitate to use them against Israel, and living under the constant threat of an Iraqi attack was unbearable. But the reports of India's "pre-emptive" plan first surfaced in 1982, when Indian and Pakistani leaders had just recently met for the first bilateral talks in over a decade.[98] Relations did not start to deteriorate until January 1984, by which time the plant had already been in operation for at least two years, giving the Pakistanis' enough time to obtain enough enriched uranium for at least a primitive bomb.

Interestingly, the main source for the *Washington Post* claimed that Indira Gandhi's decision to "defer the pre-emptive strike" was a concern that India's nuclear facilities might be vulnerable to a retaliatory Pakistani air strike.[99] Without corroborating evidence, we cannot assess the veracity of this claim. However, it might make sense, since Pakistan would still have had the capability to attack using conventional means. One might note that in the Israeli case, Iraq was distracted by the Iran-Iraq war, and was thus seen as less likely to retaliate. However, if Gandhi had indeed "deferred" the attack, instead of dismissing it outright, one might wonder if she somehow believed that Pakistan would not have the ability to retaliate in the future. The more likely explanation was that the decision to defer the attack was related to the improvement in Indo-Pakistani relations, and Gandhi decided against the attack, deferring it as a hedge against a future deterioration in relations.

The second period discussed is the 1990 crisis, by which time both countries had the ability to produce nuclear bombs, and possibly even possessed a small stockpile of such weapons. The region seems to have been on the brink of war, even by conservative estimates. After a war started, there was no way of knowing whether or not it would escalate to the nuclear level, but there was at least a good possibility that it might do so. Besides, one might note that the BJP's demands for preventive strikes against terrorist training camps seem reasonable, and in fact is now the avowed policy of the United States. Why then did India not decide upon such a course of action? The crisis in 1990, along with the Brasstacks crisis in 1987, had heightened tensions between the two countries to the point where the region was perched on the precipice of war. Even if Indian leaders had desired only a limited preventive strike against terrorist training camps in Pakistan, they would have had to balance that out against the probability that such an action would most likely escalate into a major war. It is unlikely that Pakistan would have sat back and let India conduct raids in their territory. Instead, Pakistani leaders would almost definitely have taken any Indian movement across the border as a sign of the beginning of a general war and acted accordingly.

The Kargil conflict is important not so much for any consideration of preventive or pre-emptive action, but instead for its implications on the stability of nuclear deterrence in South Asia. The Kargil conflict alerted the world to the possibility that regional deterrence in South Asia was not as stable as previously believed. It also showed that Indian and Pakistani leaders were perfectly willing to initiate a limited conflict under the "protective umbrella" of nuclear weapons. That Pakistan initiated such action likely justified Indian suspicions that Pakistan was "reckless" and "aggressive." The continuous hardening of these "enemy images" has dangerous implications for future action. Instead of confidence-building measures that might over time break the cycle of the inherent bad faith relationship, both countries are only solidifying each other's perceptions.

The last scenario, preventive war planning from 2001 onward, is interesting in that it occurred during the same time period as the U.S. announcement of its strategy of preventive action. However, unlike the United States, India does not have to deal with the question of where to take the battle next. India knows where the terrorists are and it knows which state is aiding them. Why then, has it not acted? It is possible that it is out of a fear of destabilizing the Musharraf government. Musharraf's government is notoriously unstable, and India might consider it to be better than an unknown alternative. However, the distinction must be made between terrorism in Kashmir and the terrorist attack against the Indian parliament. Terrorism and violence in Kashmir, as awful and despicable as it is, has become almost the status quo. In addition, it must be obvious even to Indian leaders that Pakistani support would have no traction were it not for the desires of at least some of the Kashmiris to be independent from India. However, a strike against the parliament of any country is tantamount to an act of war, and monumentally different from border clashes.

Again, Indian leaders would have a difficult time separating a preventive strike against *terrorists in Pakistan*, from the larger conflict with the *state of Pakistan*. However, it is difficult to imagine that the Indian public (as well as leaders) would be able to withstand another attack against the "heart" of India without responding forcefully. The diplomacy of the United States, and efforts by Musharraf to curb terrorism, have been able to restrain India thus far, but it is doubtful whether it would be able to restrain it in the future if another attack of the magnitude of the parliament attack occurred, and could be directly linked to Pakistan.

This case illustrates the difficulty of constructing a comprehensive, yet at the same time concise, theory of preventive war. India's reasons for not striking preventively in 1982 were different than their reasons for not doing so in 1990, which in turn were different from their reasons in 2001. This case highlights the importance of a close examination of the principal decision-makers and their individual perceptions. Such an examination is not always easy, but without it, any theory of preventive war would sacrifice explanatory power for brevity.

6

Preventive War as a Grand Strategy? George W. Bush and "Operation Iraqi Freedom"

On March 19, 2003, the U.S. military, along with a "coalition of the willing," began their invasion of Iraq. At the time, roughly two-thirds of those polled in the United States approved of the war.[1] However, a significant and vocal minority opposed it. President Bush took the United States to war in a climate of division within the United States itself, and between the United States and many of its traditional allies. The initial phase of the war was completed relatively quickly, though a resilient insurgent movement within Iraq still threatens the safety of those within its borders.

This chapter explores the motivations behind President Bush's decision to wage preventive war against Iraq.[2] The use of force, especially in the case of a ground invasion, is one of the most complex and difficult decisions that any administration can face. Numerous factors are necessarily involved, and the relative importance of economics, geopolitics, natural resources, public opinion, and relative military strength should not be overlooked. However, it is undeniable that even in democracies, and especially in the administration of George W. Bush, personality and leadership play a significant role in the decision-making process. The Iraq War seems in many important respects leader-driven, and driven by George W. Bush in particular. That fact is the focus of this case study. What were the most important factors in his decision? Does this case fit into the theoretical framework of preventive war as set out in the first chapter?

In fact, the theoretical framework for preventive war decisions already developed provides clear explanatory power in understanding President Bush's decision to invade Iraq. As was the case in the four previous chapters, not every single "preventive war factor" is visible in this case. In this case too, some factors are more visibly important than others. Moreover, it is important to keep in mind that in each case, each leader is different, and the factors that influence decisions to go to war preventively are given different weight and relative importance by each decision-maker.

That said, the strong personality and bold leadership of George W. Bush accentuate the "personality factors" that drove the preventive war decision-making in this case. Bush's personal worldview—that the world is a dangerous place—his sense of the nature of the threats confronting the United States and the best means to combat them, his stark moral outlook, his resilience to criticism from others, and his propensity for ambitious, high-risk strategies are all important elements in the Iraq War decision. These psychological factors, which have appeared to some extent in other cases, appear in sharp relief in this particular case.

In addition to these psychological traits, other preventive war factors are also evident. Four of the five other factors already discussed in other cases of preventive war seem to be significant in this case. First, there is without a doubt an inherent bad faith relationship with the adversary. Bush's perception of Saddam Hussein as both undeterrable and unable to be trusted to comply with international law were important factors in his decision to act preventively. Second, the link made in Bush's mind between the larger War on Terror and Iraq as a "rogue regime," led him to see preventive action against Iraq as part of a war that was already in progress. Thus, he viewed the conflict with Iraq as somewhat inevitable because of the clash of interests and the beliefs that underlay them. Coexistence was increasingly seen as an unlikely option.

One other particularly important factor that is evident in this case is the belief that the situation favors the offensive. President Bush's somewhat revolutionary doctrine of prevention (as opposed to previous strategies of containment and/or deterrence) is testament to his perception of the necessity of taking the offensive in certain cases. After September 11, the presumption of the importance of offensive thinking became quite clear.

As in all other cases discussed in this book, the individual leader's worldview, his perceptions, and his frames of analysis play an important role. The ongoing controversy over the decision to invade Iraq testifies to the fact that not everybody processes the available evidence, or perceives threats, in the same way. The decision to go to war against Iraq preventively in 2003 was a direct result of President Bush's particular worldview. Thus, it is only by examining his assumptions about the nature of the threat, the relative safety of the global environment, and the optimal means to achieve U.S. goals (in addition to exactly what those goals should be) that we can understand the decision to act preventively against Iraq.

GEORGE W. BUSH AS THE PRIMARY DECISION-MAKER

This book's analysis began with the tentative formulation that the individual leader matters, especially in cases involving preventive war. But how accurate is this presumption? The previous four case studies provide ample support for the view that a leader's perceptions, beliefs, and psychology matter in the decision to launch a preventive war.

However, there has been and remains much debate on the specific question of whether George W. Bush is the prime decision-maker in the United States. Books such as *Bush's Brain: How Karl Rove Made George W. Bush Presidential* as well as many others put forth the proposition that Bush is merely a figurehead for those individuals who really run the country—alternately Karl Rove, Richard Cheney, Donald Rumsfeld, the "Vulcans," the Israeli lobby, the Christian Right, George Bush Sr., or even the Saudi Royal Family.

However, there is overwhelming evidence that refutes the claim that Bush is merely a puppet. Hugh Heclo, for instance, describes Rove's significance as merely "complementing" Bush's own political mind and providing the benefit of his longer experience in the political world.[3] Similarly, even Ivo Daalder and James Lindsay, who are in general critical of Bush's foreign policy, argued that his cabinet—often referred to as "the Vulcans"—were significant not because they directed policy, but rather because their selection signaled Bush's own predispositions in the realm of foreign policy.[4] Likewise, presidential scholar Fred Greenstein talks convincingly about "the vision thing" as one of the central themes of Bush's presidency.[5] Certainly, it would be difficult to find evidence of Bush being railroaded into doing anything that he did not specifically want to do in either of Bob Woodward's books that follow the Bush administration.[6] This evidence points to President Bush as being very much in charge of his own policies.

PRE-SEPTEMBER 11 POLICY TOWARD IRAQ

The decision to invade Iraq did not take place in an historical or political vacuum. In 1991, at the conclusion of the first Gulf War, the United Nations passed Resolution 687, which required Iraq to end its weapons of mass destruction (WMD) programs, recognize Kuwait, account for missing Kuwaitis, and end support for international terrorism. Iraq accepted the terms of the resolution, and on April 18 declared that it no longer had a biological or nuclear weapons program. Later, Iraq was forced to admit that it still had a nuclear weapons program (which had produced about 1 lb of enriched uranium) and four times more chemical weapons than had first been admitted.[7]

The official policy of the Clinton administration when it took office was "regime-change."[8] This policy was made into law in the 1998 Iraq Liberation Act (H.R. 4655), which provided up to $97 million in military assistance to opposition forces in Iraq toward the goal of removing Saddam Hussein from power in Iraq and "promoting the emergence of a democratic government."[9]

In one of President-elect Bush's first security briefings, he was informed that the U.S. and U.K. patrols in the Iraqi no-fly zones had been fired upon or threatened by the Iraqi air defense system in almost every mission. Bush was informed that the Pentagon had five "graduated response options" in response to Iraq firing at patrol planes, ranging from automatic air strikes to more serious options involving multiple strikes against more strategically important targets outside the no-fly zone. The patrols were expensive, putting million-dollar jets at risk every day.[10] There was also a plan named Desert Badger which was the planned response to a U.S. pilot being shot down; it involved measures to prevent the pilot from being captured by Iraqi troops.[11]

Bush was dissatisfied because he felt that U.S. policy was not accomplishing anything besides putting U.S. fighter planes at risk. However, the initial "Iraq planning" that took place within the administration was solely a re-evaluation of the viability of no-fly zones, as well as a push to tighten sanctions against Iraq. In February of 2001, Colin Powell toured the Middle East touting a new plan for "smart sanctions." These new sanctions would target Saddam's military more specifically than had been the case under the previous sanctions regime. The resolve of the allies enforcing the old sanctions was beginning to crumble as evidence mounted that sanctions hurt Iraqi people more than Saddam Hussein.[12]

However, even before the terrorist attacks of September 11, and even while Bush and his team discussed more sanctions, there were indications that the Bush presidency would depart from the policies of the past. Before Donald Rumsfeld became Bush's secretary of defense, he had a talk with the incoming president. Rumsfeld told Bush that the country's "natural pattern" when attacked had been "reflexive pullback." Rumsfeld said he believed that, in contrast, the Bush administration should be "forward leaning," and Bush agreed.[13] This concept of a "forward leaning" policy, as the preventive war against Iraq illustrates, was probably something of an understatement: subtle changes in language can prefigure substantial differences in actual policy.

PRE-SEPTEMBER 11 FOREIGN POLICY

President Bush's foreign policy pre-September 11 lacked a big, organizing paradigm for his views. Bush had strong instincts, but without the broad paradigm of the Cold War to give direction and coherence to his policy decisions, they gave the impression of piecemeal decisions instead of a "grand strategy." Yet, at the same time, his early pre-September 11 foreign policy decisions clearly did show some of the core values and principles that would later form the basis for the Iraq war.

President Bush's general distrust of international institutions and agreements was clearly visible in the pre-September 11 period. One example of this was President Bush's determination to move past the Cold War relationship between the United States and Russia, embodied by the Anti-Ballistic Missile

Treaty (ABM Treaty). The treaty, signed in 1972, was based on the belief that both sides would ultimately be more secure if neither had defensive capabilities, thus assuring "mutually assured destruction." Bush saw the treaty as a relic of the Cold War relationship between the two suspicious superpowers, and hoped to move on toward the type of strategic relationships where neither state would be threatened by the other's nuclear arsenal. It might seem to be a simple observation—that the Cold War was over, and Russia was more an ally than an adversary—but it was a bold one nonetheless, and drew criticism from many corners, including Russian and South Korean leaders.[14]

The Bush administration is intensely skeptical of international institutions that might place limitations on America's ability to act in the national interest. President Bush's withdrawal from the ABM treaty signaled his reluctance to allow international agreements/institutions to impede the United States' freedom of action.[15] It was obvious to Bush well before the terrorist attacks of September 11 that Russia was no longer the major threat facing the United States. Yet, the end of the Cold War had left a void in U.S. grand strategy, which was later filled by the administration's campaign against terrorism. One wonders if another leader would have been as open to seeing the broad paradigm shift from the Cold War to the War on Terror, and the implications of rogue states and WMD as clearly as Bush saw it—after all, the Cold War had been over for twelve years before a U.S. president withdrew from the ABM treaty.

Bush's pre-September 11 foreign policy also suggested the importance and limits of various neoconservative thinkers in his administration. Many of his foreign policy advisors shared similar beliefs and values. Among these beliefs is that American power is ultimately a force for good in the world. Connected to that is the belief that the United States should use its position of unparalleled global dominance to spread the values of liberal democracy overseas.[16] Bush did not necessarily take every option presented to him by his foreign policy advisors, but there was certainly a congruence in basic beliefs about the nature of American power, and the responsibilities and opportunities it conferred on the United States.

Bush famously remarked that he did not need anybody to tell him what to believe, but he did need somebody to tell him where Kosovo was.[17] Overall, it seems that Bush's pre-9/11 foreign policy decisions were generally based on deeply-held personal views and values, but were not formed into a coherent grand strategy for the United States.

His pre-September 11 policy indicates some of the qualities which were later a factor in the decision to go to war preventively with Iraq, such as a reluctance to bind the United States to international institutions and a willingness to challenge conventional wisdom regarding U.S. security policy. However, it would be going too far to see the "seeds" of the Iraq decision in Bush's first few months in office. It is unlikely that without the dramatic impact of the September 11 attacks, the "threat nexus" of Iraq, terrorism, and WMDs would have crystallized as potently as did. However, a glance at Bush's early foreign-policy decisions does show that the basic worldview of President Bush was in place, even if it had not yet focused on the dual threats of terrorism and rogue regimes.

BUSH AS A LEADER

It is not within the scope of this case study to fully examine the character and personality of President Bush. There are numerous biographies and analytical works that do so.[18] However, a brief examination of some of his most important qualities, as they relate to the decision to go to war in Iraq, is certainly necessary. Some of the most important of these qualities are his resilience to criticism, his worldview, which is Manichean in its outlook, and his propensity toward risk-taking in the pursuit of far-reaching and ambitious goals.

Bush's ambitious plans for the United States are readily apparent. In an interview in 2003, Bush revealed that he greatly admired President Lincoln, saying: "He inspires me...the toughest job for a president is to unite the country, to achieve objectives, and I believe the president must set big objectives. And I set big objectives."[19]

The ambitious scope of President Bush's plans is evident in his desire to reshape the Middle East. John Lewis Gaddis, the distinguished historian who heads the Yale Grand Strategy Program, wrote:

> If I'm right about this, then it's truly a *grand* strategy. What appears at first glance to be a lack of clarity about who's deterrable and who's not turns out, upon closer examination, to be a plan for transforming the entire Muslim Middle East.... There's been nothing like this in boldness, sweep, and vision since Americans took it upon themselves, more than half a century ago, to democratize Germany and Japan.[20]

Similarly, Philip Gordon speaks of Bush's plans to "reshape the Middle East" through the application of American power and ideals.[21] And political pundits seem to agree. Allan Murray of the *Wall Street Journal* described Bush's "agenda for remaking the world" as rivaling those of Harry Truman and Woodrow Wilson in its ambition, scope, and idealism.[22] Unlike many politicians who stick to the status quo even while speaking of great changes, Bush's actions have demonstrated his very real commitment to following through on his bold plans.

Even those who disagree vehemently with the policies and vision of the president agree that his goals are striking in their objectives. Thus, Ivo

Daalder and James Lindsay write about a "revolution" in American foreign policy, and assert that Bush's worldview is "radical in its claims and ambitious in its reach."[23] There is little doubt about either; Bush is nothing if not ambitious, and the controversy that has surrounded many of his actions is an indicator of just how sweeping his plans may be.

Paired with President Bush's grand vision for the future of the world is a propensity for taking risks. There are numerous examples of this in his policies. Perhaps the most obvious of these risk-taking actions is the decision to go to war with Iraq. Immediately before the conflict with Iraq began, a loyal Bush strategist noted, "It seems hard to imagine that if the war goes badly, he'll be reelected. This is almost sheer risk from a political calculus."[24]

Putting yourself in President Bush's place in 2002–2003, there were many ways that a war with Iraq could be politically devastating. American casualties might have been high and turned the tide of public opinion against Bush. Other countries might have balked at helping, forcing the president and the United States to stand alone. The war itself might have gone badly in many ways. Evidence of WMD or WMD programs might not be found. Transatlantic relations might be badly, or irreparably, damaged. The Muslim world might have erupted with violence or displeasure. It seemed clear that if the war turned out badly, Bush would have severe difficulties being reelected. This is as big a political risk as any president can take: the willingness to give up their own power in pursuit of a risky policy they believe to be right. There were similar issues at stake in Menachem Begin's decision to strike Iraq in 1981; an election hung in the balance, and Israeli casualties would likely have cost Begin the election. Similar to Begin, Bush made the risky decision of acting preventively and risking lives in a very public manner and very close to an election.

Chief of Staff Andy Card warned the president in February 2002 that congressional elections were coming up in a few months, as well as the presidential election later on—factors that should be taken into account in the planning of a possible war with Iraq. Bush responded: "That is no consideration at all. If we go to war, it will be because the security of America requires it. Timing will have nothing to do with congressional elections or polls."[25]

Part of Bush's resilience—his ability to do what he thinks is right even if doing so subjects him to strong or harsh criticism—comes from the strong belief that he is "on the right side." Richard Perle, a former Defense Department official with ties to the Bush administration, believes that Bush's serenity "comes from the conviction he's on the right course."[26] The same article declares that Bush's confidence in his own decisions "is consistent with his character, which draws sharp lines between good and evil, black and white."[27]

This resilience is also partly rooted in Bush's belief in the role of the president. That is, Bush understands the necessity of having public support for a given policy, but believes that it is the role of the president to create public support and to lead the public. Thus, in a speech made before he became president, Bush declared that "unless a president sets his own priorities, his priorities will be set by others—by adversaries, or the crisis of the moment, live on CNN...."[28]

And just as Bush believes the role of the president is to set the objectives—the "grand strategy" of the country—he also believes that it is just as important not to change those policies because of "bad reviews."[29] Those bad reviews, whether they are from political opponents, other world leaders, or even his own constituents, should not distract a leader from the right course. When that happens, a foreign policy becomes "random and reactive, untethered [to the national interest]."[30]

This resilience to criticism, as well as confidence in decision-making, has very important implications for the decision to wage preventive war. Preventive war decisions are inherently controversial because it is very difficult to obtain the relevant information that "proves" that such action is necessary.[31] Because the risks involved in preventive war lie in the future, such decisions necessarily rely on interpretations of the available evidence. Unlike decisions to attack preemptively, there is unlikely to be public evidence in the form of armies massing on the border, planes on the ground, or missiles in the air to justify preventive action. This is even more true in the realm of catastrophic terrorism and rogue regimes. In the case of terrorism, decisions must be based on judgments of whether human intelligence and "tips" are credible, and rely on the difficult task of distinguishing "signals" from "noise."

Preventive war decisions not only rely on real-world evidence, but also necessarily on the cognitive makeup of the decision-maker. In the case of rogue regimes and WMD, there is rarely any obvious evidence as to the capabilities. The realm of dual-use equipment, nuclear, chemical, and biological weapons programs, is enormously complex, and also relies upon the judgment of decision-makers as to the purpose of the equipment. Machinery that advances peaceful scientific research can also be used to produce weapons of murder. Thus, preventive war decisions rely on the inexact science of divining intent.

Decisions to go to war preventively rely upon the filtering of smaller, less obvious bits of evidence filtered in turn through a leader's worldview and individual perception of threat. An example of this dynamic can be seen in the fact that the Western powers could have stopped Hitler's advance after Germany remilitarized the Rhineland in 1936. Hindsight provides us with poignant evidence that suggests that a preventive attack then would have saved millions of lives, and at a much lower cost than was later required in World War II. However, such a decision, taken in March 1936, would have had to rely on much less evidence than is available retrospectively, and would have required a very specific worldview and threat perception to see Hitler for what he was as early as 1936. Even though Churchill was later famous for recognizing the threat that Hitler represented very early on, he was the lone voice. Not only must the leader appreciate the danger, but also the country must be at least somewhat prepared to follow. How many Americans would have backed an invasion of Iraq before 9/11?

BUSH'S WORLDVIEW

The last of the psychological factors that has relevance in this case is Bush's worldview, or belief system. The questions that help to define a worldview for the purposes of this analysis are a modified version of George's operational code: First, how dangerous a place is the world? Second, what is the role of the United States? Third, what are the greatest threats to American security, and what are the best means of combating them?

Bush sees the world as a dangerous place, a world in which America is threatened by powerful and dangerous enemies. He also sees these enemies as implacable and evil, and therefore sees force as the appropriate tool to combat them. The last aspect of this worldview that is relevant is Bush's perception of the War on Terror as part of a historical trend of good versus evil, and the stark morality implied by such a conflict.

In an address to Congress nine days after the terrorist attacks, Bush described Al-Qaeda, and other terrorist organizations, as heir to the "murderous ideologies of the 20th century," such as fascism, totalitarianism, and Nazism.[32] Thus, in a manner similar to the fight against Nazism in World War II, the fight against extremist and terrorist ideologies was a fight for the future of civilization.

Similarly, only days after the terrorist attacks, Bush spoke at the National Cathedral, and declared, "Just three days removed from these events, Americans do not yet have the distance of history, but our responsibility to history is already clear; to answer these attacks and rid the world of evil."[33]

This remark clearly illustrates Bush's view of America's war on terror as a struggle of "good versus evil." However, it also shows that Bush feels the "responsibility to history," the sense that the United States stands at a pivotal moment in history, and must act not just for the present, but also for the future.

The events of September 11 confirmed Bush's view that the world is a dangerous place, but they did more than that. They made the world seem much more dangerous than it had been before. Whereas before Saddam Hussein might be able to be contained, in the light of September 11, his actions and intentions looked much more menacing. In an interview two years after 9/11, Bush spoke of the effect of the terrorist attacks: "Saddam Hussein's capacity to create harm . . . all his terrible features became much more threatening. Keeping Saddam in a box looked less and less feasible to me."[34]

The second aspect of Bush's worldview that is significant for his Iraq decision is his stark sense of morality. This is the "with us or against us" mentality that has been so often criticized. For Bush, there is no neutrality in the war against terror, no "shades" or "degrees" of cooperation. It follows from this that there could be no distinction between the actual terrorists and countries that harbor terrorists. For Bush, any shades of gray are simply ways of obfuscating what is readily apparent to him: there is good and there is evil, and all of the degrees in between just confuse the issue.[35]

This has particular bearing for preventive war decisions. A stark, black-and-white sense of morality has two effects. It tends to throw into starker relief the dangers and risks of a given threat once a leader like Bush decides that such a threat exists. The lack of degrees, in essence a lack of gradation or subtlety in viewing adversaries, also exacerbates the effects of the "inherent bad faith image" of one's adversary. Evil is evil, and one simply cannot negotiate with evil, especially if its goal is your destruction. By invoking the specter of Nazism in his speeches, Bush consciously or unconsciously equated both the *type* of threat and the *implications* of that threat. The type of threat is *dire*, and the implication of this is that negotiation is not possible, and the conflict will end only when one side has been defeated decisively.[36]

The second effect of this type of worldview is the implication for Bush's view of the United States in this matter. If terrorism—embodied in the threat of Osama Bin Laden and Al-Qaeda—is evil, then it follows that the United States is on the other side, the side of good. This imbues the actions of the United States with an inherently virtuous quality. This contributes to Bush's resilience to criticism, discussed earlier. For Bush, "knowing" that he is on the right side, fighting evil, makes him more resilient to outside critics, whom he believes simply do not see the threat in the same way as he does.

There is a last element that merits attentions here, which is Bush's view of the role of the United States. Throughout the history of the United States, a common metaphor used to describe America's mission is as a "city upon a hill." Based upon John Winthrop's seventeenth-century speech, this metaphor envisions America as an example for the entire world to emulate. After the United States declared its independence from Britain, the metaphor took on an even more profound meaning: the United States, an "empire of liberty," would serve as an example to all the less-democratic countries in the world.

Ronald Reagan—whose legacy President Bush has invoked many times—was fond of this metaphor.[37] However, this metaphor prescribes a *passive* role for the United States. In this metaphor, the United States is a model to be emulated, not a country crusading to bring its values to the rest of the world. A contrast to this is provided in a speech made by Tom Ridge, the former director of Homeland Security, at the London School of Economics in 2005. Ridge made the comment that "freedom is a *conquering* ideal."[38] Whether or not Ridge meant to do so, he unwittingly put his finger on President Bush's conception of America's role, its responsibility to spread, and not simply model, freedom.

George W. Bush's view of the proper role for the United States is far more active than the "city on the hill" formulation. It is not enough for the United States to sit back and merely serve as an example for other nations; it must play a more active role. As will be illustrated later in this chapter, the events of September 11 played an important role with regard to Bush's view of the proper role of the United States. Even if the United States could be content to sit back and be less involved in world affairs before September 11, it certainly could not do so after. As John Lewis Gaddis wrote, "the world, quite literally, must be made safe for democracy."[39] The implication of this in Bush's mind, as evinced by his actions, is that the United States could no longer afford to wait on the rest of the world; it must go out into the world and transform it in order to preserve its security.

There are elements of Bush's worldview—in particular his Manichean outlook—that are remarkably similar to Reagan's outlook. The "with us or against us" policy of the White House following September 11 was partly a product of Bush's sense of the world as divided into two camps, good and evil. This parallels both John Foster Dulles' and Ronald Reagan's view of the nature of the Cold War. Similar to these two leaders, Bush sees the world (especially after 9/11) as divided into opposing camps of good and evil; for him there is no political middle ground because this is more a moral than a political issue. This has implications for Bush's propensity for "inherent bad faith images," which are closely associated with the tendency to see problems in moral rather than political terms.[40]

THE IRAQ WAR AS "INEVITABLE"

In January 2004, former treasury secretary Paul O'Neill published his recollections of his time in the administration of George W. Bush. O'Neill had served as secretary of the treasury for almost three years before being fired by President Bush. In his book, *The Price of Loyalty: George W. Bush, the White House and the Education of Paul O'Neill* (written with Ron Suskind), he detailed a number of accusations against President Bush, including his belief that Bush had come into office with the intention of attacking Iraq and that the events of September 11 merely gave him the opportunity, or excuse, to do so.

O'Neill's account details in dramatic fashion what he perceived as the administration's focus, right from the inauguration, on removing Saddam Hussein from power. In one of his vignettes, O'Neill recalls a meeting that took place ten days after the inauguration in which those present focused on the threat that Iraq posed to the region. O'Neill wonders in his memoirs whether or not the meeting was "scripted," perhaps as part of some elaborate ruse to convince him that action against Saddam was necessary. O'Neill's suspicions aside, there seems little evidence that the meeting was about anything more than rethinking the traditional approach toward the Iraq regime, which even Clinton's cabinet admitted was not working.[41]

Similarly, O'Neill complains that there was never any "rigorous talk" about the "sweeping ideas" that were driving the administration's planning with regard to Iraq.[42] However, the "sweeping ideas" that were being discussed were really not sweeping at all. In fact, Bush had simply come into office and decided that U.S. policy—a contradictory program of sanctions against the Iraqi people, risky flights into the no-fly zone, and talk of both removing Saddam from power and at the same time "containing him"—was not working. This realization was not revolutionary. In fact, one might argue that what was surprising was that it took almost a decade for the U.S. government to realize how ineffective its policy was toward Iraq.

Besides Paul Wolfowitz, whose predisposition toward invading Iraq was well known, there is no evidence that the administration was doing anything more than attempting to reformulate a policy that was not working. O'Neill even grudgingly admits that at that meeting Rumsfeld declared specifically that his objective was *not* to get rid of Saddam Hussein.[43]

O'Neill's accusations of an administration dead-set from the beginning on invading Iraq has been picked up by many others.[44] An article published in the prestigious journal *International Security* simply takes for granted that O'Neill's accusations are true. Chaim Kaufmann wrote, "Postwar revelations have made clear that President Bush and top officials of his administration were determined from early 2001 to bring about regime change in Iraq."[45]

Yet, without any corroborating evidence, it is difficult to give much weight to these accusations. The information available to date suggests strongly that Iraq was certainly on the agenda immediately after Bush took office (O'Neill was right about that). However, the evidence also suggests that to the extent that it was on the agenda, discussion of U.S. policy toward Iraq was based solely on the premise that the current policy of sanctions and no-fly zone patrols was putting U.S. planes at risk while accomplishing little. Thus, President Bush and his advisors (some of whom no doubt would have preferred Saddam Hussein be toppled) discussed the different options available to the United States, including "smart sanctions," funding opposition leaders within Iraq, and military plans should U.S. planes be shot down in the no-fly zone. Bob Woodward writes (from the recollections of several in attendance at the meeting) that in the first meeting with the Joint Chiefs of Staff concerning Iraq, Richard Cheney fell asleep several times, and President Bush seemed preoccupied with the mints on the table; not what one would expect if Cheney and Bush had indeed already decided to remove Saddam from power.[46]

In the end, the best argument against O'Neill's argument, and those that are similar in nature, is that the war against Iraq did not begin until March 2003. In the first part of Bush's presidency, pre–September 11, there was very little said about Iraq; the administration's tax-cut proposal was its major priority. In the aftermath of September 11, when 81 percent of those polled *supported* military action to remove Saddam Hussein, the United States attacked Afghanistan, which arguably presented a tougher challenge for the U.S. military.[47] And finally, after a quick, decisive victory in Afghanistan, the Bush administration waited for well over a year—including two major and time-consuming diplomatic pushes at the United Nations—until it launched a preventive war against Iraq.

There is always a temptation to read history backward, to start from what happened and then see "clues" that reveal how a given event was inevitable. However, reality is often both complicated and messy, and one would need considerably more proof than either O'Neill or his proponents can provide in order to demonstrate that the Iraq War was in any way inevitable. Rather, the events of September 11 dramatically altered President Bush's worldview, and made the Iraqi threat appear far more urgent than it had been previously.

SEPTEMBER 11 AND THE TRANSFORMATION OF THE BUSH PRESIDENCY

On Tuesday, September 11, 2001, the United States was attacked by terrorists linked with Al-Qaeda, a loosely organized network of Islamist extremists. This act of terrorism had profound consequences for the United States, as well as the rest of the world. The most immediate consequence was the U.S.-led invasion of Afghanistan, and the toppling of the Taliban.[48] However, the events of September 11 also started America down the path that ultimately led to the invasion of Iraq two years later. This section analyzes the ways in which September 11 transformed the Bush presidency, and brought to the fore many of the factors (both psychological and strategic) that led ultimately to the preventive war against Iraq.

Some of those closest to Bush insist that September 11 did not change anything in his character. His wife, Laura Bush, for instance, insisted that the qualities that came to the fore in the aftermath of the attack—"decency, firmness, resolve, patience—were already formed in his character."[49] It would be hard to argue that any of the commentators who disagree with Laura Bush know the president better than his own wife; however, there was an overwhelming sentiment in the wake of 9/11 that Bush had somehow been "transformed."

Perhaps it is enough to say that the Bush presidency, as well as his public persona, was changed dramatically by the events of September 11. It is useful to think of the transformation in terms of these two separate, but linked, elements. It is almost impossible to argue that the public persona of President Bush—the leadership skills, vision, and the confidence that the public sees—was not transformed. This theme of transformation was picked up on almost immediately in the aftermath of the terrorist attacks. After a prime-time news conference on October 11, an editorial in the *New York Times* declared:

> The George W. Bush who addressed the nation at a prime-time news conference yesterday appeared to be a different man from the one who was just barely elected president last year, or even the man who led the country a month ago. He seemed more confident, determined and sure of his purpose, and was in full command of the complex array of political and military challenges that he faces. . . .[50]

Many others agreed. Noted presidential scholar Fred Greenstein declared that there had been a "quantum jump in Bush's mastery of policy specifics"; that in contrast to the first phase of his presidency, where he had seemed "strikingly out of his depth in the Oval Office," there had been a "dramatic increase in competence," comparing his growth to the on-the-job growth of Harry Truman.[51] John Lewis Gaddis compared Bush's transformation to that of "Prince Hal" into King Henry V.[52] Bush himself, when asked if the terrorist attacks had changed him, characteristically answered: "I'll give you a hint, I liked coming to the ranch before September the 11th; I like coming to the ranch after September 11th."[53] But Bush's typical reticence cannot change what others have observed: a dramatic change in Bush as a leader.[54]

However interesting the personal growth of Bush is, what is most relevant to the question at hand on preventive war is the way in which the events of September 11 transformed the presidency of George Bush. September 11 transformed the Bush presidency in two ways: by giving Bush an historic sense of purpose and direction, a sense of his place in history, and also by changing the administration's perception of the major threats facing the United States.

In the first months of his presidency, Bush had been struggling. He had lost the popular vote during the presidential election and won the office of the president only through the intervention of the U.S. Supreme Court. Five months into his term, Bush's approval ratings had dropped to 50 percent.[55] He had some policy successes, most notably his $1.35 trillion tax cut, but overall his first months in office seemed to be marked by the lack of an integrated vision. Stephen Hess of the Brookings Institute noted that when the Republican Party lost Senator James Jeffords of Vermont, Bush lost control of the Senate as well as of the legislative agenda.[56] A former speechwriter of Bush's, David Frum, put it succinctly: the administration lacked a "big, organizing idea."[57]

However, the terrorist attacks of September 11 gave George W. Bush both an "organizing principle" for his administration and the sense of "mission" which drove him to accomplish his new goals. A sense of mission implies something very specific in this case. The events of September 11 not only gave Bush a purpose and direction for his administration—to secure the future safety of the United States—but a sense of urgency as well. An aide of Bush's said of him "he never wants to stand again on another pile of rubble. He'll err on the side of being overly vigilant."[58] That is where the "sense of mission" comes in. As Fred Greenstein put it, the events of 9/11 have contributed to Bush's somewhat remarkable growth as a leader in the immediate aftermath of the terrorist attacks. Some evidence of his sense of mission is provided by Greenstein, who points out that Bush met with his NSC twenty-four times in the month following the terrorist attacks.[59] This immersion in policy details, as illustrated vividly by Woodward's *Bush at War*, from a president previously disinterested in the details of policy-making, is evidence of the urgent sense of purpose felt by Bush after September 11.

September 11 not only gave Bush a hypercharged sense of mission, but radically realigned the threat perception of the administration with regard to Iraq. Of the United States' pre-9/11 policy toward Iraq, Bush said: "I was not happy with our policy. Prior to September 11, however, a president could see a threat and contain it or deal with it in a variety of ways without fear of that threat materializing on our own soil."[60]

Similarly, while before the oppressive and aggressive regime of Saddam Hussein was mainly a problem for those living in that region, it had now become a problem for the United States as well. Once Bush made the link in his mind between terrorism, rogue regimes, and the spread of democracy in the Middle East, the implication was that the status quo in the Middle East was no longer acceptable.[61] It had been acceptable to some degree for Clinton, who did not feel any direct threat from Iraq, and thus felt little sense of urgency for his stated policy of regime change, which explains his reliance for the most part on the much more conservative strategy of dual-containment. Even Condoleezza Rice argued that "time was on the side of the United States" with regard to Iraq in 2000.[62] However, after September 11, a sense of urgency was unquestionably present in Bush's mind.

This is a clear illustration of one of the most important and lasting effects of the 9/11 terrorist attacks: the way in which they transformed the Bush presidency by shifting his most fundamental perceptions of threat, and forcing the administration to reevaluate its basic assumptions about the nature of the world. This had drastic consequences for issues like Iraq even though there had been little empirical change. If he were asked, even President Bush might admit that Saddam Hussein was no more dangerous on September 12, 2001 than he had been on September 10, 2001. What had changed was not the material circumstances of the threat, but the lens through which that threat was viewed.

There is ample evidence of this change in perception. In an article written before taking office, Condoleezza Rice acknowledged that Saddam Hussein would always pursue WMD, but that his regime "was living on borrowed time" and a "classic statement of deterrence" was the most effective strategy for dealing with Iraq.[63] But, as Richard Cheney put it, American action in Iraq was due not to new evidence, but old evidence viewed in a new light, "through the prism of our experience on September 11."[64] Similarly, in a joint press conference with Tony Blair in 2003, President Bush commented:

> Actually, prior to September the 11th, we were discussing smart sanctions. We were trying to fashion a sanction regime that would make it more likely to be able to contain somebody like Saddam Hussein. After September the 11th, the doctrine of containment just doesn't hold any water, as far as I'm concerned. . . . *My vision shifted dramatically after September the 11th, because I now realize the stakes.* . . .[65]

Without the events of September 11, the Bush administration might have relied on previous strategies of containment and deterrence to "keep Saddam in the box," but not anymore.

In fact, Bush, and his administration, seemed to have avoided a major psychological pitfall. The tendency of political leaders when confronted with new information that might contradict central beliefs is to focus on the "idiosyncratic acts of a few individuals," in order to preserve the consistency of their belief system.[66] Had he taken this psychological route, Bush might be expected to blame Osama Bin Laden, and Al-Qaeda, and stop there. Instead, Bush seems to have exhibited enough cognitive flexibility to assimilate new information almost seamlessly into a modified cognitive framework, instead of changing the information to fit an outdated framework.

THE TRANSFORMATION OF THE U.S. SECURITY STRATEGY

Along with transforming Bush's presidency, the events of September 11 pushed President Bush to reconsider the fundamental assumptions underlying the grand strategy of the United States. The product of that reassessment was the National Security Strategy (NSS) of the United States released in September 2002. It was a fundamental reformulation of U.S. security doctrine, and drastically reordered the major threats against the United States. Though the NSS was not written as a rationalization or justification of action against Iraq, an understanding of the assumptions underlying it provide key insights into the motivations for later preventive action against Iraq.

The NSS wastes little time in asserting the changed nature of the global environment. In the letter accompanying the doctrine, President Bush asserted:

> Enemies in the past needed great armies and great industrial capabilities to endanger America. Now, shadowy networks of individuals can bring great chaos and suffering to our shores for less than it costs to purchase a single tank. Terrorists are organized to penetrate open societies and to turn the power of modern technologies against us.... The gravest danger our Nation faces lies at the crossroads of radicalism and technology.[67]

Therein lies the first of the fundamental shifts that are contained within the document: the greatest threat that faces the United States is no longer the specter of Communism and the "evil empire," nor is it the ethnic conflict and civil wars that immediately followed the end of the Cold War. Instead, the most dangerous threat to the United States is that posed by networks of terrorists, potentially armed with the weapons of mass destruction. The shift enumerated in the previous quotation is a shift in the sources of threat, it does not (yet) say anything about the implications of that shift.

Even if the NSS had done nothing more than reorder the priority of threats facing the United States, it would have been an important document. However, that was merely a taking-off point for the more ambitious and transformational aspects of the document. The following section, also contained in Bush's letter accompanying the NSS, enunciates the implications of the shift in threats:

> [A]s a matter of common sense and self-defense, America will act against such emerging threats before they are fully formed. We cannot defend America and our friends by hoping for the best. So we must be prepared to defeat our enemies' plans, using the best intelligence and proceeding with deliberation. History will judge harshly those who saw this coming danger but failed to act. In the new world we have entered, the only path to peace and security is the path of action.[68]

This, then, is the most revolutionary aspect of Bush's new formulation of America's security strategy: the doctrine of prevention.[69] Security studies scholar Lawrence Freedman writes that the collapse of Soviet power followed by the "apparent rise of super-terrorism—together suggested that deterrence was no longer relevant as a strategy."[70] This is a bit of an overstatement, and

Freedman later pulls back to say that in fact, the NSS of 2002 did not relegate the twin strategies of containment and deterrence to the dustbin, but rather focused on prevention only as one strategy among many.[71]

Which situations would require preventive action? Was there any blueprint for when such action would be necessary, a set of conditions that would mark a state for preventive action, as opposed to containment, deterrence, bargaining, or another strategy? In fact, the fine print of the NSS, as well as numerous statements made by President Bush, indicate that there was a very rough yardstick by which potential threats might be measured. The acid test of a threat would be whether or not the United States believed a given adversary to be deterrable.

Gone was the old assumption that deterrence was a "catch-all" strategy. Giving the graduation address at the U.S. Military Academy at West Point in 2002, shortly before the publication of the NSS, President Bush provided a rationale for the "new thinking" of his administration:

> For much of the last century, America's defense relied on the Cold War doctrines of deterrence and containment. In some cases, those strategies still apply. But new threats also require new thinking. Deterrence—the promise of massive retaliation against nations—means nothing against shadowy terrorist networks with no nation or citizens to defend. Containment is not possible when unbalanced dictators with weapons of mass destruction can deliver those weapons on missiles or secretly provide them to terrorist allies.[72]

Thus, the difference between the "old" threats to the United States (Soviet Union, spread of Communism, rise of China, etc.) and the "new" threats was that the new threats were undeterrable; terrorism is undeterrable. However, this was always true, and September 11 was not the first incident of terrorism against the United States, nor even the first to take place on American soil. The difference, pointed out by Bush in his West Point address as well as in the NSS, was that the proliferation of technology allowed small groups access to planes and weapons that had previously been the exclusively domain of states, thus giving rise to the fear of "catastrophic terrorism." And while the United States was not always pleased that other states had access to WMD (i.e., U.S.S.R. and China), they were seen as "deterrable."[73]

Here one can see the importance of global norms of accepted behavior. Thomas Schelling wrote, "Khrushchev [and the Soviets] understood the politics of deterrence."[74] Therein lies the problem: it takes some type of mutual understanding for deterrence to work. The logic of mutually assured destruction (MAD) provided a measure of safety because both the United States and the Soviets believed it to be true. The understanding of deterrence was that while the United States would not be able to prevent an attack, it would retaliate and inflict harm on the perpetrator, thus deterring potential aggressors by the threat of harsh retaliation.

The NSS of 2002 proposes that there can be no mutual understanding between the United States and terrorists. How does one deter suicide bombers whose goal is to die? Does the logic of deterrence work on extraterritorial groups such as loosely linked terrorist networks? Robert Jervis writes of terrorists that "[they] cannot be contained by deterrence. Terrorists are fanatics, and there is nothing that they value that we can hold at risk."[75] Historian of the Cold War John Lewis Gaddis agrees, asking, "How does one negotiate with a shadow? . . . How does one deter somebody who's prepared to commit suicide?"[76] This was certainly the conclusion of George W. Bush in the aftermath of September 11.[77]

THE LINK BETWEEN DETERRENCE, TERRORISM, AND ROGUE REGIMES

The most important aspect of the NSS was the link that it drew between terrorists and rogue regimes. The NSS declares that the link lies primarily in the intentions of the two—both are undeterrable, both pursue WMD, and both have the potential ability to strike without warning (through the use of biological or chemical weapons, or a "dirty bomb" released in the United States). Of these two positions, the most controversial conclusion is that these "rogue regimes" are undeterrable.[78] The NSS assumes them to be so because they are risk-prone (in contrast to the supposedly more risk-averse Soviet Union), and thus more likely to develop and use WMD (which are considered by them to be a "weapon of choice").[79] These conclusions, though controversial, provide the foundation for the rationale of possible preventive action against both terrorists and rogue states.[80]

The Bush Doctrine also highlights a number of motivations that are factors in decisions to act preventively. These arguments, as enunciated in the National Security Strategy, are not specifically focused on Iraq, yet they form the core of the arguments that were later used by the Bush administration to explain their preventive action. We have already seen these factors in our other cases.

First, the NSS makes clear that the Bush administration believes the situation to favor the offensive. Bush's comment—"the only path to peace and security is the path of action"—makes clear the importance (in the minds of the administration) in taking the initiative. In fact, it is not just that the situation favors the offensive, but in fact requires the offensive. In fact, the implication of this argument for Iraq is clearly spelled out in the NSS; the scale of destruction made possible by rogue states (and terrorists) equipped with WMD makes preventive action necessary. The risk is too great to wait on events.

The NSS groups terrorists and certain "rogue states" (Iraq, Iran, and North Korea) together in declaring that the nature of these new threats means that the United States "can no longer rely on a reactive posture." Terrorism and these rogue states are inextricably linked in that there is always the possibility that rogue states which have or are pursuing WMD would give these weapons over to terrorists and attack western countries by proxy. In fact, this possibility is mentioned specifically by Bush in his commencement address at West Point, when he declared, "Containment is not possible when unbalanced dictators with weapons of mass destruction can deliver those weapons on missiles or secretly provide them to terrorist allies."[81] Bush's use of the term "unbalanced" indicates his perception that there is something intrinsic to the psychology of leaders like Saddam Hussein which makes any kind of mutual understanding impossible, and makes deterrence impossible to achieve.

The second "preventive war factor" that the NSS illustrates is the notion of an inherent bad faith relationship with the adversary. Part of this image of the adversary is illustrated by the view that they are undeterrable. There are two important components of Bush's bad faith image of these enemies. The first is the view that conventional strategies of deterrence will not work against terrorists and rogue regimes because they play by a fundamentally different set of rules (or norms). In order to make this dichotomy clear, Bush takes a bit of creative license in declaring:

> In the Cold War, weapons of mass destruction were considered weapons of last resort whose use risked the destruction of those who used them. Today, our enemies see weapons of mass destruction as weapons of choice. For rogue states these weapons are tools of intimidation and military aggression against their neighbors.[82]

However, it is debatable that U.S. leaders during the Cold War would have completely agreed with this assessment of the "restraint" of the Soviet Union, especially in the years immediately following World War II. The earlier chapter on preventive war thinking in the Truman and Eisenhower administrations makes clear that many elements of the bad faith image were present there as well.

The other aspect of the bad faith image of the adversary is that the United States cannot trust either terrorists or rogue states to stand by any agreement that is made. This belief, especially in regard to Iraq, is made clear by the many statements by President Bush stating that Saddam Hussein cannot be trusted to keep his word on any inspection agreements.[83]

In his West Point address, Bush foreshadowed the conflict with Iraq by declaring: "We cannot defend America and our friends by hoping for the best. We cannot put our faith in the word of tyrants, who solemnly sign nonproliferation treaties, and then systemically break them."[84]

This image of the adversary—as one with whom no agreements can be made and who does not conform to the norms of international conduct—will be explored in further depth shortly, but at this point, it is striking how clearly this imagery is enshrined in America's National Security Strategy.

The last factor that is illustrated by the NSS is the view that war, or serious conflict, is inevitable. In a striking parallel to similar declarations by leaders in several of the previous four cases, the NSS is clear in enunciating that not only is war inevitable, it has already begun. However, this "war" is different in nature than previous wars. Unlike wars of the past, the war described in the NSS is not against a single adversary, country, group, or individual. Instead, this broad-based war is a "war on terror."[85]

It is clear from Bush's actions and words that this was not just a clever turn of phrase meant to make a point. Rather, Bush seems to feel that the United States really is in a state of war, whether or not others agree with him. The implication of this is that it is not "business as usual"; the rules and even laws that govern peacetime do not necessarily apply anymore. Whether or not one agrees with the policies they embody, the passage of the Patriot Act in 2001, the controversy over the status of detainees and their treatment, the semantic wrangling over the issue of torture, and the status of "enemy combatants" indicate clearly that Bush perceives the United States to be in a time period of extraordinary circumstances which require something more than the usual methods.

A clue to the transition from a domestic war on terrorism to the focus on rogue regimes and proliferation of WMD can perhaps be found in the anthrax attacks of October 2001. As Bush scholar Alexander Moen points out, the anthrax attacks reinforced the view that terrorists would eventually strike with biological, chemical, or nuclear weapons in an "asymmetric" manner. Another attack on the homeland of the United States had some influence, therefore, in driving home the point that the administration needed both an "offensive" and a "defensive" option in the War on Terror. A strategy tailored to dealing with immediate threats (or tailored to retaliation) would not protect the United States.[86]

PLANNING FOR WAR WITH IRAQ

Immediately after the terrorist attacks of September 11, the question was raised as to whether Iraq should be included in a list of possible targets in the new "war against terror." In an NSC meeting on September 12, Secretary of Defense Rumsfeld raised the question of Iraq. Rumsfeld was speaking for both himself and Paul Wolfowitz, his deputy and a well-known advocate of regime change in Iraq when he wondered whether "they should take advantage of the opportunity offered by the terrorist attacks to go after Saddam immediately."[87] Secretary of State Powell could not contain his displeasure at the thought of going after Iraq, and later complained, "What the hell, what are these guys thinking about?"[88]

One of Powell's main concerns was the stability of the international coalition that was being put together for the War on Terror. Powell was sure that the coalition was ready to go after Al-Qaeda, but was worried that it would begin to fall apart if the president extended the scope of the war so soon. The disagreement between Powell and Bush was emblematic of the larger issue concerning the nature and importance of coalitions. The president replied to Powell that he did not want other countries dictating any terms or conditions for the War on Terror. He said, At some point, we may be the only ones left. That's okay with me. We are America.[89]

It is sometimes tempting to make too much of isolated comments, and give them significance after the fact because they fit in with a particular theory. However, there is no doubt that this comment is significant, as it fits in not only with a theory, but also with Bush's own actions. The divergence between Powell and Bush over the relative importance of coalitions and multilateralism highlights Bush's take it or leave it attitude toward these strategies. In Bush's view, they were useful for the help and legitimacy they provided. However, he did not want the desire for a large coalition to dictate policy direction; Bush's willingness to go it alone, if necessary, was insurance against that happening.

In the beginning, the discussion of whether or not to invade Iraq was closely tied to worries over whether fighting in Afghanistan would be too difficult, and turn into a quagmire, as it had for the Soviets. Wolfowitz made the point in NSC meetings that attacking Afghanistan would be uncertain and risky. He worried that hundreds of thousands of American troops would wind up bogged down in the mountains of Afghanistan with no end in sight. He also estimated that there was a "ten to fifty percent" chance that Saddam had been involved in the September 11 attacks. Iraq, he argued, was a "brittle, oppressive regime" that would break easily. For these reasons, Wolfowitz actually argued for going after Iraq instead of Afghanistan.[90]

Yet, aside from Wolfowitz, few in the administration seemed to be pushing hard for action against Iraq. Powell argued that options should be kept open—including Syria, Iraq, and Iran—but only if there was evidence found linking them to September 11. Rumsfeld declared that "any argument that the coalition wouldn't tolerate Iraq argues for a different coalition" but stopped short of recommending action against Iraq. Vice President Cheney also argued against action in Iraq, noting that the United States would "lose momentum" in the War on Terror and "lose our rightful place as good guy."[91]

In a September 17 meeting with the NSC, President Bush ended debate on the issue of Iraq for the time being. Bush declared that, while he believed Iraq was involved in September 11, he did not have the evidence to back up his assumptions, and would not strike them at that point. He ordered his military advisors to keep working on plans for action against Iraq, but indicated that nothing would happen in the near future, the near future was Afghanistan.[92] An indication of Bush's desire to maintain focus in the war against Afghanistan came later when the president turned down a routine request to strike Iraqi targets in the no-fly zone. "If you strike close to Baghdad, which turns on all the warnings in Baghdad, then the clarity of the mission becomes confused."[93]

Though the Bush administration had decided to go after Afghanistan in the aftermath of 9/11, the problem of Iraq was still in the back of everybody's mind. After the president's September 17 decision, Secretary Rumsfeld ordered Gen. Tommy Franks not to "forget about Iraq." However, this should not be taken as evidence of a broader conspiracy to target Iraq. Rather, Rumsfeld's warning was meant to remind General Franks of the almost daily U.S. flights in the Iraq no-fly zones. General Franks took the comment in exactly this way, later recalling that "at some point I knew America would have to change or abandon its containment strategy, which had not succeeded in ensuring Saddam Hussein's compliance with U.N. sanctions. . . . Planning for that day . . . was the only wise course of action."[94]

OIL AND THE MOTIVATION FOR WAR IN IRAQ

One common charge against the U.S. war in Iraq is that it was motivated by oil. This accusation generally takes one of two forms. The first is that President Bush invaded Iraq to secure oil supplies for the United States; the second is that he went to war to secure oil contracts for the huge oil conglomerates that have a close relationship with the Bush family. This motivational attribution is incorrect, and it only takes a short glance at some of the facts to dispel notions of a "blood-for-oil" conspiracy.

Iraq was the first country in the Middle East region to have commercial oil development. Iraqi oil reserves are the third largest in the world at around 112 billion barrels, behind Saudi Arabia's 260 billion barrels and Canada's 175 billion.[95] However, in the Middle East region, Iraqi production capacity is nowhere near that of Saudi Arabia's. Saudi Arabia produces 8m barrels a day, with the "spare capacity" for 2.5m barrels a day more in emergency situations.[96] Iraq produces only about 2.5m barrels a day. Even at its peak in 1980, when Saddam pushed production capacity to pay for the Iran-Iraq war, output was only 3.5m barrels a day. In 2002, Iraq represented only 3 percent of total global daily production.[97]

The first accusation leveled against President Bush—that the invasion of Iraq was designed to secure more oil for the United States—faces a number of problems. First, it is not at all clear that the invasion of Iraq would help the United States in any appreciable way. Energy experts have estimated that it will take a $5 billion infusion of cash just to keep the oil infrastructure from falling apart in the near future. In order for Iraq to increase its production capacity to 4 million barrels a day, it is estimated that it will take $30+ billion and at least a decade.[98] That is an optimistic estimate; Deutsche Bank placed the number at closer to $40 billion and two decades time.[99] This is a very large expenditure for not very much in the way of potential gains. While the United States imports significant amount of oil from the Middle East, Iraq by itself represents little of the U.S. import totals.

Immediately prior to the war, the United States imported 463,000 barrels a day from Iraq, which was the United States' sixth-largest supplier behind Canada, Saudi Arabia, Mexico, Venezuela, and Nigeria. Thus, immediately prior to the war, Iraq represented only 3.9 percent of U.S. oil imports, and only about 2.27 percent of total U.S. oil demand.[100] While not insignificant, the United States could easily stop importing oil from Iraq completely and not experience any major setbacks. After the United States invaded, U.S. imports of Iraqi oil rose to 706,000 barrels a day in November 2003, but then fell back to 596,000 in November 2004.

Second, there was a significant possibility that Saddam Hussein would destroy the oil infrastructure and wells before being defeated. In 1991, while retreating from Kuwait, Saddam blew up nearly 700 wells, causing an environmental disaster and more than $20 billion in damage. There was the significant possibility that Saddam would do the same to his own country if he felt his own defeat was imminent.[101]

The second criticism leveled against Bush is that the war against Iraq was motivated by the desire to gain lucrative oil contracts for Bush's friends in the oil business. However, this charge disregards the general rule that war is not good for oil companies. If war benefits any major segment of the business world, it is arms manufacturers. The price of oil itself might go up when there is uncertainty, but the shares of oil companies do not necessarily follow. In fact, falling share prices in oil companies during the buildup to the war indicate that the major oil companies were quite apprehensive about military action in the Middle East.[102] Halliburton, the much-criticized company that Richard Cheney ran from 1995 to 2000, received only $50 million in contracts for oil-related work orders out of the predicted $100 billion in reconstruction work needed in the aftermath of the invasion.[103]

To believe that U.S. action was motivated primarily by oil, one would have to believe that the United States was willing to spend upwards of $100 billion (for the war and resulting occupation), as well as tens of billions of dollars just to return the oil fields to previous production capacities to facilitate—if all went well—a moderate increase in supply and a few oil contracts, all at least a decade away.

Iraq has significant amounts of oil in reserve, and the Middle East in general is a very important part of the globe in geopolitical terms. There is little doubt that President Bush and his advisors took into account the region's oil production capabilities in their decision-making process. However, such thoughts were generally directed at making sure that a U.S. war did not destabilize the entire region or cause short-term prices to skyrocket. Almost all references to Iraqi oil in Woodward's account of the decision-making process are instances of Bush and General Franks trying to devise a strategy to prevent Saddam from immediately torching the Iraqi oil fields, or of Bush's hopes that Iraqi oil revenues would help "fast-track" any new regime's entrance into the global economy.[104]

PHASE TWO OF THE WAR ON TERROR: IRAQ

Toward the end of December 2001, military planning for Iraq—which had been going on quietly in the background—began to become more focused. I. Lewis "Scooter" Libby Jr., a longtime Washington insider and member of the Bush administration, told Bob Woodward that it was around this time that he became convinced that Bush was "determined to deal with the issue of Iraq." He believed that the president was "well on the road to deposing Saddam Hussein."[105] It is clear, at the very least, that much work was being done in the military to revise old war plans for a potential conflict with Iraq. War plans for Iraq had not been updated since the Gulf War, and Gen. Tommy Franks had been ordered to rethink the entire plan, essentially starting from scratch.[106] However, the only options explored at this point were those that would *not* commit the nation to war.[107]

Publicly, Iraq was put in the crosshairs of the Bush administration during the State of the Union address on January 29, 2002. In that speech, eight months before the publication of the NSS (2002), and fifteen months before the war on Iraq, President Bush foreshadowed those two events. In his speech, Bush referred to an "axis of evil," comprising Iraq, Iran, and North Korea. However, Iraq received much more attention in the speech than did those two other regimes:

Iraq continues to flaunt its hostility toward America and to support terror. The Iraqi regime has plotted to develop anthrax, and nerve gas, and nuclear weapons for over a decade. This is a regime that has already used poison gas to murder thousands of its own citizens—leaving the bodies of mothers huddled over their dead children. This is a regime that has agreed to international inspections—then kicked out the inspectors. This is a regime that has something to hide from the civilized world.

In addition to beginning to make the case against Iraq, Bush added that "time is not on our side. I will not wait on events, while dangers gather. . . . Our War on Terror is well begun, but is only begun. . . ."[108] David Frum, one of the writers of that speech, later claimed that it was designed to specifically target Iraq, with Iran and North Korea being added on later, almost as an afterthought.[109] What the speech accomplished was to link together the War on Terror with Iraq; the conceptual link between the two was the notion that both were concerned with the pursuit of WMD; and "rogue" states such as Iraq might give WMD, or provide other forms of aid, to terrorist groups. Additionally, the sense of time running out and not waiting while "dangers gather" reflected the urgency felt and presage the later concept of a doctrine of preventive action.

Days after the State of the Union speech, Secretary of Defense Rumsfeld had a meeting with General Franks in which they discussed the progress of Iraq war plans. Franks had finished the new plan, which could be executed as a unilateral U.S.-only war. Op Plan 103 called for an eventual ground force of 300,000 troops. Franks explained that he would be comfortable starting the war on approximately ninety days' notice.[110]

However, for the moment, plans for a potential invasion of Iraq were in the form of concepts—like "shock and awe"—and ideas, not specific dates and plans. On February 13, President Bush said only that he would "reserve whatever options" he had.[111] Later in the month, however, abstract plans became more concrete.[112] On February 28, General Franks provided Secretary of Defense Rumsfeld with a list of 4,000 possible targets in Iraq. Around the same time, Vice President Cheney, while planning a March trip to the Middle East, asked General Franks what countries might be "ripe for solicitation" for help in a potential war against Iraq.[113]

About a month later, on March 21, General Franks met with commanders of the Army, Navy, Air Force, and Marines—those who would be in charge of the war—and told them to review the war plans with an eye toward realistic planning. "Don't let yourself believe that this won't happen," he told them. Franks had become convinced by this time that the United States was going to war. Nothing short of Saddam and his family fleeing the country would stop the countdown—and, as a practical matter, that was not going to happen.[114] However, Franks does remember that Secretary Rumsfeld repeatedly made sure that military planning had not, and would not, bring them beyond the "point of no return."[115]

In the summer, Bush foreshadowed the upcoming publication of the NSS by declaring at West Point Military Academy that containment of, and deterrence against, the new threats were no longer possible. Though the speech did not specifically mention Iraq, it was hinted at in a section where Bush spoke of not being able to defend America by "hoping for the best," a none-too-subtle jab at Clinton-era foreign policy. Furthermore, the "word of tyrants" could no longer be taken as a guarantee of America's safety. This speech presaged the NSS, which was released in September 2002.

The release of the NSS marked a turning point in the administration's public rhetoric. This is partly because of the links drawn in the NSS between the War on Terror and the possible acquisition of WMD by terrorists and "rogue regimes" such as Iraq that are also pursuing WMD and are no longer considered to be "deterrable."

In September 2002, Bush and members of his administration began much more vocal and strident calls for "action" against Iraq. This period marks the beginning of a concerted strategy of coercive diplomacy against Iraq. Coercive diplomacy is best understood as a strategy that seeks to compel a certain behavior through the threat of potential consequences and the use of "carrots" or incentives for compliance.

Between September 2002 and March 2003, the Bush administration worked to form an international coalition to pressure Saddam, first to allow inspectors back in, then to abdicate power and leave the country. The "stick" of this diplomatic approach was the threat of American military action. While the NSS was the theoretical embodiment of the Bush strategy, the White House wasted little time in moving forward in a very practical manner.

On September 3, the White House Iraq Group (WHIG) met for the first time. The group, composed of senior staffers, cabinet members, and advisors, formulated a plan for "selling" the Iraq war in the months of September and October. This was not a cynical plan to deceive the public, but rather a discussion of the steps needed to prepare the U.S. public, and the rest of the world, for the possibility of war.

The first decision made was to ask Congress for a resolution formally authorizing the use of force. The next morning, Bush met with eighteen influential Senate and House representatives in the White House to discuss the issue of Iraq. In this meeting, Bush made clear his desire for Congress to vote on a resolution before the October 11 recess, less than five weeks away. Foreshadowing later arguments against the war, Senator Dianne Feinstein (D-CA) declared that she did not see any new evidence against Saddam that warranted going to war at that point.[116]

On September 12, Bush announced to the United Nations General Assembly that he would ask the Security Council for a new resolution on Iraq. He referred to the regime as a "grave and gathering danger," and demanded that it stop support for terrorists and destroy its weapons of mass destruction. Though seeking a diplomatic solution, Bush warned that the UN must act within weeks. It is interesting to note that Bush did not mention resuming weapons inspections in Iraq, though his aides later leaked that the United States would not oppose inspections, so long as they resumed within a few months and resulted in the "immediate destruction" of Saddam's weapons.[117]

Though Bush's UN speech did not specifically mention the use of force, the White House soon made clear its backup plan should the diplomatic route not work. On September 19, President Bush asked Congress for a resolution formally authorizing the use of force against Iraq. In his speech to Congress, Bush asked for authority to "use all means, including force" to disarm Iraq and dislodge Saddam Hussein from power. In a telling comment to a reporter later that day, Bush noted that "if you want to keep the peace, you've got to have the authority to use force."[118]

It seems clear that from at least September 2002, the Bush administration was engaged in an effort to coerce Saddam Hussein to allow unfettered access for new weapons inspections, or failing that, to leave the country. Thus, the increase of public rhetoric threatening the use of force, even the actually military planning for an invasion, can be viewed from two perspectives. It can be viewed as supporting the credibility of the coercive diplomacy the White House was engaged in, as providing Saddam Hussein with evidence of what might happen should he not comply with the international community. Alternately, the public diplomacy aspect could be viewed as a smoke screen to divert attention from a decision that had already been made.

It is likely that both played a role in Bush's thinking. In fact, it seems clear that Bush's decision to remove the threat of Saddam Hussein had already been made by September 2002. "Removing the threat" meant either allowing inspectors back in to verify the destruction of all weapons—not as some had argued to find them[119]—destroying all weapons, or removing Saddam from power. As Colin Powell declared in a comment to reporters, "one way is perhaps with inspectors playing a role. We see regime change as another way." Powell went on to describe the latter as the more "effective and desirable outcome."[120] Similarly, General Franks stated the "policy goal" as removing Saddam from power. This goal would hopefully be accomplished by diplomacy, but that diplomacy had to be backed up by a credible threat of force in order for it to work.[121] The administration believed that as long as Saddam Hussein remained in power, there was always the possibility that he might change his mind, kick out inspectors, and begin a WMD program again. In fact, this was the specific analysis of an NSC official.[122]

It is not possible to pinpoint the exact moment of decision, a meeting where Bush decided to act against Iraq. It is only possible to document the dual nature of Bush's strategy—the diplomatic push for inspections and then regime change, and the military planning for an invasion that took place simultaneously. There is no doubt that had Saddam left there would have been no war. On the other hand, there was little doubt that barring that unlikely development, there would be.

In early October, the House and the Senate voted approval for a resolution authorizing the use of force in Iraq, by a margin of 296–133 and 77–23, respectively.[123] Though President Bush still maintained in public that a military option had not been decided upon, the Joint Resolution passed by Congress gave Bush authority to use force against Iraq should he deem it necessary.[124]

On November 8, the United Nations Security Council voted unanimously for a new resolution that threatened "serious consequences" should Iraq not comply with a new inspections regime. The vote came after several weeks of difficult negotiations over the language of the resolution. In particular, France and Russia provided major obstacles to U.S. efforts to toughen up the language of the resolution. In the end, the unanimous passage of the resolution (even Syria, Iraq's neighbor and ally, voted for it) was a major diplomatic coup for the United States.[125]

However, the unanimous declaration could not disguise that there was a growing divergence between the United States and other countries. Some countries seemed to view a war as justified only if Iraq "flagrantly violated" the new inspections regime. For Bush, the resolution was a step, but only a step, toward the larger goal of regime change. For the time being, the White House was content to wait until Iraq had submitted its list of weapons programs. Iraq had agreed, grudgingly, to the resolution and promised to allow new UN weapons inspectors into the country on November 18.[126]

On December 8, the United States took possession of Iraq's weapons declaration. The United States was so impatient that it insisted on seeing the reports immediately—scrapping plans to have the reports screened for information that might potentially be used to make a nuclear weapon. Iraq's weapons declaration was nearly 12,000 pages long, and "proved" (according to Iraq) that it had no prohibited weapons program. The Bush administration thought differently.

Vice President Cheney insisted that the president declare Iraq in "material breach" of the UN resolution without even reading the report, so convinced was he that it was a smoke screen. Rice, Rumsfeld, and Bush, however, agreed that they should carefully inspect the document before making any public pronouncements as to its veracity. The UN resolution that was passed the previous month required a false declaration and a failure to cooperate before serious consequences were considered. On the surface, Iraq appeared to be cooperating, even if its report was incomplete and misleading.[127]

While the public debate over the inspections regime raged on, military preparations continued in the background, out of the public eye. On November 26, General Franks had sent Secretary Rumsfeld the plan for mobilization of troops for war. Franks requested the deployment of 300,000 soldiers. However, notifying 300,000 troops that they would be deployed to the Middle East in a few months could not be done quietly. President Bush stepped in, declaring that he did not want the deployment of forces to limit U.S. options. If 300,000 troops were deployed, diplomacy would be over. Rumsfeld solved the problem by issuing deployment orders in smaller segments, "dribbling out" the orders. The numbers that did reach the press, such as the 60,000 soldiers that the *New York Times* reported on December 8 were enough to keep pressure on Iraq without committing the United States to war.[128]

Even by the end of December, Bush's private and public comments maintained two separate and somewhat contradictory notions. Bush told Spanish president Jose Maria Aznar that "at some point, we will conclude enough is enough and take him out. He's a liar and he has no intention of disarming." However, in the same breath he used to scoff at the Iraqi weapons statement, Bush insisted that the United States would be "measured in its response."[129]

On Thursday, December 19, Secretary of State Powell declared Iraq to be in material breach of the UN disarmament resolution. Powell called the 12,000-page declaration a "catalogue of recycled information and flagrant omissions." Chief UN weapons inspector Hans Blix was slightly more cautious in his assessment, but also agreed that there were "inconsistencies" in the report, which contained "little new information." Blix added that the lack of evidence means that "one cannot have confidence that there do not remain weapons of mass destruction."[130]

On December 21, DCI George Tenet met with Bush and the principals to present the case for WMD in Iraq. The presentation included nothing new, and Bush commented that he did not think the public would understand the examples given by Tenet, which were "underwhelming." Tenet defended his presentation, and declared that it was a "slam dunk case" against Iraq. Though the presentation itself needed work, Tenet's reassurance carried a great deal of weight with Bush and Cheney, who ordered more work done on the presentation.[131]

By Christmastime, there seemed to be a growing consensus within the White House that the inspections regime was not working. The international coalition that had voted for the first UN resolution was beginning to fracture. The pressure that had been put on Iraq initially seemed to be letting up. Bush believed that Hussein was figuring out how to "work" the UN inspectors, buying more and more time. In a meeting with Rice immediately after Christmas, Bush declared: "He's getting more confident, not less. He can manipulate the international system again. We're not winning. Time is not on our side here. Probably going to have to, we're going to have to go to war."[132]

In a cabinet meeting on January 6, Bush's tone was more subdued, and he only declared that it did not appear as if Saddam was complying, but added that there was still time. However, in a later meeting with Republican leadership, Bush was more candid, admitting that there was a "good chance" he would have to commit U.S. troops to war.[133]

For the month of January, Bush stuck closely to the same script; in public, he told the press that Hussein must disarm, or there would be serious consequences. In private meetings, the tone was much harsher, and Bush often barely stopped short of declaring war.[134]

In retrospect, it seems clear that by early January, the decision to go to war had been made. By this time, all of the principals seemed to believe that the United States would eventually go to war. In early January, Bush had taken Cheney aside and said, "Look, we're going to have to do this, I'm afraid. I don't see how we're going to get him to a position where he will do something in a manner that's consistent with the UN requirements, and we've got to make an assumption that he will not."[135]

On January 13, Bush asked Secretary of State Powell for his support in his decision to go to war. Powell assented.[136]

On January 27, Hans Blix made his final report to the UN Security Council. It concluded that Iraq had not complied with the previous UN resolution, and had not given conclusive evidence that they had dismantled their weapons programs. However, France, Russia, and China continued to argue that the inspections were working, and should be continued.[137]

The White House was uniformly against going to the UN for a second resolution on Iraq. Even Powell thought that it was not necessary. However, British prime minister Tony Blair had promised his political party in the UK that he would get a second resolution, and was confident that the United States and the UK could rally support for it. In a meeting on January 31, Blair asked Bush, as a favor, to ask the UN for a second resolution. Bush agreed.[138]

On January 5, Secretary of State Powell made the case for war to the United Nations.[139] Powell asked DCI Tenet to sit behind him while he made his presentation, as further validation of the intelligence being presented. Powell asserted that Iraq possessed "biological weapons-factories on wheels," and had possibly produced up to 25,000 liters of anthrax. Powell also asserted that intelligence reports showed that Hussein "was making nuclear weapons, and rockets and missiles to deliver them."[140] He also highlighted the links between Al-Qaeda and Iraq, after being pushed to do so by Cheney throughout the week.[141]

In mid-February, Bush told Secretary Rumsfeld to slow down troop deployments, as it was not yet clear when war would start. Bush's main allies, the UK, Australia, and Spain, were all having domestic political trouble that necessitated a second UN resolution. However, the United States and the UK found that they would likely not get a majority vote in the Security Council for the second resolution, and certainly not the unanimous vote they had gotten the first time. After almost a month of diplomatic wrangling, the United States was still unable to gain a majority for the second resolution. The final straw seems to have been Bush's conversation with the leaders of Chile and Mexico, both of whom indicated that they would not vote for the second resolution.

On March 17, in a public address, President Bush gave Saddam Hussein an ultimatum: Leave the country within forty-eight hours or the U.S.-led coalition would invade and remove the current Iraqi regime from power. Bush cited as reasons for the invasion Saddam Hussein's flouting of international law and the thirteen resolutions passed by the United Nations; the Iraqi regime's previous use of biological weapons against its own people; the regime's continuing efforts to obtain WMD; its reckless aggression against neighboring countries and its own people; and its links with terrorist groups such as Al-Qaeda.[142] Saddam defiantly replied that he would not leave, and on March 19, the U.S.-led invasion of Iraq began.[143]

THE RHETORIC OF WAR: REVISITING
THE PREVENTIVE WAR FACTORS

What can we say at this point of the psychological factors that influenced Bush's decision to go to war? One of the most apparent factors was Bush's perception of Saddam Hussein. His image of Hussein had several important facets. He believed the Iraqi leader to be untrustworthy, he believed him to be aggressive, and he believed him to be a risk-taker. These three separate convictions combined to imply to Bush that Saddam was not deterrable, in any conventional sense. His untrustworthiness implied that any inspections regime, any international agreement that was signed, was not enough. Bush's perception of Saddam as deceitful was so ingrained that any conflicting information (Saddam appearing to comply with UN resolutions) would be either ignored or rationalized as a ploy. Thus, in an interview with Diane Sawyer, Bush declared: "I wouldn't trust a word he said. He—he's deceived and lied to the world in the past. He's not going to change his stripes."[144]

Similarly, after Hussein agreed to comply with UN inspections in early September 2002, Bush declared: "All they've got to do is look at his record, his latest ploy. He's not going to fool anybody."[145] What Bush really meant was that he would not be fooled by Saddam Hussein.

That Bush believed Saddam to be aggressive is indicated by his repeated reference to Saddam's invasions of Kuwait and Iran, his attempt to assassinate a former U.S. president, and his use of biological weapons against Iraqi citizens. Secretary of Defense Rumsfeld, in making the case for war, declared that no other living dictator matched Saddam's record of aggression.[146]

The third notion, the supposed irrationality of Saddam Hussein, reinforced the belief within the Bush administration that Hussein could not be deterred any longer. Bush's repeated characterization of Saddam as a "madman" implies a certain lack of rationality.[147] As noted, deterrence involves a degree of mutual understanding. It can therefore only work when the party being deterred understands and cares about the costs and risks of disobeying. If two states have drastically different ideas of what will happen if one of them "cheats" or disobeys, then deterrence cannot work. For Bush, Saddam's repeated noncompliance with UN resolutions indicated that he (Saddam) believed he could do so with impunity.

These different facets of Bush's view of Saddam Hussein—his bad faith image of the Iraqi leader—combined to produce a conclusion, and with that a prescription for action. The conclusion was that because of a variety of factors—Saddam was deceitful, aggressive, and irrational—Saddam must give up power or have it taken from him. The implication, or prescription, of this conclusion was that, given past experience, Saddam would not leave peacefully, he was dangerous, and the United States must therefore act to remove him from power.

The second factor that was evident in this case was Bush's belief that a serious conflict was inevitable. There are two elements to this. The first is the more general belief that the United States was already involved in a war on terror, and had been since September 11, 2001. The second is the more specific idea that a conflict with Iraq was inevitable, in addition to being part of the larger war on terror. A critic could argue that a conflict with Iraq was inevitable only because Bush pushed the country to the brink of war, and it was therefore bound to invade Iraq eventually. However, for Bush, a conflict with Iraq was inevitable because of the combination of Iraqi intentions and capabilities. Iraq might not have WMD yet (though Bush clearly believed they did), but once their capabilities matched their aggressive intentions, it would be too late for the United States to act. Bush's perception of Saddam's intentions was that he was so aggressive and evil that a world in which Saddam was the leader of Iraq was simply too big a risk to take. Furthermore, Bush's public declarations make clear that his image of Saddam had become calcified, and there was little chance that his perceptions would change significantly, even if Saddam's behavior had.

This view that conflict with Iraq was inevitable had important implications for the third preventive war factor that appeared in this case; the belief that there were significant advantages in taking the offensive. The Bush administration had already argued that, in the more general sense, preventive action was warranted against terrorists simply because they could not be deterred in the conventional sense, nor could a war be fought against organizations without territory, without a state apparatus. How did that argument come to be applied to Iraq as well?

For Bush, the link between the two was the issue of weapons of mass destruction. If a rogue regime such as Iraq came to possess WMD—and given his assumption that deterrence was unlikely to work against Saddam—the only effective solution was to act preventively to make sure that Saddam never acquired WMD. The nature of delivery for WMD—the possibility that

Iraq might give WMD to terrorists, or use a "dirty bomb"—meant that an attack might come without warning. The threat of the Cold War—a nuclear missile launch—was no longer the "doomsday scenario." Instead, it was a suitcase bomb in an airport, or a small amount of smallpox leaked into the air. The high level of threat from such a scenario, combined with the small amount of warning and the relative difficulty of tracing such an attack, implied that there was little that could be done once Iraq acquired these weapons. Thus, the only way to contain the new type of threat against the United States was to act before the threat fully materialized. In essence, if the United States waited until it had irrefutable proof, it would be too late. This is not an argument likely to garner universal support, but such is the nature of preventive war.

The last factor that was significant in this case was the logic of Bush's worldview, which was the lens through which all of the other factors were viewed. As discussed previously, Bush's worldview had a number of important components. First, it was defined by a stark moral code—a Manichean outlook—that envisioned the United States as embroiled in a historic battle against evil, whether embodied in the form of terrorists or Saddam Hussein. Second, Bush saw the world as a particularly dangerous place, a view that was confirmed after the events of September 11.

The last important aspect of this worldview was Bush's view on the use of force. Specifically, Bush saw the use of force as an important tool in defending the United States against the threat of terrorism and WMD. This might seem to be a matter of common sense, but there is a wide spectrum of views on the utility of force, as well as how comfortable leaders are with its use. Some leaders see the use of force as a last resort, or even as not a viable option. For Bush, force might be an option of last resort if regular and coercive diplomacy failed, but it was definitely an option.

This particular worldview had some very important implications in the decision to go to war preventively. The first effect was to amplify the other factors found in this case. Bush clearly believed Saddam Hussein to be dangerous, and to either have WMD or to be actively pursuing them. But for somebody possessed of a significantly different worldview, such beliefs would not necessarily lead to the decision to go to war. Indeed, that was the conclusion of many opponents of the war, who did not agree that war was necessary. Without the particular outlook that characterized Bush's psychology, one might believe that Saddam was not an imminent threat who required immediate action. In effect, Bush processed the available evidence in a manner very different from those who did not support the war. The logic of Bush's worldview suggested that preventive war was an eminently reasonable option when confronted with the threat posed by Saddam Hussein.

Thus, those who argue that there was no new evidence are missing the point in explaining Bush's actions. It was true that the evidence had not changed significantly in the past ten years. However, what had changed was the sense of urgency brought on by September 11, which reinforced Bush's perceptions of the world as a dangerous place, and thus magnified threats, especially those that were connected with terrorism and WMD.

CONCLUSIONS

The 2003 war against Iraq was an historic occasion, the first application of the Bush administration's revolutionary doctrine on the preventive use of force. It is not the first time that a preventive war has been fought, but it is the first time a country has published a justification for preventive action before the fact.

This case illustrates many of the preventive war factors that were present in the previous chapters. There was an inherent bad faith image of the adversary, the view that conflict was inevitable, and the view that the situation favored (in this case, demanded) taking the offensive. This case thus provides further support that these factors are linked to preventive war decisions. However, just as in other cases, these were contributing factors, and cannot alone explain the war. The psychology of the individual decision-maker plays a very important role, and can either work against these factors (by dismissing them or playing them down) or fortify them. In this case, these preventive war factors interacted with President Bush's worldview, acting as catalyst so that one reinforced and strengthened the other.

The important elements of Bush's belief system for this case were: his view of the world as a particularly dangerous place, his sense of the nature of the threats confronting the United States and the best means to combat them, and his stark moral outlook. These component values and beliefs acted as a prism, magnifying and amplifying the threat of Iraq in the mind of George W. Bush (as well as many others). All of these different elements—the different facets of his worldview combined with the other preventive war factors—coalesced to produce the decision to initiate preventive war against Iraq.

Of course, one need not replicate the exact psychological makeup of President Bush for preventive war to occur. His exact thought processes and the events that led to the Iraq War were unique. What is important is to separate the idiosyncratic factors from those that are generally linked to preventive war decisions. In this case the most salient aspects of Bush's worldview were already in place before September 11, but it took an act of catastrophic terrorism to drastically change both the administration's perceptions of threat and the strategy best suited to combat those threats.

7

Conclusion:
Preventive War
in Perspective

A THEORY OF PREVENTIVE WAR

One purpose of analysis is to draw useful theoretical inferences. What inferences can we draw from these case studies? Although they are drawn from disparate regions of the world and different time periods, a closer inspection suggests that there are continuities.

Leadership, Psychology, and Preventive War

One particularly important point that comes out of these case studies is the significance of individual leaders and their perceptions. In the three instances of preventive action discussed in this book, it was individual leadership that was ultimately responsible for the decisions. All of the factors discussed throughout the cases are important, but leaders—their psychology, their leadership styles, and their judgments—play key roles. Thus, it was Menachem Begin's unique psychology—in particular the experience of the Holocaust—that made the threat of a nuclear Iraq seem more dire, and international institutions seem less reliable. The information available suggests strongly that, in a similar situation, Shimon Peres would not have ordered the attack on Osiraq.

It is apparent that preventive action requires the leadership of decisive individuals. Preventive action, to a greater extent than pre-emption, is a positive action. Pre-emption is a response to an imminent threat, and it would likely require special circumstances for a leader to choose *not* to pre-empt given the opportunity. For a leader to order a preventive action, however, requires a high degree of self-confidence. In Begin's case, his confidence (even certainty) in his own actions came from his understanding of the lessons of the Holocaust. The comparison of the threat of a nuclear Iraq with the Holocaust implicitly justifies almost any action necessary to stop the development of nuclear weapons, especially those that might one day be aimed and used against the Jews and Israel. This belief not only makes it legitimate to destroy the Osiraq reactor, but makes such action a *moral duty*. It was this view—that it was his duty as a leader to destroy the reactor—which gave Begin the self-assurance to order the strike.

Anthony Eden provides another example of a decisive leader with strong views of the nature of the threat facing Britain, and the "right" course to choose. Eden's decisiveness came primarily from the belief that Nasser represented a newer incarnation of the tyrannical dictators his country had appeased before World War II. Eden's comparison of Nasser to Hitler and Mussolini suggests that he had made up his mind to use force; one does not use such powerful analogies to recommend negotiation. In addition, Eden took the nationalization of the canal very personally, turning a conflict between Egypt and Britain into a personal battle between Nasser and Eden in which there was "only room for one."

In the case of the Iraq War, it was clearly President Bush's confidence in his own assessment of the threat and decision-making ability that led to the preventive war decision. That this decision was as controversial as it was provides further evidence for the importance of individual threat perceptions. Preventive war requires individuals to interpret the available evidence, which is, by necessity, never conclusive. Leaders who decide to take preventive action must have interpreted that evidence—often circumstantial—in the light of their own beliefs, worldviews, and threat perceptions. Because not everybody will process the available evidence in the same way, or see the threat as such a potential danger, preventive war decisions require a leader with strong confidence in his actions as well as the ability to weather strong criticism. This is clearly illustrated in the case studies of the three leaders who ordered preventive action.

But is the opposite true? Are leaders who decide against preventive action "weak?" The answer is that they most certainly are not—at least intrinsically. Even in cases where a decision-maker did not initiate preventive action, the "strong leader" factor was evident. Thus, it was President Eisenhower's unique insight into the nature of the Soviet threat that changed U.S. strategic planning. Previous planning, for the "crisis" or "danger" year, had emphasized windows of opportunity, and spurred preventive war thinking within the government and military. Eisenhower's contribution was to see that the conflict with the Soviet Union would last decades, not years. This was a significant insight, and dramatically altered U.S. national security policy. His confidence in his own vision and beliefs led him to push his New

Look defense policy through the bureaucracy, and ultimately led to the decision not to pursue a strategy of prevention.

Leadership as a Catalyzing Factor

An explanation for preventive war that focuses on the individual leader must necessarily take into account leaders' perceptions of power, morality, stakes, reputation, and threats. Thus, declining power is significant, but it is the *fear* of declining power that is ultimately relevant for individual decision-makers. Based on pure capabilities, the declining power factor is not present in the Suez case. And yet, it is obvious that the perception of Britain's loss of influence, status, and prestige weighed heavily on Eden's mind.

The inherent bad faith image is also very important, and it is unlikely that preventive action would occur without this factor being present. It is this perception—of a hostile, unpredictable, untrustworthy adversary—which forms the basis for preventive war thinking. Without this factor, none of the other factors would assume much importance at all in decision-makers' minds.

One possible gauge of the strength of the bad faith image is the use of particular historical analogies that compare an enemy to a historical figure such as Hitler or Mussolini. Such analogies, if they are used in earnest, il- lustrate that an adversary is someone with whom there can be no negotiation, no appeasement. The use of such analogies suggests that forceful action must be taken, and any plan of action that resembles appeasement must be avoided at all costs. Again, this factor is heavily dependent on individual psychology. Thus, evidence suggests that the bad faith image the Indian Bharatiya Janata Party (BJP) politicians (certainly those who advocated preventive strikes) held of Pakistan in 2000 was significantly stronger than the one held by Indira Gandhi in 1982 when she decided not to strike the Pakistani nuclear plant.

The "bad faith image" factor is also closely linked to the idea that war or serious conflict is inevitable. It is possible that a state may see competition with a friendly state as inevitable. But, a *war* is seen as inevitable only against a state that is thought to have hostile intentions. This view, that war is inevitable, leads to preventive war when leaders feel that they ought to attack at once while they have some advantage—window thinking. This type of thinking was particularly notable in the case of the United States, where advocates of preventive war suggested that if war with the Soviet Union was inevitable, then the United States should initiate it at "the most propitious moment."

A situation in which there is perceived to be an advantage in the offense can be an important factor, but is not necessary to a general explanation of preventive war. It can undoubtedly help to explain some instances of preventive action, World War I for instance, but as the analysis here suggests, this situation is clearly not necessary or sufficient to explain all preventive action. In the first U.S. case, for instance, the belief that the offense held an advantage led to the doctrine of pre-emption—preventive war thinking in that case was based on entirely different arguments.

Risk-Taking and Preventive War

In Chapter 1, I pointed out two schools of thought regarding risk-taking in international politics. This is an important subject, and has particular relevance for preventive war. Preventive war decisions—because of their reliance on incomplete information, assessments of an adversary's intent, and interpretations of material circumstances—inherently require a leader to take on a certain amount of risk, but how can we explain differences in different leaders' willingness to accept this burden? Is it dependent upon the situational context of a situation? Or is the willingness to accept risk a quality that can be attributed to an aspect of a leader's psychology?

One point that this analysis makes clear is that it is not just the decision to initiate preventive action that requires a degree of risk-acceptance. Obviously, such decisions do require this, but so do some decisions not to initiate preventive action. Of course, leaders may not initiate preventive action because they are unwilling to bear the risk associated with such a venture. But there is also a certain amount of risk that accompanies the decision *not* to initiate preventive action. As an example, President Eisenhower's decision to more or less abandon planning for a possible preventive war in favor of the "long-haul" strategy carried with it a great deal of risk. What if Eisenhower had misinterpreted the available evidence? What if future events suggested that a preventive war waged in 1954 might have averted something much worse later on? The point here is that we should not fall prey to the false assumption that only decisions to *initiate* war involve risk, or the opposite, but equally false assumption that all decisions to *not* initiate preventive action are made by leaders who are risk-averse.

What other conclusions can we draw about the relationship between risk-taking and preventive war? While this work cannot put to rest the debate over which factor, context, or personality, is more important with regard to risk-taking behavior, it does strongly suggest that both must be taken into account. Here is why: Any discussion of preventive war is *inherently framed in terms of losses.* By the time leaders have decided to consider preventive action, they have already framed a given issue in terms of something bad that may happen in the future, that is, they are in the domain of losses. This is as true of the two cases where preventive action did not happen as the three cases in which it did. If this is true, and it applies to all discussion of preventive action, then it cannot (alone) explain instances where leaders choose to initiate preventive war. This conclusion then brings us back to the importance of individual psychology, where we must determine not just whether something is framed in terms of losses or gains, but how a "reference point" is calculated, whether an individual is predisposed toward taking or avoiding risks, how dire the risks of action or inaction are perceived to be, along with numerous other variables.

Democracies and Preventive War

All of the states examined in this work—Britain, Israel, the United States, and India—are mature representative democracies. Randall Schweller asserted in a 1992 article that democracies are less likely to initiate preventive war than nondemocracies. His theory is that the "costs of war" are spread out more in democracies than nondemocracies, and thus "prior to risking the high domestic political costs of large-scale war, democratic elites require something more than the assumption of a potential future threat based on the projection of an irreversible decline in relative power."[1] He thus argues that leaders of democracies require evidence of a "clear and present danger," as well as repeated provocations, before initiating preventive war. It is possible that regime type has a contributory effect on the likelihood of preventive war, but such a claim cannot be substantiated by cases that examine only one type of domestic structure, as in this book.

Nonetheless, the case of President Bush is instructive in that there was no "clear and present danger" to the safety of the United States—or at least not an uncontroversial one. Additionally, the Iraq War seems to show that circumstances, such as the September 11 attack, can make a democratic populace feel sufficiently threatened that a preventive war becomes a possibility. At the very least, the Iraq case shows that there is likely not anything about democratic regimes that makes them inherently less likely to wage preventive war, if the nexus of threat, opportunity, and leadership converge.

Previous research has not considered the moral aspect of preventive war. However, it is clearly an important factor in the decision to initiate or refrain from preventive war. Both Eisenhower and Truman cited morality as a major reason for not initiating preventive action against the Soviet Union. They both believed that such action was "un-American" and immoral. However, Eden, Bush, and Begin's framing of the threat had the opposite effect: it was highly moral to initiate preventive war in the circumstances they believed Britain and their states to be in. Thus, it seems clear that anything that makes preventive action seem more "moral" in the minds of decision-makers has the effect of taking away one major restraint, and making preventive action more likely.

Reputation and Preventive War

Another factor that deserves mention is the importance of state reputation to decision-makers. In at least two of the cases, the individual leader's perception of their state's reputation was central to their decision, though it had different implications for each. In the case of the United States, Eisenhower and Dulles firmly believed that a major problem of a strategy of preventive war would be that the United States would end up destroying the very ideals it purported to be fighting for. They believed that such aggression would forever tarnish the ideals of the United States—which they believed deeply in—even if it succeeded in defeating the Soviet Union.

In the case of Britain, one of Eden's primary concerns was for Britain's reputation in the international arena. He was convinced that if Britain let Nasser "get away with it," then that would be the end of British influence throughout the world. However, Eden's strong desire to keep secret the collusion with Israel and France also suggests that he anticipated adverse effects on Britain's reputation should they be "found out." However, even the factor of reputation is reliant on the perception of the individual leader. For Eden, the possibility that Britain would gain the reputation of a weak country outweighed the possibility that it might be thought to be an immoral country.

PREVENTIVE WAR FACTORS: A COMPARISON

There is no single factor that can explain all instances of preventive action. In each case, different factors take on different levels of importance, according to the priorities and perceptions of individual leaders. That said, it is important to understand how other factors contribute to individual leaders' decisions to initiate preventive action. Table 1 provides a visual illustration of the ways in which each of the factors played out in the circumstances of the different cases.

DECLINING POWER IN RELATION TO AN ADVERSARY

The most comprehensive discussion of motivation for preventive war, Levy's "Declining Power and the Preventive Motivation for War," focused almost exclusively on this factor. In fact, this factor did appear in three of the five cases, although it did not have the effect that Levy predicted when it appeared. An important reason is that leaders calculate relative, not absolute decline. In the cases of India and the United States (Cold War case), the issue was parity, not imbalance. Thus, the important issue here was not the fact of the decline, but what the end result of the decline

Table 1
Preventive War Factors*

	Britain (1956)	Israel (1981)	The United States (1946–1954)	India (1982–2002)	The United States and Iraq (2003)
Declining power in relation to an adversary	✓**		✓	✓	
Inherent bad faith relationship with adversary	✓	✓	✓	✓	✓
A belief that war or serious conflict is inevitable	✓	✓	✓	✓	✓
A belief that there is only a short "window" in which to act		✓	✓	✓	
A situation that is perceived to favor the offensive	✓		✓	✓	✓
Black-and-white thinking	✓	✓			✓
Preventive Action?	**YES**	**YES**	**NO**	**NO**	**YES**

* Check marks indicate that the factor was manifested clearly by the key decision-makers of a case.

** In this case, the perception of declining power was not in relation to an adversary, but relative to a bygone era of British hegemony.

was going to be. Though leaders did fear the consequences of the decline, the threat of rough equality was not sharp enough to induce preventive action.

In the case of British action in the Suez Canal Crisis, the "declining power" factor was present, but not in the sense envisioned by Levy. By 1956, British power had already been in decline for decades. The trend toward decolonization, and the destruction wrought by two successive world wars, had already greatly diminished British capabilities and influence. In addition, there was no real competition for relative power between Egypt and Britain, certainly not in the way envisioned by Levy's theory. Though it is true that Nasser's seizure of the canal did change the power equation between Egypt and Britain, that, as I have argued, was not what spurred Eden to initiate preventive action. In addition, it was not really Britain's "military power and potential," as Levy puts it, that was Eden's concern, but rather Britain's worldwide influence and prestige.

In the first U.S. case, the declining power factor was present, albeit in a limited way. The United States was not concerned that its own military power was declining, but rather that the Soviet Union's military power was increasing to the point of rough equality between the two states. The United States was not really concerned that it might lose a war later on—by the mid-1950s nobody believed that a thermonuclear war was "winnable"—but that the world would be living in "armed camps." For some, even this threat was enough. Thus, the constant threat of nuclear war (as a result of rough atomic parity) was seen by many leaders as an untenable position for the United States, which is why many advocated preventive war.

The declining power factor was not present at all in the case of Israel in 1981. The development of an Iraqi nuclear weapon would indeed have changed the relative power equation in that region. However, Israeli leaders were not concerned about regional hegemony, or a "rising power" that might eventually threaten them. Nor were they worried that the situation was moving toward a time when Iraq would eventually be more powerful than Israel. The primary issue for Israeli decision-makers was not their relative influence in the region, or their position in the international system. If declining power could be said to have been a factor at all, it was so only insofar as the manner in which Iraq was planning to increase their "power" had serious security implications for Israel.

In the case of India, the "declining power" factor might be said to be present in the first period, from 1982–1984, when India considered preventive strikes against Pakistani nuclear facilities. Similar to the case of the United States and the Soviet Union, the development of a Pakistani nuclear program would have affected the relative power relationship by bringing India and Pakistan into a roughly equal relationship. Though Indian leaders would likely have preferred Pakistan not to have a nuclear program, and feared its consequences to a certain extent, the fear of parity was not sharp enough to impel Indian leaders to order preventive action.

The case of the United States and Iraq (2003) is instructive on the issue of declining power. The United States did not fear a change in the relative power balance between the United States and Iraq. Given the overwhelming U.S. military superiority, even if Iraq had possessed WMD programs, as the Bush administration feared, the relative power balance would hardly have changed. After the terrorist attacks of September 11, the United States came to realize the danger posed by "asymmetric threats." These types of threats will never fit into Levy's framework of the "declining power motivation," because they are inherently not a threat to the balance of power, which focuses on traditional measurements of military power and force. To take "asymmetrical threats" into account would be impossible, since the very nature of such threats is that they rely on surprise methods of delivery and often do not fit into traditional state-centric power calculations.

Additionally, the primary threat of such attacks is that they will cause mass hysteria, terror, and confusion. Thus, the United States was not fearful of a nuclear missile attack from Iraq, but rather of a dirty bomb (or biological agent) smuggled into the country by a terrorist affiliated with or aided by Saddam's regime.

INHERENT BAD FAITH RELATIONSHIP
WITH ADVERSARY

This factor was present in every one of the five cases. In fact, this factor appears to be inextricably linked to preventive war decisions. The evidence in these cases, as well as common sense, supports such a view. After all, it is the leader's perception of their adversary, and their intentions, that acts as the prism through which other factors are viewed and calculated. One particularly important question is how strong, and how rigid, the "enemy image" is. Is the other state thought of as a rival? An opponent? A mortal enemy? Does it seem as if there is the chance for any reconciliation? For example, think of the many European wars of the nineteenth century, when alliances constantly shifted. The strength of the bad faith images present in that time period may have been considerable, but they were for the most part relatively fluid.

The evidence presented in this book indicates that there is a strong positive correlation between the bad faith image and preventive war. However, is there a causal relationship between the two? Because the bad faith image shows up in all of the five cases, including two where a leader decided against preventive action, it is probably more accurate to postulate a link between a particularly rigid and intense bad faith image and preventive action.

In the case of Britain, the primary bad faith image present was Eden's view of Nasser. Eden's perception of Nasser was highly emotional, and very personal. Eden was convinced that Nasser had embarked on a "planned campaign... to expel all Western influence and interest from Arab countries."[2] In addition to the seizure of the canal, Eden held Nasser personally responsible for Glubb's dismissal in Jordan.[3] Perhaps because of the personal nature of Eden's feelings, they were very strongly held. The seizure of the canal appeared to have hardened Eden's image of Nasser, which was already overwhelmingly negative as a result of Nasser's previous behavior. Nutting recalls that on the day of the seizure of the canal, "he [Eden] decided that the world was not big enough to hold both him and Nasser."[4]

Eden's perception of Nasser—as hostile, untrustworthy, and power-hungry—was instrumental in the decision-making process. Capabilities were important, and had Nasser not nationalized the canal, Eden might have left Egypt alone. But it was his personal view of Nasser that made preventive action necessary in his own mind. In his memoirs, he wrote that "a man with Colonel Nasser's record could not be allowed to have his thumb on our windpipe."[5] The image is one of mortal danger for England.

In the case of Israel, Begin's bad faith image was also intensely personal. However, it was slightly different in that it was directed not only at an individual—Saddam Hussein—but also at an entire group of people (Arabs). Perlmutter wrote that Begin did not comprehend the customs, culture, and aspirations of the Arab people, but only the dire threat they represented to Israel.[6] It was this general perception of the Arab world that, in this case, was embodied in Saddam Hussein. After the raid, a government spokesman declared that the raid was carried out because Begin (and the Israeli government) was convinced that Iraq was planning to build atomic bombs, and that Saddam Hussein was "an unstable person who would not necessarily be deterred from a first strike...."[7] The element that links Begin and Eden is that both perceived their threats to be "mortal" threats. For Begin, the threat was that his people might be destroyed, whereas for Eden, his concern was for the end of British influence throughout the world, in essence the "death" of an entire era.

Capabilities were also important in this case. We might never know what Begin would have decided had Iraq had a different leader. But capabilities alone did not decide the issue. Instead, it was Begin's bad faith image of Arabs in general, and Hussein in particular, that led him to the belief that Israel simply could not live in a world in which Saddam Hussein had the power to order a nuclear attack on Israel. Indeed, it might easily have been Begin who could have said that a man with Hussein's record could not be allowed to have his thumb on Israel's windpipe.

There was also a bad faith image of the adversary in the case of the United States (Cold War case), and yet it did not lead to preventive action. There is no shortage of quotes and memoirs that make the point that both Truman and Eisenhower believed the Soviet Union to be a hostile adversary, one that was both unpredictable and untrustworthy. However, this bad faith image was balanced out by the belief that war could still be averted, and that preventive war was morally wrong. Additionally, Eisenhower possessed a sense of hope for the future, which was not present in either the British or the Israeli case. There is no evidence that either Eden or Begin's image of their enemy was balanced out by any hope for reconciliation. The very fact that both decided on preventive action serves as evidence, after the fact, that neither held much hope for rapprochement. But, for American leaders, there was hope. In the late 1940s and early 1950s, the United States was only at the very beginning of a new era. There were numerous possibilities— a hot war against the Soviet Union, a cold war, or something completely different. Thus, after Stalin's death in 1953, Eisenhower recalled in his memoirs, "The new leadership in Russia, no matter how strong its links with the Stalin era, was not completely bound to blind obedience to the ways of a dead man. The future was theirs to make."[8] He then wrote that a "major preoccupation" of his mind throughout 1953 was the "development of approaches to the Soviet leaders that might be at least a start toward the birth of mutual trust...."[9] What is particularly interesting is that such hope could exist alongside the bad faith image that Eisenhower also held. Thus, it is important to emphasize that two contrasting perceptions—a bad faith image tempered by some measure of hope—did exist, which helps to explain the unwillingness of Truman and Eisenhower to initiate preventive action.

There is definitely a bad faith relationship between India and Pakistan. The numerous wars that the two countries have fought against each other, combined with religious tension, communalism, and almost constant border skirmishes, have created and hardened both states' images of each other as hostile, warlike, and untrustworthy. Certainly, the comments of Indian leaders in the press have portrayed this image of Pakistan. However, it seems as if that image is mediated to a certain extent by a desire to avoid a general war, especially given that both countries possess nuclear weapons. Thus, even though India could have preventively attacked Pakistan's nuclear program in 1982, the diplomatic reconciliation between the two countries likely gave Indira Gandhi the hope that the future might be better than the past—even if she hedged her bets by only postponing the preventive strike.

In the case of the Iraq War, the bad faith image was undeniably evident. President Bush's perception of Saddam Hussein was characterized by intense mistrust, as well as a hardened belief in the "evil" intentions of Hussein. This was solidified over time by Iraq's repeated violations of UN resolutions, as well as his general history, which was well known to Bush. This bad faith image of Hussein led Bush to see regime-change as the only viable option, even if the preventive war itself was not decided upon until relatively late in the decision process.

A BELIEF THAT WAR OR SERIOUS CONFLICT
IS INEVITABLE

This factor was also present in every case. In addition, in every case in which it was present, there was also an "inherent bad faith" relationship. Indeed, this seems logical, as decision-makers are more likely to believe that war is inevitable if their image of another state is one of hostility and suspicion. Thus, we might postulate that if a state's bad faith image of their adversary is strong enough, then they are much more likely to see war as inevitable. The implication of this, which was borne out in three of the five cases, is that preventive action is more likely once war is believed to be inevitable.

In the Suez case, the issue was not that conflict was seen as inevitable, but that it was perceived as already having begun. British preventive action in this case was to prevent Egypt from using its new influence to blackmail or humiliate Britain. For Eden, the beginning of the conflict likely began as soon as Nasser nationalized the Canal. Eden's frequent use of historical analogies comparing Nasser to Hitler and Mussolini provides more evidence that Eden believed conflict to be inevitable. These are powerful analogies, and are meant to both prescribe and justify action against aggression. Eden believed that Nasser, like Hitler, would not be satisfied after his first act of aggression, and would keep demanding and taking more until he was stopped. Additionally, the use of these analogies suggests that not only is conflict inevitable, but that preventive action is morally justified.

In other cases too, leaders felt that their state was already at war. Because of Iraq's refusal to sign armistice agreements with Israel after three separate wars, a state of war already existed between the two countries.[10] In the first American case, NSC-68 freely admits that arguments that the United States and the Soviet Union were already at war were "compelling."[11] In the second American case, the "War on Terror" was well underway by the time Iraq came to be targeted by the Bush administration. Once the cognitive link was made between terrorism, rogue regimes and WMDs, it allowed a preventive war against Iraq to be framed as part of the conflict already in progress. Whether or not Iraq was itself responsible for September 11, or even directly linked to those who were, the Bush administration came to see war against Iraq as intrinsically linked to the War on Terror. Thus, the Iraq War was merely an extension of a conflict already being fought all over the world. This view allowed Bush to see the war as less offensive and more defensive than those who had not made that particular cognitive link.

In the case of India, leaders often voiced similar opinions concerning a perpetual state of war. India and Pakistan have fought three major wars, one small-scale conflict, and innumerable border skirmishes. In addition, there is evidence that, in between the major wars, Pakistan has (and continues to) sponsor and train terrorists operating in Kashmir. In 1990, leaders of the BJP asserted that "India and Pakistan are in effect already at war, and what remains is for India to take the war into Pakistani territory."[12]

A BELIEF THAT THERE IS ONLY A SHORT "WINDOW" IN WHICH TO ACT

This belief was present in several of the cases. However, it is unlikely that there is any direct, causal connection between "window thinking" and whether a state initiates preventive action. Certainly, by itself, it is not a critical factor. There are windows opening and closing all of the time, most of which we are not even aware. This factor is important to the extent that it interacts with, and reinforces, other factors such as a declining power situation, or the belief that conflict is inevitable. Additionally, it creates a time pressure for decision-makers, which might impact the process of decision-making.

In the case of Israel, there were two deadlines that created time pressures, though only one might properly be called a "window of opportunity." The first deadline was the date when the reactor would go online, and the second was the impending elections, which Begin believed might be won by Shimon Peres. The first of these factors can properly be described as a window of opportunity—a period of time in which there was a strategic advantage over another state. Interestingly, this window of strategic opportunity did not seem to have any effect on whether or not the strike occurred. The possibility that the reactor might go online merely dictated the time frame in which a preventive strike would be effective (and not lead to radioactive fallout); not whether or not Begin should order the strike. It was the second deadline—the impending elections—that influenced Begin's view of whether or not he should order the strike.

This is interesting and important because the window of opportunity that seems to have had the greatest effect was not military at all, but political. Peres' private note to Begin in May of 1981 made clear that, were he to be elected prime minister, he would never order the strike.[13] These two factors combined to make the window of opportunity a short one—elections were to be held within a month, and the reactor would go on-line soon after that (Begin was convinced). But neither of these factors would have led to the strike if the other factors (bad faith image, Begin's personal experience with the Holocaust) had not been present.

In the case of British action, window thinking was not present. This is not to suggest that British leaders did not see time as a factor, they did—the longer they waited, the better the chance that the passage of time would transform Nasser's aggression into the status quo.[14] As the weeks and months passed, the "danger" described by Eden seemed to be imminent. The feeling that "something must be done soon," no doubt, had an important effect on Eden's decision to go along with the notorious scheme concocted at Sevres. However, there was no window, or period, when Britain possessed a significant military or strategic advantage.

Window thinking in the United States case was not a unitary idea, but referred to different things, and changed over the years. At first, the term applied to the American monopoly on atomic weapons. By 1949, the Soviets had detonated an atomic bomb, and the window changed accordingly. After 1949, window thinking had taken the form of leaders speaking of a "danger year," after which time the Soviets "would assume complete command of the world situation (if nothing was done *now*)."[15] Sometimes, leaders and academics used the same language, but asserted that the window of opportunity was the Soviet Union's window. For instance, Hans Morgenthau asserted in an article that the United States was already in the "danger period," and should act cautiously until it was over.[16] Thus, "window thinking" in this case actually inspired increased prudence, and not preventive action.

Even in the United States case, which was dominated by window thinking and changing capabilities, window thinking alone did not lead to preventive war thinking. "Window thinking" by itself only refers to the idea that there is a short period of time in which it is possible to act. By itself, such thinking does not necessarily imply that the state should act. This is an important distinction, and thus window thinking is neither a necessary nor a sufficient condition for preventive action. Rather, it is when such thinking is combined with the belief that an adversary is hostile and war is inevitable, that this factor becomes increasingly significant.

The window of opportunity factor was present in the case of India. However, it does not appear to have been an important factor in Indian decision-making. This suggests that decision-makers might not see the same window that scholars, in retrospect, can identify. Theoretically, the conditions for such thinking existed in the early period covered in the case, in 1982. Then, the Pakistani nuclear facility was about to go online, and was vulnerable to attack. However, there did not seem to be any references to a window of opportunity by Indian leaders in the press, though we cannot know what was said in private. The reason that India did not strike the atomic plant was that a potential upswing in relations between the two countries seemed to have overshadowed the idea of a window of opportunity. In fact, the window of opportunity for improved relations between the two states seems to have been more important than any opportunity that India had to destroy Pakistan's nuclear capability.

In the case of the United States and Iraq, there was no evidence of a closing window of opportunity. Time was a factor, but the United States did not have any military or strategic advantage that the passage of time would erase. The best evidence that George W. Bush did not see a closing window of opportunity is the circuitous route that he took to war. The pressures and constraints imposed by a closing window of opportunity would probably have led Bush to push the country toward war much more quickly than actually occurred.

A SITUATION THAT IS PERCEIVED TO FAVOR THE OFFENSIVE

This factor was present in three of the cases examined in this book, two of which did not end in preventive action. Of course, the presence of this factor certainly does not preclude preventive action. However, the absence of this factor in the two cases where preventive action did occur suggests that its presence is not a necessary condition for preventive war.

In the case of the United States and the USSR, the belief that there was an advantage in offensive action affected decision-making, but did not lead to preventive action. In fact, in this case, the main implication that decision-makers drew from the "advantage of the offensive" was the need for pre-emptive action. For instance, a JSSC report written in 1945 reported that the nature of the atomic bomb made conventional defense inherently inadequate.[17] Eisenhower made reference to the fact that an atomic threat was the only threat that might, without notice, endanger the existence of the United States. He thus asserted his intention to launch SAC upon "trustworthy evidence" of an attack.[18]

However, the belief that atomic weapons favored the offensive did not seem to have any impact on preventive war thinking. In all the statements by various leaders that advocated preventive war, none used the argument that nuclear weapons favored the offense. The arguments in favor of preventive war did refer to the destructive nature of nuclear weapons, but only to make the point that the United States should not allow hostile states to acquire them. In fact, there seems to be a noticeable aversion to admitting that preventive action requires going on the offensive. This makes some sense, as preventive action can be defensive, and certainly explanations to an international audience would focus on that aspect. But even in closed meetings of the president and his top advisors, there seems to be an unwillingness to admit that there is an aspect of offense involved in the proposition of preventive war.

The belief that there was an advantage to the offense was also present, in a more limited way, in the India-Pakistan case. For the most part, it seems that both Indian and Pakistani leaders were focused on the immediate prospect of a conventional war, not a nuclear confrontation. However, there was, in fact, a situation that favored the offensive. Both India and Pakistan were nuclear powers, but neither had a secure second-strike capability. In fact, it is not even clear whether either country had weapons assembled during some of the time period covered in the case. If it destroyed most of Pakistan's nuclear capability, India's significantly larger size would, theoretically, allow it to absorb a small nuclear attack. The United States was deterred by the threat of Soviet conventional forces. Pakistan has no such advantage to deter a preventive attack by India.

In the case of the Iraq War, the factor was clearly present. Numerous references were made by all the principal decision-makers referring to the need to "take the offensive" against rogue regimes, proliferation of WMD, and catastrophic terrorism. This seems to have been a relatively important factor, as the nature of the threat faced by the United States was not easily dealt with by traditional methods. Though the threats to the United States during the era of the Cold War were just as dire, decision-makers had some confidence in their ability to deter Soviet aggression. Not only did these threats not prescribe offensive action, but they also actively warned against it. The end of the Cold War, however, brought a paradigmatic shift in the nature of security threats. For George W. Bush, the answer to these new threats lay in taking the offensive, first in Afghanistan and then in Iraq.

BLACK-AND-WHITE THINKING

Black-and-white thinking, the last of the preventive war factors, was present in several of the cases. In fact, the three cases in which such thinking occurs were the same three cases in which preventive action occurred.

Why is this the case? What implications does a black-and-white view of the world have for preventive war? First, the tendency to see the world in stark moral contrasts—good and bad, virtuous and evil—means that enemies (once they have been identified) are seen as more threatening. Black-and-white thinking obscures and blocks any potential mitigation that might have been perceived. An offer to negotiate, a hopeful remark in a public speech; neither of these are likely to be recognized by a leader who has a propensity for black-and-white thinking. Similarly, the behaviors linked in most people's minds with the concept of "evil" mean that decision-makers' views of their adversary will be accompanied by a host of associated emotions and associations that stack the deck against compromise.

Second, the propensity to see the world in black-and-white, good and evil, has a direct impact on a leader's ability to make a decision. Hard decisions are often surrounded by doubt and uncertainty, but a leader's view that they are on the "right" side makes hard decisions much easier.

It is also interesting to note the correlation between black-and-white thinking, preventive war, and the use of historical analogies. We should be careful not to assume a causal link between the use of historical analogies and preventive action. However, it is also true that the three cases in which preventive war was initiated were the same three cases where the use of analogies was prevalent. These analogies, comparing a leader to Hitler, Mussolini, or other authoritarian dictators, certainly did not *cause* preventive action. But the frequent use of such analogies by Menachem Begin, Anthony Eden, and George W. Bush suggests that these analogies were relevant to the decisions they made, and more generally that they might provide insight into the thinking of political leaders. Analogies that refer to past situations, or compare one figure to another, are informative of a leader's framing of the situation, and their perception of the best way to "solve" a problem. Once a leader becomes convinced that such strong analogies are relevant, negotiation or compromise is no longer an option.

CONCLUSIONS

The purpose of this book was to examine the motivations of decision-makers with regard to preventive action. The five cases used here provide a small window into the decision-making process of individuals contemplating preventive action. In three of the cases, preventive action was initiated, while in the other two, it was not. What separated those cases from each other? How can we explain the different decisions?

The most obvious point to emerge from the analysis of these cases is the importance of individual leaders and their perceptions. Previous explanations of preventive action have, for the most part, focused on material capabilities, with only a slight acknowledgment of the role played by intentions. However, these theories fall short of providing a full explanation because intentions are almost never as easy to deduce as some have assumed. Even if they could be, they would not be as important as the individual's perception of their adversary's capabilities and intentions. This is the key to any explanation: an examination of the decision-making process focusing on individual leadership and perception. These factors have, in these five case studies, cut across boundaries of time, geography, culture, and ethnicity. It is the study of leaders and their perceptions of the world—including capabilities, intentions, risk assessments, and emotions—that provide the fullest explanation of decisions to initiate preventive action.

The fact that individual leaders—their psychology, beliefs, and judgments—are central to preventive war decisions is the start of understanding, not its conclusion. Much remains to be done and understood. How does risk and uncertainty enter into the leader's calculations? What role do different forms of bureaucratic advisory systems play in encouraging or constraining a leader's inclinations? To what extent is public opinion important in preventive war decisions?

All of these are important questions that await further study and analysis. One thing, however, is certain. In an age where rogue states and individuals can cause catastrophic terror without warning, leaders will come under increasing pressure to strike before being struck first. How the states respond to the changing circumstances of an increasingly dangerous and unpredictable world has consequences of the highest importance.

Epilogue:
Preventive War in the Age of Terrorism and Rogue States

THE FUTURE OF PREVENTIVE WAR

The Bush Doctrine, and the subsequent war against Iraq, brought preventive war to the forefront of the world's attention. However, like many important events in history, the after effects for the future of preventive war are not yet apparent, and will not be for some time. Will the Iraq War be viewed as successful by later generations? Will world and American public reluctance to support such ventures in the future prove insurmountable? Does a successful exercise of preventive war lessen the need for such strategies in the future, or does it guarantee future conflict? Certainly, the lethal mix of WMD, rogue regimes, and catastrophic terrorism will remain a dire threat. But will preventive war continue to be utilized as a strategy?

Preventive Wars and Deterrence

One of the most important questions raised by the Iraq War is what effect it will have on the stability of deterrence in the future. Deterrence theory is inextricably linked to questions of preventive war, since it is the failure of deterrence that leads to strategies of prevention. More specifically, it is the perception that a specific threat cannot be deterred that leads decision-makers to consider (and sometimes take) preventive action. This is true in all cases examined in this book. A strategy of preventive war is the result of the perception that deterrence is likely to fail. Note that it need not have failed already, but there must be the perception that it is likely to fail, combined with the belief that the consequences of such a failure would be unacceptable. Here is the sliding scale of decision-making: the potential consequences of an event balanced against the likelihood of that event occurring.

Preventive war is linked to deterrence in another critical way as well. Preventive war may help to strengthen a state's deterrent ability for the future, especially in cases where states had previously been thought of as weak, or unwilling to suffer casualties. Recall that Osama Bin Laden specifically called attention to the weak American response in Lebanon, Vietnam, and Somalia as evidence that the United States was, if not a "paper tiger," then at least a timid one. A determined and clear-cut willingness to go to war and stay there, despite intense difficulties and international pressure is one method of revitalizing one's credibility, and with it the viability of future deterrence.

More generally, preventive war may affect deterrence in any of three ways: it may damage it, strengthen it, or not have any effect. Historical example suggests that there is no single answer to the difficult question of which is more likely. Different circumstances will bring different outcomes. The Israeli attack on Osiraq is generally deemed a "successful" preventive strike.[1] And it is true that doing so brought a measure of relief for Israel's leaders. Yet, Israel still lived in perpetual fear of missiles fired from Iraq. In the aftermath of World War II, the United States chose not to initiate preventive action against the Soviet Union, and yet a relatively stable deterrence evolved. Anthony Eden's preventive war against Egypt likely destroyed any moral credibility that Britain had left after the decline of its empire, and its forced departure from Suez, at the insistence of the United States, did nothing to burnish its credentials as a power to be reckoned with. In a similar vein, the U.S. action in Iraq might have increased the credibility of American will and resolve, but the perception that the United States is "bogged down" in Iraq, and weakened by an overstretched military, might negate any potential gains from the war in terms of benefits to future deterrence, surely a somewhat paradoxical effect.

It seems likely that if preventive war does have a positive effect on deterrence, its benefits would primarily be in the short term. Certainly, demonstrating commitment and resolve (will) is one likely consequence of preventive action. But what is the shelf life of resolve? Is one precision strike enough? Is one major war enough? Do preventive actions (whether strikes or wars) have to be followed up by other actions to sustain credibility? Do these follow-up actions risk labeling the actor as a bully, or worse, an aggressor? In short, how much "maintenance" does deterrence require?

There is another shelf-life question: Do the deterrent effects of a preventive war outlive an administration? Assume that President Bush has demonstrated his resolve to potential adversaries. Will his successor need to do so as well? There is reason to suppose that this credibility is nontransferable. President Eisenhower demonstrated his resolve by threatening to bomb the North Koreans, breaking the stalemate in talks about ending the Korean

War. Yet, when Kennedy succeeded to the presidency, the Soviet Union's Nikita Khrushchev immediately tested him. Eisenhower's credibility did not carry over to the next administration, and there is no good reason why it should in other circumstances. The nature of democratic government means that the credibility of any one administration is destined to be short-lived. Authoritarian governments do not suffer from this problem, and it is conceivable that their deterrent capability might improve and last for quite a while. As long as a dictator remains in power, there is no reason to believe that their deterrent capability would diminish without some precipitating event (such as failing health).

Still another issue is whether credibility gained by preventive war (and the benefit to a state's deterrent ability) is transferable over geographical and political circumstances. Some have argued that Syria's withdrawal from Lebanon was a short-term result that followed from the change in risk calculations brought on by Bush and his policies. On the other hand, the preventive war against Iraq does not seem to have had much of an effect on North Korea's behavior to date. In retrospect, it seems mistaken to assume that preventive war will work to compel changed behavior in all circumstances, but there is, as yet, no delineation of those circumstances that favor it and those that do not. Consider the situation of North Korea. President Bush has repeatedly stated that he favors a diplomatic solution. Why? Is it that North Korea is thought to already have multiple nuclear weapons? That it has large numbers of soldiers stationed a few miles from the capital of South Korea? That its leader, Kim Jong-Il, is considered by many to be wildly unreliable and unpredictable, possibly even unbalanced? What separates situations that are perceived to require preventive action from those that do not?

The Likely, the Unlikely, and the Improbable

In considering the future of preventive war, one point is very clear after September 11: leaders must worry about the unlikely and the implausible, especially if the consequences of inaction are high. Nineteen terrorists hijacking four planes simultaneously and using them as missiles to attack the United States was unlikely, and yet it happened. That they lived for years in the United States undetected by American intelligence services is even more unlikely, yet it too happened. In fact, the entire course of events that led to September 11 might be considered, at best, unlikely. And yet, they happened. Catastrophic consequences lower the threshold at which leaders must take the unlikely seriously.

There are two types of events that fall into this high-impact, (relatively) low-probability category: the proliferation of nuclear weapons to "unstable" regimes, and potential terrorist attacks. After the end of the Cold War rivalry, it appears as if these two threats have emerged as two of the most pressing problems of the twenty-first century. It is worth exploring why it is precisely these types of threats that tend to recommend themselves to preventive action.

The Appeal of "Positive" Action: From Deterrence to Prevention

This study has focused on what leads individual decision-makers to consider and choose a strategy of preventive action. Certainly, critical elements to consider are the types of threats that recommend themselves to strategies of preventive action, and under what circumstances they do so.

In order for preventive action to be a viable choice, the threat must entail particularly disastrous consequences, such that the decision-maker sees guaranteed conflict immediately on their own terms (even with the risks it carries) as better than possible conflict later. But it is not enough for the stakes to be high. After all, the stakes were as high as they go during the Cold War, when the fate of the world rested upon the restraint of two opposing superpowers.

In addition to drastic, severe consequences, deterrence must not be an option in order for preventive war to appeal to leaders. In the case of terrorism, it is generally accepted that deterrence is not possible against suicide terror attacks. Deterrence is, at its heart, an understanding between two parties, where one party deters the other by threatening retaliation against something of value. To the extent that deterrence worked during the Cold War, it did so because the Soviet Union and the United States shared some core values and an understanding of the rules of the game.

There are numerous reasons for a leader to believe, given some circumstances, that deterrence will not work against another state. A leader might believe that their adversary is irrational and unpredictable, that they are risk-prone in their decision-making, that at some basic level, there is no agreement on fundamental values (such as the sanctity of human life), or that the adversary will find some indirect way to attack (such as giving WMD to terrorist groups) that would make retaliation difficult. For any of these reasons, once a leader believes that deterrence is no longer viable, there are few options left. The leader may do nothing, in the hope that an "unlikely" scenario will not become reality, or he may take positive action to either realign the balance of power or capabilities (as in Israel's strike on the Osiraq reactor) to remove a threat completely (as in the war in Iraq).

The Future of U.S. National Security Strategy

The Iraqi insurgency and the difficulties of nation rebuilding have proved to be much more difficult than the administration anticipated. Saddam

Hussein is gone, and a new elected government is in place, but the long-term prospects are hardly a given. Even more than the long-term effects in Iraq, the immense costs of the war (in terms of political capital, relationships with allies, money, and lost lives) for the United States raise the question of whether another American-led preventive war is likely in the future.

The presidency of George W. Bush has been remarkable in the enormous consequences that followed from one initial judgment. The recognition that terrorism represents a unique type of threat, wholly different from that faced by the United States during the Cold War, was arguably an inevitable conclusion after 9/11. However, the implications drawn from that one conclusion were far-reaching and controversial. That Bush linked terrorism, weapons of mass destruction, and rogue regimes together in the National Security Strategy was enormously significant for its post–9/11 stance toward the world. Yet, his decision to use Iraq as a "test case" for preventive action was equally significant. Many policy makers agreed that the United States and its allies must actively prevent acts of terrorism and that deterrence would not suffice to keep the United States safe from further attacks. However, it was a huge risk, both for the country and his own political career, for President Bush to have initiated preventive war not because of a direct and immediate terrorist threat, but because of his judgment that Iraq posed a long-term threat.

If the Iraq War was a test case for preventive action, then did it pass the test? Will this preventive war be an isolated incident, an anomaly in the history of modern U.S. foreign policy? Or does President Bush's National Security Strategy signal a major and long-lasting change of grand strategy? Will the Iraq War mark the beginning of a descent into a new era of international conflict and suspicion, marked by more and more states acting preventively? Will the policies of George W. Bush outlast his presidency?

How we answer these questions in the future will depend on a great many factors: how well the war in Iraq goes and how deeply democracy takes root there, how successful the United States and its allies are in eradicating the most dangerous terrorist cells throughout the world, and how well the United States can help other countries deal with some of the root causes that allow terrorists to flourish by earnestly helping countries on the path to economic and political development. What is certain, however, is that in the near future, the United States will face severe threats from a number of quarters that will force dire situations and stark choices upon our leaders. Underestimating the threat might lead to catastrophe. And yet, preventive war is a blunt instrument, not a panacea. If utilized unwisely, or without any thought given to the likely consequences, its effects may be more detrimental than beneficial.

American presidents and allied leaders will be forced to make decisions with profound consequences, and yet they will often be required to do so on the basis of incomplete or imperfect information—this is inevitable. As a result, the security of the United States will ultimately hinge on the best judgments of leaders and their advisors. These decisions will engage their motivations, worldviews, perceptions, and emotions. To the extent that there are "answers" to the questions posed in this epilogue, they will be found in the recesses of the human mind, and not solely in material circumstances. It is critical, therefore, in examining preventive war to focus substantial attention there.

Notes

Preface

1. "National Security Strategy of the United States of America," September 2002 [www.whitehouse.gov/nsc/nss.pdf].

2. John Lewis Gaddis, for instance, argues in *Surprise, Security and the American Experience* (Cambridge: Harvard University Press, 2004) that a doctrine of prevention has been the typical American response to great national security threats. A.J.P. Taylor argues in a similar vein that every war between the Great Powers in the years 1848–1918 "started as a preventive war, not as a war of conquest." *The Struggle for Mastery in Europe, 1848–1918* (Oxford: Clarendon Press, 1954), 166.

Chapter 1

1. George W. Bush, graduation speech, U.S. Military Academy at West Point, June 1, 2002.

2. "National Security Strategy, 2002" [www.whitehouse.gov] (accessed February 5, 2005).

3. Quoted in Linda D. Kozaryn, "Cheney Says Grave Threats Require Preemptive Action," *American Forces Press Service*, August 26, 2002.

4. "Preventive War: A Failed Doctrine," *New York Times*, September 12, 2004.

5. "Statement of Senator Edward M. Kennedy on the Bush Doctrine of Preemption," October 7, 2002 [www.senate.gov/~kennedy] (accessed October 1, 2005).

6. Arthur Schlesinger, "Seeking Out Monsters," *Guardian*, October 19, 2004.

7. Senator Arlen Specter, "Remarks During the Senator Debate on Iraq," *Congressional Record*, September 5, 2002, S8246.

8. Paul Craig Roberts, "Is the Bush Administration Certifiable?" *Washington Times*, December 8, 2004 [www.washingtontimes.com] (accessed December 9, 2004).

9. Henry Kissinger, "America's Assignment—Pre-emption," *Newsweek*, November 8, 2004, 35.

10. I use the term "preventive action" to underscore the point that "prevention" may include a range of actions that stop short of war. One important reframing of the concept, therefore, is to decouple *prevention* from *war*.

11. An adversarial relationship may result for many different reasons, such as economic competition, territorial disputes, ideological disputes, "sphere of influence" conflicts, ethnic conflicts, historical events, access to trade routes or resources, etc.

12. Lawrence Freedman, "Prevention, Not Pre-emption," *Washington Quarterly* 26, no. 2 (Spring 2003): 106.

13. For this line of argument, see Michael Walzer, *Just and Unjust Wars: A Moral Argument with Historical Illustrations* (New York: Basic Books, 1977), 75–80.

14. Samuel P. Huntington, "To Choose Peace or War: Is There a Place for Preventive War in American Policy?" *United States Naval Institute Proceedings* 83, no. 4 (April 1957): 360.

15. Jack S. Levy, "Declining Power and the Preventive Motivation for War," *World Politics* 40, no. 1 (October 1987): 87.

16. Walzer, *Just and Unjust Wars*, 76.

17. For another such explanation, see Robert Gilpin, *War and Change in World Politics* (Cambridge: Cambridge University Press, 1981), 191.

18. Interestingly, Levy and Gilpin do make a distinction between the "preventive motivation" for war and "preventive war" as a *type* of war. However, both authors still overemphasize balance of power calculations in their explanations.

19. James Steinburg, "Preventive Force in U.S. National Security Strategy," *Survival* 47, no. 4 (Winter 2005–2006): 59–62.

20. Huntington, "To Choose Peace or War," 360.

21. Robert Gilpin writes that the "greatest danger inherent in preventive war is that it sets in motion a course of events over which statesmen soon lose control." Gilpin, *War and Change in World Politics*, 191.

22. In fact, a recent graduate thesis hypothesizes that the primary benefit of preventive strikes is that they "buy time" and attract international attention. However, there are also very serious, potential negative consequences: a strike may *reinforce* a proliferation's desire to acquire WMD, and it might create an international backlash against the state that initiated preventive action. Peter S. Ford, "Israel's Attack on Osiraq: A Model for Future Preventive Strikes?" (Master's dissertation, Naval Postgraduate School, 2004), 3.

23. Gilpin, *War and Change in World Politics*, 201.

24. Neta C. Crawford, "The Best Defense: The Problem with Bush's 'Preemptive' War Doctrine," *Boston Review* 28, no. 1 (2002). For another example of a scholar linking preventive war to aggression, see Chris J. Dolan, "The Bush Doctrine and U.S. Interventionism" [www.americandiplomacy.org] (accessed April 30, 2005).

25. Levy, "Preventive Motivation for War," 87.

26. Thomas C. Schelling, *Arms and Influence* (New Haven, CT: Yale University Press, 1966), 2–6; Daniel Byman and Matthew Waxman, *The Dynamics of Coercion: American Foreign Policy and the Limits of Military Might* (Cambridge: Cambridge University Press, 2002), 3.

27. Byman and Waxman, *Dynamics of Coercion*, 5.

28. Lawrence Freedman, *Deterrence* (London: Polity Press, 2004), 27.

29. *General* deterrence is a long-term strategy that seeks to prevent a *type* of action (i.e., aggressive military action). *Immediate* deterrence (alternatively referred to as "pure" deterrence), by contrast, is directed at preventing a specific action. For more on this important theoretical distinction, see Jack S. Levy, "When Do Deterrent Threats Work?" *British Journal of Political Science* 18, no. 4 (October 1988): 488–489; and Patrick M. Morgan, *Deterrence: A Conceptual Analysis* (London: Sage Publications, 1983), 30.

30. Morgan, *Deterrence*, 31.

31. The cognitive aspect of deterrence, while important, is too large a category to describe in detail here. However, there are numerous studies of the cognitive biases that lead decision-makers to misunderstand or misinterpret warnings. For example, see Robert Jervis, *Perception and Misperception in International Politics* (Princeton, NJ: Princeton University Press, 1976), 58–117.

32. Scott D. Sagan, "The Perils of Proliferation: Organization Theory, Deterrence Theory and the Spread of Nuclear Weapons," *International Security* 18, no. 4 (Spring 1994): 66.

33. There is a great deal of literature on the "proliferation optimism/pessimism" issue. For a more detailed account of this debate, see David J. Karl, "Proliferation Pessimism and Emerging Nuclear Powers," *International Security* 21, no. 3 (Winter 1996–1997): 87–119; Kenneth Waltz, *The Spread of Nuclear Weapons: More May Be Better*, Adelphi Paper No. 171 (London: International Institute of Strategic Studies [IISS], Autumn 1981); Scott D. Sagan, "The Perils of Proliferation in South Asia," *Asian Survey* 41, no. 6 (November–December 2001): 1064–1086; Scott D. Sagan and Kenneth Waltz, *The Spread of Nuclear Weapons: A Debate Renewed* (New York: W. W. Norton, 2003).

34. Sagan, "The Perils of Proliferation," 74.

35. UN Charter, Chapter I, Article 2 (4) [www.un.org] (accessed May 10, 2004).

36. UN Charter, Chapter VII, Article 51, emphasis added [www.un.org] (accessed May 10, 2004).

37. "Anticipatory self-defense" is a legal term used to discuss the "right" to pre-emption in international law. Because the charter of the UN only allows states the right to act in self-defense, the term anticipatory self-defense has arisen to highlight the defensive nature of pre-emption. As far as I am aware, the term refers exclusively to pre-emption, though technically it might apply to any action taken to defend oneself in anticipation of a future attack (and thus might actually include prevention).

38. UN Charter, Chapter VII, Article 39 [www.un.org] (accessed May 10, 2004).

39. Michael Bothe, "Terrorism and the Legality of Pre-emptive Force," *European Journal of International Law* 14, no. 2 (2003): 229.

40. Letter from Secretary of State Daniel Webster to Lord Ashburton of August 6, 1842, reprinted in John Bassett Moore, *A Digest of International Law, Volume II* (Washington, DC: Government Printing Office, 1906), 412.

41. Thomas M. Franck, "Who Killed Article 2(4)? Or: Changing Norms Governing the Use of Force by States," *American Journal of International Law* 64 (October 1970): 821.

42. Ibid. (Emphasis added.)

43. "A More Secure World: Our Shared Responsibility," United Nations, 62–64 [www.un.org] (accessed February 20, 2005).

44. For an interesting take on the implications of "imminence" for international law in the twenty-first century, see Terrence Taylor, "The End of Imminence?" *Washington Quarterly* 27, no. 4 (Autumn 2004): 57–72.

45. For a full explanation of prospect theory, see Daniel Kahnneman and Amos Tversky, "Prospect Theory: An Analysis of Decision under Risk," *Econometrica* 47, no. 2 (March 1979): 263–292.

46. Jack S. Levy, "An Introduction to Prospect Theory," *Political Psychology* 13, no. 2 (1992): 171.

47. Nathan Kogan and Michael Wallach, *Risk Taking: A Study in Cognition and Personality* (New York: Holt, Rinehart and Winston, 1964), 214.

48. Margaret G. Hermann and Paul A. Kowert, "Who Takes Risks? Daring and Caution in Foreign Policy Making," *Journal of Conflict Resolution* 41, no. 5 (October 1997): 630.

49. See Hans J. Morgenthau, *Scientific Man vs. Power Politics* (Chicago: University of Chicago Press, 1946), 192, 200.

50. In fact, this is very close to Levy's definition.

51. Jervis, *Perception and Misperception in International Politics*, 288–291.

52. Douglas Stuart and Harvey Starr, "The 'Inherent Bad Faith Model' Reconsidered: Dulles, Kennedy, and Kissinger," *Political Psychology* 3, no. 3/4 (Fall/ Winter 1981–1982): 1. Much of the work on inherent bad faith relationships and enemy image is derived from the pathbreaking work of Ole Holsti, who examined the belief system of John Foster Dulles in a graduate dissertation. Holsti noted that "the more his [Dulles'] image of the Soviet Union was dominated by ethical rather than political criteria, the more likely it would be that the image would resist any change." See Ole Holsti, *The Belief System and National Images: John Foster Dulles and the Soviet Union* (Doctoral dissertation, Stanford University, 1962), 231–232.

53. Arthur Gladstone, "The Conception of the Enemy," *Journal of Conflict Resolution* 3, no. 2 (June 1959): 132.

54. Heikki Luostarinen, "Finnish Russophobia: The Story of an Enemy Image," *Journal of Peace Research* 26, no. 2 (May 1989): 125.

55. Hermann and Fischerkeller correlate an enemy image with the perception that the enemy will be exposed as a "paper tiger" if met with strong opposition.

However, the results of the cases in this book indicate that the enemy image is often associated with the opposite belief: that capabilities of an enemy are greater than what empirical evidence suggests. See Richard K. Hermann and Michael P. Fischerkeller, "Beyond the Enemy Image and Spiral Model: Cognitive-Strategic Research after the Cold War," *International Organization* 49, no. 3 (Summer 1995): 428.

56. David J. Finlay, Ole R. Holsti, and Richard R. Fagen, *Enemies in Politics* (Chicago: Rand McNally Press, 1967), 21.

57. For two opposing points of view on this issue, see Stephen van Evera, "Causes of War" (PhD dissertation, University of California, Berkeley, 1984), 61–71, 89–95, 330–339, 650–654; and Richard Ned Lebow, "Windows of Opportunity: Do States Jump through Them?" *International Security* 9, no. 1 (Summer 1984): 149.

58. This is the theory underlying Jack Snyder's work *The Ideology of the Offensive: Military Decision Making and the Disasters of 1914* (Ithaca, NY: Cornell University Press, 1984). This is also the premise behind Stephen Van Evera's *Causes of War: Power and the Roots of Conflict*, which explores the different reasons for which the offensive comes to be favored by leaders (Ithaca, NY: Cornell University Press, 1999).

59. Nathan Leites, *The Operational Code of the Politburo* (New York: McGraw-Hill, 1951) and *A Study of Bolshevism* (New York: Free Press, 1953).

60. Alexander George, "The 'Operational Code': A Neglected Approach to the Study of Political Leaders and Decision-Making," *International Studies Quarterly* 13, no. 2 (June 1969): 191.

61. James David Barber, *The Presidential Character: Predicting Performance in the White House* (NJ: Prentice-Hall, 1972), 8, 11.

62. Alexander George, "Assessing Presidential Character," *World Politics* 26, no. 2 (January 1974): 244–245.

63. Betty Glad, "Black-and-White Thinking: Ronald Reagan's Approach to Foreign Policy," *Political Psychology* 4, no. 1 (Spring 1983): 33.

64. Stephen G. Walker, "The Interface between Beliefs and Behavior: Henry Kissinger's Operational Code and the Vietnam War," *Journal of Conflict Resolution* 21, no. 1 (March 1977): 131.

65. Juliet Kaarbo and Ryan K. Beasley, "A Practical Guide to the Comparative Case Study Method in Political Psychology," *Political Psychology* 20, no. 2 (June 1999): 380–382. For an extensive treatment of the comparative use of case studies for theory building, see Alexander L. George and Andrew Bennett, *Case Studies for Theory Development in the Social Sciences* (Cambridge, MA: MIT Press, 2005).

Chapter 2

1. Henry Kissinger, *Diplomacy* (New York: Simon & Schuster, 1994), 523.

2. Levy, "Preventive Motivation for War," 87.

3. Ibid.

4. Quoted in David Carlton, *Britain and the Suez Crisis* (New York: Basil Blackwell, 1989), 27.

5. Quoted in Anthony Gorst and Lewis Johnman, *The Suez Crisis* (New York: Routledge Press, 1997), 41.

6. Selwyn Lloyd, *Suez 1956: A Personal Account* (New York: Mayflower Books, 1978), 28.

7. This will be discussed in greater detail in another section of this case study, as it seems to have had a very significant effect on Eden's views of Nasser.

8. Kissinger, *Diplomacy*, 529.

9. Anthony Nutting, *No End of a Lesson: The Story of Suez* (New York: Clarkson N. Potter, 1967), 44.

10. Kissinger, *Diplomacy*, 530.

11. Keith Kyle, *Suez: Britain's End of Empire in the Middle East* (London: I. B. Tauris, 2003), 133.

12. Quoted in Gorst and Johnman, *Suez Crisis*, 58.

13. Lloyd, *Suez 1956*, 83–85.

14. Nutting, *No End of a Lesson*, 46.

15. Ibid., 47.

16. In fact, the cabinet of July 27 conceded that, from a legal point of view, the nationalization of the canal "amounted to no more than a decision to buy out the shareholders." Quoted in Keith Kyle, "Britain and the Crisis, 1955–1956," in *Suez 1956: The Crisis and Its Consequences*, ed. Wm. Roger Louis and Roger Owen (Oxford: Oxford University Press, 2003), 112.

17. Quoted in Gorst and Johnman, *Suez Crisis*, 57. (Emphasis added.)

18. Anthony Eden, *Full Circle: The Memoirs of Anthony Eden* (Boston: Houghton Mifflin, 1960), 476. (Emphasis added.)

19. Eden, *Full Circle*, 477.

20. Quoted in Gorst and Johnman, *Suez Crisis*, 58.

21. Derek Varble, *The Suez Crisis 1956* (Oxford: Osprey, 2003), 15.

22. In 1920, the British Empire included Australia, India, Canada, Iraq, Malaysia, Borneo, Papua New Guinea, New Zealand, Sierra Leone, and stretch of Africa that ran uninterrupted from Egypt in the north down to the tip of South Africa. However, by 1956, most of these territories were on the road to independence, if not independent already. The "crown jewel" of the empire, India, had been made independent in 1947. For more information, see table in Lloyd, *The British Empire 1558–1995* (Oxford: Oxford University Press, 1996), 427–433.

23. Anthony Adamthwaite, "Suez Revisited," *International Affairs* 64, no. 3 (Summer 1988): 450.

24. Nutting, *No End of a Lesson*, 18.

25. Ibid.

26. Adamthwaite, "Suez Revisited," 450.

27. Nutting, *No End of a Lesson*, 17.

28. Jerrold Post and Robert Robins present some evidence that Anthony Eden was "addicted to the powerful stimulant amphetamine" during some of his tenure in office. They report that it was Eden's self-medication which "robbed him of his good judgment" during the Suez crisis. However, we should be careful not to rely too heavily on medical diagnoses to explain political judgments. A medication might impair judgment (aside from the fact that what is "bad" judgment is in itself a subjective matter), but so do a host of other psychological and physical elements. How then to know which one is operative? One answer is to gather as much evidence as possible and try to see how a behavior (or judgment) fits in with past actions and current context before deciding what "caused" a particular action. In this case, Eden's behavior seems to fit in with a general pattern of behavior and beliefs. We should be careful not to completely divorce the pathologies of political leaders from the context of politics itself. His attitude toward Nasser, for instance, was not changed because of medication, but rather because of a series of events that Eden interpreted in a particular way. Jerrold M. Post and Roberts S. Robins, *When Illness Strikes the Leaders: The Dilemma of the Captive King* (New Haven, CT: Yale University Press, 1993), 68–69.

29. Alistair Horne, *Harold Macmillan Volume 1: 1894–1956* (New York: Viking Press, 1988), 396.

30. Evelyn Shuckburgh, *Descent to Suez: Diaries, 1951–1956* (New York: Random House, 1986), 341.

31. Kissinger, *Diplomacy*, 523.

32. Nutting, *No End of a Lesson*, 8.

33. Horne, *Harold Macmillan*, 397.

34. The willingness of major or declining powers to take ever-increasing risks to avoid the loss of prestige or status by initiating risky and often self-defeating incursions into the "periphery" is not unique to this particular case. See Jeffrey Taliaferro, *Balancing Risks: Great Power Intervention in the Periphery* (Ithaca, NY: Cornell University Press, 2004).

35. Kyle, *Suez: Britain's End of Empire in the Middle East*, 10.

36. Karl W. Deutsch and Richard Merritt, "Effects of Events on National and International Images," in *International Behavior: A Social-Psychological Approach*, ed. Herbert C. Kelman (New York: Holt, Rinehart and Winston, 1965), 182–183.

37. Quoted in Kyle, "Britain and the Crisis, 1955–1956," 114.

38. Eden, *Full Circle*, 535.

39. Gorst and Johnman, *Suez Crisis*, 57.

40. Daniel Yergin, *The Prize: The Epic Quest for Oil, Money, and Power* (New York: Free Press, 1992), 480.

41. Ibid., 580.

42. Eden, *Full Circle*, 475.

43. Nutting, *No End of a Lesson*, 10.

44. Varble, *Suez Crisis 1956*, 11.

45. Though Eden is admittedly not an expert on energy resources, his account on the importance of the Suez Canal for the transportation of oil is nevertheless an important source. This passage illustrates the importance of the canal *in the mind of Eden*, the primary decision-maker in this case.

46. Eden, *Full Circle*, 478.

47. Nutting, *No End of a Lesson*, 55.

48. Lloyd, *Suez 1956*, 15.

49. Shuckburgh, *Descent to Suez*, 155.

50. Ibid., 341.

51. Quoted in Ann Lane, "The Past as Matrix: Sir Ivone Kirkpatrick, Permanent Under-Secretary for Foreign Affairs," in *Whitehall and the Suez Crisis*, ed. Saul Kelly and Anthony Gorst (London: Frank Cass, 2000), 206.

52. Lloyd, *Suez 1956*, 54.

53. Horne, *Harold Macmillan*, 112.

54. Kyle, *Suez: Britain's End of Empire in the Middle East*, 11.

55. Scot Macdonald, *Rolling the Iron Dice: Historical Analogies and Decisions to Use Military Force in Regional Contingencies* (Westport, CT: Greenwood Press, 2000), 113. (Emphasis added.)

56. William Clark, *From Three Worlds: Memoirs* (London: Sidgwick & Jackson, 1986), 184.

57. Eden, *Full Circle*, 519–521.

58. Jervis, *Perception and Misperception in International Politics*, 240.

59. Nutting, *No End of a Lesson*, 52.

60. Eden, *Full Circle*, 485.

61. Ibid., 487.

62. Nutting, *No End of a Lesson*, 54.

63. Quoted in Kyle, *Suez: Britain's End of Empire in the Middle East*, 184.

64. Kyle, *Suez: Britain's End of Empire in the Middle East*, 199.

65. Nutting, *No End of a Lesson*, 54–55.

66. Eden, *Full Circle*, 509.

67. Macdonald, *Rolling the Iron Dice*, 125.

68. Kissinger, *Diplomacy*, 536.

69. Lloyd, *Suez 1956*, 130.

70. Moshe Dayan, *Moshe Dayan: The Story of My Life* (New York: William Morrow, 1976), 193–194.

71. Ibid., 195.

72. Ibid.

73. Nutting, *No End of a Lesson*, 92.

74. Ibid., 93.

75. Ibid., 95.

76. Ibid., 97.

77. Carlton, *Britain and the Suez Crisis*, 63.

78. Avi Shlaim, "The Protocol of Sevres, 1956: Anatomy of a War Plot," *International Affairs* 73, no. 3 (July 1997): 514.

79. Ibid.

80. Dayan, *Moshe Dayan*, 219.

81. For details of the planning discussions, see Dayan, *Moshe Dayan*, 214–225; and Shimon Peres, *Battling for Peace: A Memoir* (New York: Random House, 1995), 110–113.

82. Quoted in Gorst and Johnman, *Suez Crisis*, 98.

83. Ibid., 100–101.

84. Mordechai Bar-On, *The Gates of Gaza: Israel's Road to Suez and Back 1955–1957* (New York: St. Martin's Griffin, 1994), 263.

85. Carlton, *Britain and the Suez Crisis*, 162.

86. Horne, *Harold Macmillan*, 440.

87. Quoted in Carlton, *Britain and the Suez Crisis*, 163.

88. Quoted in Edward Vose Gulick, *Europe's Classical Balance of Power: A Case History of the Theory of One of the Great Concepts of European Statecraft* (New York: W. W. Norton, 1955), 28–29.

89. John G. Stoessinger, *Nations in Darkness: China, Russia, and America* (New York: Random House, 1981), 240.

90. Hans J. Morgenthau and Kenneth W. Thompson, *Politics among Nations* (New York: Alfred A. Knopf, 1967), 111–145.

91. Ibid., 151.

92. Eden, *Full Circle*, 510.

Chapter 3

1. Osiraq is variously referred to as "Osirak," "Osiraq," or "Tammuz." For purposes of clarity, it will be referred to as "Osiraq" in this chapter.

2. Ian Black and Benny Morris, *Israel's Secret Wars: A History of Israel's Intelligence Services* (New York: Grove Press, 1991), 332.

3. Shlomo Nakdimon, *First Strike: The Exclusive Story of How Israel Foiled Iraq's Attempt to Get the Bomb*, trans. P. Kidron (New York: Summit Books, 1987), 38.

4. Ibid.

5. Amos Perlmutter, Michael I. Handel, and Uri Bar-Joseph, *Two Minutes over Baghdad*, 2nd ed. (London: Frank Cass, 2003), xviii.

6. Edward Cody, "Israel Angered as French Send Uranium to Iraq," *Washington Post*, July 20, 1980, A15.

7. Jerel A. Rosati, "The Power of Human Cognition in the Study of World Politics," *International Studies Review* 2, no. 3 (Fall 2000): 60.

8. For instance, see Deborah Welch Larson, "Trust and Missed Opportunities in International Relations," *Political Psychology* 18, no. 3 (1997): 701–734.

9. Michael B. Oren, *Six Days of War: June 1967 and the Making of the Modern Middle East* (Oxford: Oxford University Press, 2002), 6.

10. Nakdimon, *First Strike*, 40.

11. Jed C. Snyder, "The Road to Osiraq: Baghdad's Quest for the Bomb," *Middle East Journal* 37, no. 4 (Autumn 1983): 565.

12. Its output was later upgraded to 5 MW in 1978.

13. Nakdimon, *First Strike*, 41.

14. Snyder, "Road to Osiraq," 566.

15. Ibid.

16. Quoted in Nakdimon, *First Strike*, 57.

17. Steve Weissman and Herbert Krosney, *The Islamic Bomb: The Nuclear Threat to Israel and the Middle East* (New York: Times Books, 1981), 86.

18. Peter Beaumont, "Countdown to Conflict: Last Days of Saddam," *Observer*, February 23, 2003, 18.

19. Kanan Makiya, *Republic of Fear: The Politics of Modern Iraq*, 2nd ed. (Berkeley: University of California Press, 1989), 118.

20. Marion Farouk-Sluglett and Peter Sluglett, *Iraq Since 1958: From Revolution to Dictatorship* (London: I.B. Tauris Press, 2001), 73.

21. Weissman and Krosney, *Islamic Bomb*, 86.

22. Beaumont, "Countdown to Conflict," 18.

23. Farouk-Sluglett and Sluglett, *Iraq Since 1958*, 116–121.

24. Beaumont, "Countdown to Conflict," 18; and Said K. Aburish, "How Saddam Hussein Came to Power," in *The Saddam Hussein Reader*, ed. Turi Munthe (New York: Thunder's Mouth Press, 2002), 41–43.

25. Nakdimon, *First Strike*, 31.

26. Snyder, "Road to Osiraq," 566.

27. Ibid.

28. Perlmutter, Handel, and Bar-Joseph, *Two Minutes over Baghdad*, 41.

29. Weissman and Krosney, *Islamic Bomb*, 90.

30. Shai Feldman, "Bombing of Osiraq—Revisited," *International Security* 7, no. 2 (Autumn 1982): 115.

31. Quoted in Weissman and Krosney, *Islamic Bomb*, 91.

32. Nakdimon, *First Strike*, 47.

33. Angus Deming, "What Israel Knew," *Newsweek*, June 22, 1981, 25.

34. Quoted in Nakdimon, *First Strike*, 48.

35. Ibid., 59.

36. Perlmutter, Handel, and Bar-Joseph, *Two Minutes over Baghdad*, 42.

37. Feldman, "Bombing of Osiraq—Revisited," 566.

38. Ibid., 567. This model reactor produced 40 kg of military-grade plutonium per year (Perlmutter, Handel, and Bar-Joseph, 42).

39. Weissman and Krosney, *The Islamic Bomb*, 92.

40. Perlmutter, Handel, and Bar-Joseph, *Two Minutes over Baghdad*, 42.

41. Nakdimon, *First Strike*, 57.

42. Ibid.

43. Ibid.

44. Feldman, "Bombing of Osiraq—Revisited," 116; Nakdimon, *First Strike*, 62.

45. Snyder, "Road to Osiraq," 569.

46. Feldman, "Bombing of Osiraq—Revisited," 116.

47. Ibid.

48. Snyder, "Road to Osiraq," 569.

49. "Israeli General Sees Iraq Near Nuclear Capacity," *Washington Post*, July 30, 1977, A13.

50. J. P. Smith, "Iraq's Nuclear Arms Option," *Washington Post*, August 8, 1978, A14.

51. Ibid.

52. Nakdimon, *First Strike*, 67.

53. Snyder, "Road to Osiraq," 571.

54. Ibid., 572.

55. Perlmutter, Handel, and Bar-Joseph, *Two Minutes over Baghdad*, 47.

56. *The Iraqi Nuclear Threat—Why Israel Had to Act* (Jerusalem: Ministry of Foreign Affairs, 1981), 11–12.

57. Feldman, "Bombing of Osiraq—Revisited," 117.

58. Nakdimon, *First Strike*, 74.

59. Feldman, "Bombing of Osiraq—Revisited," 117.

60. Milton R. Benjamin, "France Plans to Sell Iraq Weapons-Grade Plutonium," *Washington Post*, February 28, 1980, A29.

61. Ibid.

62. Cody, "Israel Angered as French Send Uranium to Iraq," A15.

63. Ibid.

64. Ibid.

65. Nakdimon, *First Strike*, 81.

66. For a more comprehensive picture of Menachem Begin's life, see Eric Silver, *Begin: The Haunted Prophet* (New York: Random House, 1984); Amos Perlmutter, *The Life and Times of Menachem Begin* (New York: Doubleday, 1987); and Sasson Sofer, *Begin: An Anatomy of Leadership* (New York: Basil Blackwell, 1988).

67. Sofer, *Begin*, 3.

68. Ibid., 6.

69. Ibid.

70. Silver, *Begin*, 10.

71. Ibid., 12.

72. Sofer, *Begin*, 7.

73. Ibid., 8.

74. Nakdimon, *First Strike*, 81.

75. Ibid.

76. Perlmutter, *Life and Times of Menachem Begin*, 137.

77. Silver, *Begin*, 70.

78. Perlmutter, *Life and Times of Menachem Begin*, 13.

79. Sofer, *Begin*, 165.

80. Silver, *Begin*, 65.

81. Sofer, *Begin*, 216.

82. Perlmutter, Handel, and Bar-Joseph, *Two Minutes over Baghdad*, 52.

83. Cody, "Israel Angered as French Send Uranium to Iraq," A15.

84. Although France and China did not sign the treaty, France continually and publicly asserted that it felt itself bound by it and would behave as such.

85. Richard Wilson, "Nuclear Proliferation and the Case of Iraq," *Journal of Palestine Studies* 20, no. 3 (Spring 1991): 7.

86. "The Safeguards System of the International Atomic Energy Agency" [www.iaea.org/OurWork/SV/index.html].

87. Ronald Koven, "Many Nations Ready to Break into Nuclear Club; About 15 Nations Ready to Break into Five-Member Nuclear Club." *Washington Post*, June 15, 1981, A1.

88. In addition, France's previous behavior toward Israel did not inspire confidence. In 1967, on the event of the Six Days' War, French President Charles de Gaulle announced a delay in French shipment of arms to Israel to "prevent Israel from being able to start a war." This came at a time when Egypt had already blockaded the Strait of Tiran, removed the UNEF forces from the Egypt-Israel border, and continued to receive unlimited arms shipments from the Soviet Union (Dayan, *Moshe Dayan*, 313). In 1973, after Israel was attacked by Egypt, France joined with Germany and Great Britain in not even allowing American supply planes to land in Western Europe to refuel on their way to Israel, as well as again delaying vital shipments of arms.

89. Feldman, "Bombing of Osiraq—Revisited," 121.

90. Perlmutter, *Life and Times of Menachem Begin*, 363.

91. Ibid.

92. Perlmutter, Handel, and Bar-Joseph, *Two Minutes over Baghdad*, 68.

93. Snyder, "Road to Osiraq," 581.

94. Nakdimon, *First Strike*, 171.

95. Quoted in Silver, *Begin*, 219.

96. Black and Morris, *Israel's Secret Wars*, 334.

97. Perlmutter, Handel, and Bar-Joseph, *Two Minutes over Baghdad*, 69.

98. Ibid.

99. In addition, Yehoshua Saguy, chief of IDF Intelligence Services, had warned Begin that the strike would lead to the reestablishment of the "anti-Israeli Eastern Front" composed of Syria, Jordan, and Iraq, and might even compel Iran and Iraq to forget their differences and turn their collective wrath toward Israel (Black and Morris, *Israel's Secret Wars*, 335).

100. William Claiborne, "Begin's Raid Tied Hands of U.S., Astonished His Own Cabinet," *Washington Post*, June 14, 1981, A29.

101. Quoted in Nakdimon, *First Strike*, 191.

102. Silver, *Begin*, 219.

103. Perlmutter, *Life and Times of Menachem Begin*, 365.

104. Silver, *Begin*, 218.

105. Judith Miller, "U.S. Officials Say Iraq Had Ability to Make Nuclear Weapons in 1981," *New York Times*, June 9, 1981, A9.

106. Silver, *Begin*, 219.

107. Quoted in David K. Shipler, "Prime Minister Begin Defends Raid on Iraqi Nuclear Reactor; Pledges to Thwart a New 'Holocaust,'" *New York Times*, June 10, 1981, A1.

108. Nakdimon, *First Strike*, 199–200.

109. Angus Deming, "Two Minutes over Baghdad," *Newsweek*, June 22, 1981, 22.

110. *Iraqi Nuclear Threat*, 1–4.

111. Quoted in Perlmutter, Handel, and Bar-Joseph, *Two Minutes over Baghdad*, 131.

112. Shipler, "Prime Minister Begin Defends Raid on Iraqi Nuclear Reactor," A1.

113. Ibid.

114. William Claiborne, "Begin Threatens to Destroy Any Reactor Menacing Israel; Begin Says Raid Was 'Legitimate Self-Defense,'" *Washington Post*, June 10, 1981, A1.

115. Feldman, "Bombing of Osiraq—Revisited," 136.

116. Black and Morris, *Israel's Secret Wars*, 336.

117. Arthur Gladstone, "The Conception of the Enemy," *Journal of Conflict Resolution* 3, no. 2 (1959): 132.

Chapter 4

1. Henry Kissinger, "Military Policy and Defense of the 'Grey Areas,'" *Foreign Affairs* 33, no. 3 (April 1955): 416.

2. Huntington, "To Choose Peace or War," 360.

3. Quoted in James F. Schnabel, *History of the Joint Chiefs of Staff*, vol. 1, *The Joint Chiefs of Staff and National Policy, 1945–1947* (Washington, DC: Office of the Chairman of the Joint Chiefs of Staff, 1996), 119.

4. "Report to the National Security Council by the Chairman of the National Security Resources Board (Symington)," State Department, *Foreign Relations of the United States* (hereafter "FRUS"), 1951, vol. I, 11.

5. See Arthur Fleming's (director of Defense Mobilization) memo, "Notes on National Security, *FRUS*, 1952–1954, vol. II, 782; and Hans Morgenthau, "The Conquest of the United States by Germany," *Bulletin of Atomic Scientists* 6, no. 1 (January 1950): 25.

6. George F. Kennan, *Memoirs: 1925–1950* (Boston: Little, Brown, 1967), 296.

7. "Study Prepared by the Director of the Policy Planning Staff (Nitze)," *FRUS*, 1950, vol. I, 145.

8. Marc Trachtenberg, "A 'Wasting Asset,' American Strategy and the Shifting Nuclear Balance, 1949–1954," *International Security* 13, no. 3 (Winter 1988–1989): 6.

9. Deborah Welch Larson, *The Origins of Containment: A Psychological Explanation* (Princeton, NJ: Princeton University Press, 1985), 221.

10. *FRUS*, 1951, vol. I, 17.

11. At the end of 1945, the United States had only two atomic weapons, nine in 1946, thirteen by 1947, and fifty by 1948. All of these weapons were "Mark 3" implosion bombs, which weighed 10,000 pounds and took 39 men over two full days to assemble. David Alan Rosenberg, "The Origins of Overkill: Nuclear Weapons and American Strategy, 1945–1960," *International Security* 7, no. 4 (1983): 14; David Alan Rosenberg, "American Atomic Strategy and the Hydrogen Bomb Decision," *Journal of American History* 66, no. 1 (June 1979): 66.

12. Harry S. Truman, *Memoirs by Harry S. Truman*, vol. 2, *Years of Trial and Hope* (New York: Doubleday), 306.

13. Ibid.

14. Ibid., 383.

15. Even by 1953, when the United States still had a fundamental superiority over the Soviet Union, U.S. leaders acknowledged the Soviet ability to conduct atomic strikes was, in fact, growing. See "Memorandum for the President by the Secretaries of State and Defense and the Director for Mutual Security," *FRUS*, 1952–1954, vol. II (1), 213–214.

16. "Memorandum for the President of Discussion at the 122d Meeting of the National Security Council on Wednesday, September 3, 1952," *FRUS*, 1952–1954, vol. II (1), 121. (Emphasis added.)

17. Truman, *Memoirs*, 414.

18. Ibid., 383.

19. Paul H. Nitze, *From Hiroshima to Glasnost: At the Center of Decision, a Memoir* (New York: Grove Weidenfeld, 1989), 93.

20. "A Report to the President Pursuant to the President's Directive of January 31, 1950 (NSC 68)," *FRUS*, 1950, vol. I, 281.

21. Ibid.

22. Ibid.

23. Ibid. (Emphasis added.)

24. "Memorandum of Conversation, by the Secretary of State," *FRUS*, 1950, vol. I, 207–208.

25. *FRUS*, 1950, vol. I, 238.

26. Nitze, *From Hiroshima to Glasnost*, 97.

27. *FRUS*, 1950, vol. I, 266. (Emphasis added.)

28. Trachtenberg, "A 'Wasting Asset,'" 14.

29. Nathan F. Twining, *Neither Liberty nor Safety: A Hard Look at U.S. Military Policy and Strategy* (New York: Holt, Rinehart and Winston, 1966), 49.

30. Ibid.

31. Ibid., 60.

32. George H. Quester, *Nuclear Diplomacy: The First Twenty-Five Years*, 2nd ed. (New York: Cambridge University Press, 1973), 67.

33. Ibid., 39.

34. *The Parliamentary Debates (Hansard): House of Commons, Volume 446* (London: His Majesty's Stationary Office, 1948), 561. (Emphasis Added.)

35. Charles McMoran Wilson Moran, *Churchill: The Struggle for Survival: Taken from the Diaries of Lord Moran* (Boston: Houghton Mifflin, 1966), 337.

36. Ibid., 577.

37. "Russell Urges West to Fight Russia Now." *New York Times*, November 21, 1948, 4.

38. William L. Laurence, "How Soon Will Russia Have the A-Bomb?" *The Saturday Evening Post* 221, no. 10 (November 6, 1948): 182.

39. Ibid.

40. Ibid. (Emphasis added.)

41. Hazel Gaudet Erskine, "The Polls: Atomic Weapons and Nuclear Energy," *Public Opinion Quarterly* 27, no. 2 (Summer 1963): 177.

42. Ibid., 182.

43. "Record of the Under Secretary's Meeting, Department of State, April 15, 1949," *FRUS*, 1949, vol. I, 284.

44. "Super" here refers to the thermonuclear (hydrogen) bomb then in development. The debate within the administration was whether to push forward with its development. Truman eventually decided to do so, partially spurred by the unexpected Soviet testing of an atomic bomb in August of 1949. "The Chairman of the Joint Committee on Atomic Energy (McMahon) to President Truman," *FRUS*, 1949, vol. I, 591.

45. "Memorandum of Conversation, by the Assistant Secretary of State for Far Eastern Affairs (Rusk)," *FRUS*, 1950, vol. VII, 1572–1573. (Emphasis is in original.)

46. "Significance of the H-Bomb, and America's Dilemma," *Newsweek* 35, February 13, 1950, 20.

47. Ibid.

48. "Both Parties Back Truman Arms Call," *New York Times*, September 3, 1950, 11.

49. "Memorandum by the Assistant Secretary of State for Congressional Relations (McFall) to the Under Secretary of State (Webb)," *FRUS*, 1950, vol. I, 140.

50. "Matthews Favors U.S. War for Peace," *New York Times*, August 26, 1950, 1.

51. "U.S. Disowns Matthews Talk of Waging War to Get Peace." *New York Times*, August 27, 1950, 1.

52. Austin Stevens, "General Removed over War Speech," *New York Times*, September 2, 1950, 1.

53. According to Trachtenberg, Bernard Brodie, while working at RAND, asserted that the notion of preventive war was for several years "the prevailing philosophy" at the Air War College, and quite popular at RAND as well. Bernard Brodie, "A Commentary on the Preventive War Doctrine" (RAND paper, June

11, 1953); quoted in Trachtenberg, "Strategic Thought in America 1952–1966," 314; and Stevens, "General Removed over War Speech," 1.

54. Thomas C. Schelling, *The Strategy of Conflict* (London: Oxford University Press, 1960), 207–229.

55. Quoted in David Alan Rosenberg and W. B. Moore, " 'Smoking Radiating Ruin at the End of Two Hours': Documents on American Plans for Nuclear War with the Soviet Union, 1954–1955." *International Security* 6, no. 3 (Winter 1981–1982): 27.

56. Schnabel, *History of the Joint Chiefs of Staff*, vol. 1, 128.

57. Ibid., 130. (Emphasis added.)

58. "Memorandum by the Commanding General, Manhattan Engineer District (Groves)," *FRUS*, 1946, vol. I, 1198–1199.

59. Quoted in Rosenberg, "American Atomic Strategy and the Hydrogen Bomb Decision," 67.

60. Rosenberg, "American Atomic Strategy and the Hydrogen Bomb Decision," 67.

61. Quoted in John Lewis Gaddis, *Strategies of Containment: A Critical Appraisal of Postwar American National Security Policy* (Oxford: Oxford University Press, 1982), 135. Another early reference to the "cold" war can be found in Eisenhower's diary entry from May 1, 1953. Robert H. Ferrell, ed., *The Eisenhower Diaries* (London: W. W. Norton, 1981), 235.

62. Gaddis, *Strategies of Containment*, 136.

63. Anthony Leviero, "To Build Military," *New York Times*, May 1, 1953, 1.

64. Quoted in Leviero, "To Build Military," 1.

65. "Dulles Speech to the French National Political Science Institute," Paris, May 5, 1952. Quoted in Gaddis, *Strategies of Containment*, 139.

66. Ferrell, *Eisenhower Diaries*, 307.

67. Gaddis, *Strategies of Containment*, 140–142.

68. See speech to newspaper editors in "Challenge to Soviets," *New York Times*, April 23, 1956, 26.

69. Nina Tannenwald, "The Nuclear Taboo: The United States and the Normative Basis of Nuclear Non-Use." *International Organization* 53, no. 3 (Summer 1999): 433–434.

70. "NSC Meeting, March 31, 1953," *FRUS*, 1952–1954, vol. 15 (1), 770.

71. Dwight D. Eisenhower, *The White House Years: Mandate for Change, 1953–1956* (New York: Doubleday, 1963), 181.

72. Tannenwald, "Nuclear Taboo," 450.

73. Eisenhower, *Mandate for Change*, 446.

74. "Memorandum by the President to the Secretary of State," *FRUS*, 1952–1954, vol. II (1), 461. (Emphasis in original.)

75. Robert R. Bowie and Richard H. Immerman, *Waging Peace: How Eisenhower Shaped an Enduring Cold War Strategy* (New York: Oxford University Press, 1998), 164.

76. *FRUS*, 1952–1954, vol. II (1), 460.

77. Ferrell, *Eisenhower Diaries*, 312.

78. Marc Trachtenberg, *History and Strategy* (Princeton, NJ: Princeton University Press, 1991), 209. Original in "Eisenhower, Memorandum for the Files, February 27, 1959," in the Dwight David Eisenhower Library, Kansas.

79. Ferrell, "January 22, 1952," *Eisenhower Diaries*, 209–214.

80. Dwight D. Eisenhower, "1953 State of the Union Address," in *Public Papers of the Presidents of the United States: Dwight D. Eisenhower, 1953* (Washington, DC: U.S. Government Printing Office, 1960), 17.

81. "Summaries Prepared by the NSC Staff of Project Solarium Presentations and Written Reports," *FRUS*, 1952–1954, vol. II (1), 400–401.

82. Ibid., 412.

83. Ibid., 434.

84. Ibid., 417. (Emphasis added.)

85. Ibid.

86. Ibid., 416.

87. Ibid., 397.

88. Ibid., 397–398.

89. "Memorandum of Discussion at the 157th Meeting of the National Security Council, Thursday, July 30, 1953," *FRUS*, 1952–1954, vol. II (1), 438.

90. Eisenhower, *Mandate for Change*, 446. (Emphasis added.)

91. Trachtenberg, *History and Strategy*, 162. Original in "Goodpaster Memorandum of Conference, December 22, 1954." Ann Whitman File, "ACW Diary December 1954," in the Dwight David Eisenhower Library, Kansas.

92. "Memorandum by the Staff Secretary to the President (Goodpaster)," *FRUS*, 1952–1954, vol. II (2), 1576ff. (Emphasis added.)

93. "Report of the Special Evaluation Subcommittee of the National Security Council," *FRUS*, 1952–1954, vol. II (1), 341.

94. Albert Wohlstetter, "The Delicate Balance of Terror," *Foreign Affairs* 37, no. 2 (January 1959): 212.

95. Ibid., 217.

96. Schelling, *Strategy of Conflict*, 208.

97. Nitze, *From Hiroshima to Glasnost*, 166.

98. Before the development of thermonuclear (hydrogen) weapons, atomic weapons destroyed everything within around 3 square miles. Thermonuclear weapons (first detonated on October 31, 1953), however, increased the area to around 300–400 square miles per weapon (Trachtenberg, "A 'Wasting Asset,'" 33).

99. Kenneth W. Thompson and Steven L. Rearden, eds., *Paul H. Nitze on National Security and Arms Control*, vol. XIV, W. Alton Jones Foundation Series on Arms Control (New York: University Press of America, 1990), 47–51.

100. Nitze, *From Hiroshima to Glasnost*, 204.

101. Ibid.

102. Richard K. Betts, "A Nuclear Golden Age? The Balance before Parity," *International Security* 11, no. 3 (Winter 1986–1987): 4.

103. Stevens, "General Removed over War Speech," 1.

Chapter 5

1. The first war was fought over the territory of Kashmir in 1948. The second war was begun by Pakistan in 1965 when Pakistani troops crossed the cease-fire line in Kashmir to "aid" the local populace. To their surprise, the Kashmiris notified the Indian authorities, and full-scale war broke out in September of 1965. The third war was fought when Zulfikar Ali Bhutto (leader of West Pakistan) declared martial law in East Pakistan where a pro-autonomy party had swept recent elections. India supported East Pakistan's effort to form an army, and Pakistan declared war on India in December of 1971. The war lasted only two weeks and resulted in the creation of the state of Bangladesh. See Sumit Ganguly, "India: Policies, Past and Future," in *India and Pakistan: The First Fifty Years*, ed. Selig S. Harrison, Paul H. Kreisberg, and Dennis Kux (Cambridge: Cambridge University Press, 1999), 158–163.

2. Onkar Marwah, "India and Pakistan: Nuclear Rivals in South Asia," *International Organization* 35, no. 1 (Winter 1981): 170.

3. Despite the existence of the Nuclear Non-Proliferation Treaty, these blueprints, parts, and general technology were sold to Pakistan by France, Japan, Britain, Holland, Belgium, Germany, Switzerland, and the United States (Marwah, 169).

4. Marwah, "India and Pakistan," 170.

5. Ibid.

6. Milton R. Benjamin, "India Said to Eye Raid on Pakistani A-Plants," *Washington Post*, December 20, 1982, A1.

7. Ibid.

8. William Claiborne, "India Denies Plan to Hit Pakistani Nuclear Plants," *Washington Post*, December 21, 1981, A10.

9. Benjamin, "India Said to Eye Raid on Pakistani A-Plants," A1.

10. Claiborne, "India Denies Plan to Hit Pakistani Nuclear Plants," A10.

11. Benjamin, "India Said to Eye Raid on Pakistani A-Plants," A1.

12. Pakistan had just acquired U.S.-made F-16 Fighter Jets, the same planes Israel used to attack Iraq's Osiraq reactor.

13. Benjamin, "India Said to Eye Raid on Pakistani A-Plants," A1.

14. Claiborne, "India Denies Plan to Hit Pakistani Nuclear Plants," A10.

15. Philip Taubman, "Worsening India-Pakistan Ties Worry U.S.," *New York Times*, September 15, 1984, 2.

16. Don Oberdorfer, "Pakistan Concerned about Attack on Atomic Plants," *Washington Post*, October 12, 1984, A28.

17. Ibid.

18. Ibid. (Emphasis added.)

19. William K. Stevens, "India Worried by U.S. Links to Pakistanis," *New York Times*, October 21, 1984, 7.

20. C. Raja Mohan and Peter R. Lavoy, "Avoiding Nuclear War," in *Crisis Prevention, Confidence Building, and Reconciliation in South Asia*, ed. Amith Sevak and Michael Krepon (New York: St. Martin's Press, 1955), 28.

21. Quoted in Mohan and Lavoy, "Avoiding Nuclear War," 28.

22. Staff, "Echoes of War," *Economist* 314, no. 7639 (January 27, 1990): 33.

23. Ibid., 33.

24. Rajiv Tiwari, "India: Ominous Sabre-Rattling with Pakistan," *IPS Inter Press Service*, April 12, 1990.

25. Staff, "Echoes of War," 33.

26. Ahmed Rashid, "Pakistan Fears Indian Attack over Kashmir," *Independent* (London), April 2, 1990, 12.

27. Ibid.

28. Ibid.

29. David Housego, "India Urged to Attack Camps in Pakistan over Strife in Kashmir," *Financial Times* (London), April 9, 1990, 6.

30. Ibid.

31. Michael Krepon and Mishi Faruqee, eds., *Conflict Prevention and Confidence-Building Measures in South Asia: The 1990 Crisis*, Occasional Paper No. 17 (Washington, DC: Henry L. Stimson Center, April 1994), 6. This document is a transcript of a meeting convened by the Stimson Center to discuss the 1990 crisis. Participants include the U.S. ambassadors to India and Pakistan as well as South Asian diplomats and military officers.

32. Ibid., 7.

33. David Housego and Zafar Meraj, "Indian Premier Warns of Danger of Kashmir War," *Financial Times* (London), April 11, 1990, 6.

34. Ibid.

35. Ibid.

36. Mark Fineman, "India's Leader Warns of an Attack by Pakistan," *Los Angeles Times*, April 15, 1990, A7.

37. Ibid.

38. Steve Coll, "Assault on Pakistan Gains Favor in India," *Washington Post*, April 15, 1990, A25.

39. Ibid.

40. Ibid. (Emphasis added.)

41. Ibid.

42. Staff, "The Makings of a Bloody, Old-Fashioned War," *Economist* 315, no. 7651 (April 21, 1990): 35.

43. Al Kamen, "Tension over Kashmir Called Strongest in Decade," *Washington Post*, April 21, 1990, A21.

44. Ibid.

45. Krepon and Faruqee, *The 1990 Crisis*, 8–9.

46. See comments of Ambassador William Clark in Krepon and Faruqee, *The 1990 Crisis*, 4.

47. P. R. Chari, Pervaiz Iqbal Cheema, and Stephen Philip Cohen, *Perception, Politics, and Security in South Asia: The Compound Crisis of 1990* (New York: Routledge Curzon, 2003), 106.

48. Seymour Hersh, "On the Nuclear Edge," *New Yorker* 69, no. 6 (March 29, 1993): 56.

49. Ibid., 57.

50. Ibid., 56–57.

51. Devin T. Hagerty, "Nuclear Deterrence in South Asia: The 1990 Indo-Pakistani Crisis," *International Security* 20, no. 3 (Winter 1995–1996): 80.

52. See Krepon and Faruqee, *The 1990 Crisis*, 2, 8, 14, 18–19, 20–22.

53. And it is true that Pakistan, which had stopped the production of weapons-grade uranium in 1989, re-started production as the crisis escalated in the spring of 1990. David Albright, "India and Pakistan's Nuclear Arms Race: Out of the Closet but Not in the Street," *Arms Control Today* 23, no. 5 (June 1993): 15; William E. Burrows and Robert Windrem, *Critical Mass: The Dangerous Race for Superweapons in a Fragmenting World* (New York: Simon & Schuster, 1994), 506.

54. John M. Broder and Stanley Meisler, "Terrifying Pursuit of Nuclear Arms," *Los Angeles Times*, January 19, 1992, A4.

55. Marwah, "India and Pakistan," 165.

56. One interesting note about this war is that though the three major wars occurred when Pakistan was under military rule, the Kargil conflict (as well as the first test of a Pakistani nuclear weapon in 1998) was initiated by a democratically elected prime minister.

57. "Kargil: What Does It Mean?" *South Asia Monitor*, no. 12 (July 19, 1999).

58. American officials also believed that most of the troops were from Pakistan's army, and that the entire operation was engineered and controlled by Pakistan (Pamela Constable, "Pakistan Aims to 'Avoid Nuclear War,'" *Washington Post*, July 13, 1999, A14.

59. Scott D. Sagan, "The Perils of Proliferation in South Asia," *Asian Survey* 41, no. 6 (November–December 2001): 1072.

60. Devin T. Hagerty, *The Consequences of Nuclear Proliferation* (Cambridge: MIT Press, 1998), 184.

61. Sagan, "Perils of Proliferation in South Asia," 1073.

62. Kotera M. Bhimaya, "Nuclear Deterrence in South Asia: Civil-Military Relations and Decision-Making," *Asian Survey* 34, no. 7 (July 1994): 654–655. (Emphasis added.)

63. Staff, "Omar for Pre-Emptive Strikes against Militants," *Hindu*, October 1, 2001.

64. Tony Allen-Mills, "Pakistan Panics over Threat to Arsenal," *Sunday Times* (London), November 4, 2001.

65. Ibid.

66. "Pak Fitter Case for Pre-Emptive Strike: Sinha," *Times of India*, April 10, 2003.

67. Luv Puri, "India Has Right to Pre-Emptive Strike," *Hindu*, April 7, 2003.

68. Wire Report, "India Issues Warning of Pakistan Intervention," 9.

69. Staff, "US Alarmed by India's War Threats," *Straits Times* (Singapore), April 13, 2002.

70. Firdaus Ahmed, "The Sole 'Lesson' of the Iraq War," Institute of Peace and Conflict Studies, April 28, 2003 [www.ipcs.org].

71. National Security Strategy of the United States of America (September 2002), 6.

72. Kamal Matinuddin, *The Nuclearization of South Asia* (Oxford: Oxford University Press, 2002), 47–48.

73. Edward Luce, "Pakistan Helped Organize Bombers, Says India," *Financial Times* (London), December 17, 2001, 8.

74. John F. Burns, "Pakistan Is Reported to Have Arrested Militant Leader," *New York Times*, December 31, 2001, A3.

75. John F. Burns, "Pakistan Is Said to Order an End to Support for Militant Groups," *New York Times*, January 2, 2002, A1.

76. Edward Luce, "Death Sentence for Terror Gang," *Financial Times* (London), December 19, 2002, 10.

77. Navnita Chadha, "Enemy Images: The Media and Indo-Pakistani Tensions," in *Crisis Prevention, Confidence Building and Reconciliation in South Asia*, ed. Amit Sevak and Michael Krepon (New York: St. Martin's Press, 1995), 172.

78. Ibid., 173.

79. Quoted in Anthony H. Cordesman, *Weapons of Mass Destruction in India and Pakistan* (Washington, DC: Center for Strategic and International Studies [CSIS], 2002), 11.

80. Ben Sheppard, "Ballistic Missiles," in *Nuclear India in the Twenty-First Century*, ed. D. R. SarDesai and Raju G. C. Thomas (New York: Palgrave Macmillan, 2002), 191.

81. Ibid., 194–195.

82. Ibid., 198.

83. Tellis uses the term "splendid" to describe a preventive or pre-emptive strike that would destroy the adversary's ability to retaliate with nuclear weapons.

84. Ashley J. Tellis, *India's Emerging Nuclear Posture: Between Recessed Deterrent and Ready Arsenal* (California: RAND, 2001), 311.

85. Ibid.

86. Sheppard, "Ballistic Missiles," 198.

87. Stephen Philip Cohen, "The Nation and the State of Pakistan," *Washington Quarterly* 25, no. 3 (Summer 2002): 111.

88. Ibid., 112.

89. Stephen Philip Cohen writes that in times of heightened crisis, "Pakistan has not hesitated to be the first to employ the heavy use of force in order to gain an initial advantage. This was clearly the pattern in 1965 and possibly in 1971; in both cases it was thought that a short, sharp war would achieve Pakistan's military as well as political objectives." Stephen P. Cohen, *The Pakistan Army* (Los Angeles: University of California Press, 1984), 145.

90. See Edward Luce, "India's Peaceable Premier," *Financial Times* (London), January 5, 2002, 11.

91. Jammu (Indian-controlled) is 60% Hindu, 40% Muslim; Ladakh (which is claimed by both India and China) is predominantly Buddhist; and Valley of Kashmir (Indian-held, and contains most of the region's population and resources) is 90% Sunni Muslim. Pakistan controls the areas of Mirpur and Muzzafarabad (Chari, Cheema, and Cohen, *Perception, Politics, and Security in South Asia*, 34–35).

92. Jawaharlal Nehru eloquently stated the significance of Pakistan: "We have always regarded the Kashmir problem as symbolic for us, as it had far-reaching consequences in India. Kashmir is symbolic as it illustrates that we are a secular state. Kashmir has consequences both in India and Pakistan because if we disposed of Kashmir on the basis of the two-nation theory, obviously millions of people in India and millions in East Pakistan will be powerfully affected. Many of the wounds that had healed might open out again." Ashutosh Varshney, "India, Pakistan, and Kashmir: Antinomies of Nationalism," *Asian Survey* 31, no. 11 (November 1991): 1002.

93. Varshney, "India, Pakistan, and Kashmir," 999.

94. Hagerty, "Nuclear Deterrence in South Asia," 93.

95. David Rhode, "Fighting in Kashmir Revives Rancor in Pakistan and India," *New York Times*, September 28, 2003, 8.

96. Edward Luce, "We'll Talk Only When Terror Ends, India's Leader Tell UN," *Financial Times* (London), September 26, 2003, 11.

97. One might also distinguish between two types of violence, both of which are present here. The first is state-sponsored violence, which takes the form of the three major wars fought by India and Pakistan. The second type of violence is a sort of "independent" violence, which takes the form of communalism and mass riots and killings (which the government does not officially sponsor, though it has often looked the other way).

98. Taubman, "Worsening India-Pakistan Ties Worry U.S.," 2.

99. Benjamin, "India Said to Eye Raid on Pakistani A-Plants," A1.

Chapter 6

1. "CBS News Poll, March 15–16, 2003." American Enterprise Institute Studies in Public Opinion: "Public Opinion on the War on Terrorism, the War with Iraq, and America's Place in the World," 31 [www.aei.org] (accessed February 5, 2005).

2. Two important caveats must be noted at the outset of this analysis. The first caveat is still too close to the events being analyzed for there to be a full historical record including accurate firsthand accounts. More information of this kind will undoubtedly become available over time. However, this case is important enough to proceed with even the limited information available currently, in order to provide a first-cut at an explanation of the decision-making process. The second caveat concerns the focus of this case study. There are

numerous issues that, though important, are not the focus of this case study. Some of these are: How well the Bush administration planned for reconstruction, the timeline of the transfer of sovereignty to the Iraqi people, the execution of the war plans themselves, and the wisdom of the war itself. While these factors are important for any overall assessment of the war, they are not the focus of this work.

3. Hugh Heclo, "The Political Ethos of George W. Bush," in *The George W. Bush Presidency: An Early Assessment*, ed. Fred Greenstein (Baltimore: Johns Hopkins University Press, 2003), 34.

4. Ivo H. Daalder and James M. Lindsay, "Bush's Foreign Policy Revolution," in *The Bush Presidency*, 102.

5. Fred Greenstein, "The Leadership Style of George W. Bush," in *The Bush Presidency*, 16.

6. Bob Woodward, *Bush at War* (New York: Simon & Schuster, 2002); see also Bob Woodward, *Plan of Attack* (New York: Simon & Schuster, 2004).

7. Peter Riddell, "Nuclear Arms Plan Admitted by Iraq," *New York Times*, July 9, 1991, 18; Frank J. Prial, "U.N. Team Finds Chemical Arms 4 Times Greater Than Iraq Claims," *New York Times*, July 31, 1991, A1; Elaine Sciolino, "Iraqi Report Says Chemical Arsenal Survived the War," *New York Times*, April 20, 1991, A1.

8. For more information on the conduct of Iraq after the Gulf War, see Michael Kelly, "A Chronology of Defiance," *Washington Post*, September 18, 2002, A29.

9. *Iraq Liberation Act*, HR 4655. Text of this bill is available at [thomas.loc.gov] (accessed February 5, 2005). However, it is generally acknowledged that the substance of Clinton's policy toward Iraq was actually "dual-containment," pitting Iran and Iraq against one another. Thus, though "regime change" was the official policy stance of the United States during the Clinton era, the *de facto* policy was one of containment. This fact makes Bush's continuation of Clinton's policy of regime change seem somewhat more radical than Bush would probably admit. This is essentially the difference between regime change by simply wishing it to be so (Clinton), and regime change by a pro-active policy. See Stephen Hubbell, "The Containment Myth: US Middle East Policy in Theory and Practice," *Middle East Report*, no. 208 (Fall 1998): 9.

10. Woodward, *Plan of Attack*, 10–11.

11. Ibid., 11; and "Secretary of Defense Interview with Bob Woodward," *Washington Post*, April 20, 2004.

12. John F. Burns, "Iraq Defiant as U.S. Lobbies Arabs on Shift in Sanctions," *New York Times*, February 25, 2001, 4; Stephen Fidler and Roula Khalaf, "Arab Resistance Rises to Meet Bush's Tough New Line on Iraq," *Financial Times*, April 19, 2001; Alan Sipress, "U.S. Favors Easing Iraq Sanctions," *Washington Post*, February 27, 2001, A1.

13. Woodward, *Plan of Attack*, 19.

14. John Burton and Stephen Fidler, "Seoul Sides with Moscow on US Missile Defence Plan," *Financial Times*, February 28, 2001, 1; Robert Cottrel,

Stephen Fidler, Andrew Gowers, and Andrew Jack, "Putin Hits at US Decision to Pull Out of ABM Treaty," *Financial Times*, December 14, 2001, 1.

15. David E. Sanger, "After ABM Treaty: New Freedom for U.S. in Different Kind of Arms Control," *New York Times*, December 15, 2001, 8.

16. James Mann, *Rise of the Vulcans: The History of Bush's War Cabinet* (New York: Viking Press, 2004), xiv–xv.

17. Elayne Tobin, "Dubyaspeak," *Nation* 275, no. 5 (August 5, 2002): 40.

18. See, for example, Frank Bruni, *Ambling into History: The Unlikely Odyssey of George W. Bush* (New York: HarperCollins, 2002); and Stanley A. Renshon, *In His Father's Shadow: The Transformations of George W. Bush* (New York: Palgrave Macmillan, 2004).

19. "Text of Bush Interview with Hume," September 22, 2003.

20. John Lewis Gaddis, "A Grand Strategy of Transformation," *Foreign Policy* (November/December 2002): 54–55.

21. Philip H. Gordon, "Bush's Middle East Vision," *Survival* 45, no. 1 (Spring 2003): 155.

22. Allan Murray, "Bush Seeks to Remake World Without Much Help, Discussion," *Wall Street Journal* (June 3, 2003).

23. Daalder and Lindsay, "The Bush Revolution," 100.

24. Ron Hutcheson, "Bush Risks All in Iraq Stance," *Philadelphia Inquirer*, March 9, 2003.

25. Tommy Franks, with Malcom McConnell, *American Soldier* (New York: Regan Books, 2004), 373–374.

26. Dana Milbank, "For Bush, War Defines Presidency," *Washington Post*, March 9, 2003, A1.

27. Ibid.

28. "A Distinctly American Internationalism." Speech made by Governor Bush at the Ronald Reagan Presidential Library, November 19, 1999 [www.mtholyoke.edu] (accessed February 5, 2005).

29. Daalder and Lindsay, "The Bush Revolution," 104.

30. "A Distinctly American Internationalism." Speech made by Governor Bush, November 1999.

31. Robert Jervis, "Understanding the Bush Doctrine," *Political Science Quarterly* 118, no. 3 (Fall 2003): 370.

32. "President Declares 'Freedom at War with Fear,'" September 20, 2001 [www.whitehouse.gov] (accessed February 5, 2005).

33. "President's Remarks: 'We Are in the Middle Hour of Our Grief,'" *New York Times*, September 15, 2001, 6.

34. Woodward, *Plan of Attack*, 27.

35. It should be noted that Bush is very capable of carrying out policy based on a more subtle and nuanced perception of the world. For instance, though Iran, North Korea, and Iraq were all mentioned as the "axis of evil," Bush was clear that there were very important differences between the three countries that necessitated different approaches.

36. For one of many such references by Bush, see David E. Sanger and Julia Preston, "Bush to Warn U.N.: Act on Iraq or U.S. Will," *New York Times*, September 12, 2002.

37. For some examples of this, see Paul Hendrickson, "Reagan: The Cause, the Prize and the Rendezvous," *Washington Post*, November 13, 1979, B1; Tom Shales, "Battle Hymn of the Republicans," *Washington Post*, August 24, 1984, B1; and Henry Allen, "The Sunset Side of Ronald Reagan," *Washington Post*, November 7, 1988, B1.

38. "Remarks by Homeland Secretary Tom Ridge at the London School of Economics," January 14, 2005 [www.dhs.gov] (accessed February 11, 2005). (Emphasis added.)

39. Gaddis, "A Grand Strategy of Transformation," 53. The comparison of Gaddis' phrase to Woodrow Wilson's speech declaring America's entry into World War I should not be ignored. Wilson declared that "the world must be made safe for democracy," on April 2, 1917. The similarity between Bush and Wilson is striking in this respect; both see the role of the United States in the transformative, revolutionary mold. For both, it is both a mission, and a responsibility to spread democracy. For Wilson this was primarily the result of an ideological aversion to the European colonial empires of the nineteenth and twentieth centuries. For Bush, it is the result of the perception that there was no safety to be found in the status quo; security required action, which included the democratization of the rest of the world.

40. Glad, "Black-and-White Thinking," 51; Stuart and Starr, "The 'Inherent Bad Faith Model' Reconsidered," 6, 9, and 12. See also Shoon Kathleen Murray and Jonathan A. Cowden, "The Role of Enemy Images and Ideology in Elite Belief Systems," *International Studies Quarterly* 43, no. 3 (1999): 455–481.

41. Ron Suskind, *The Price of Loyalty: George W. Bush, the White House and the Education of Paul O'Neill* (New York: Simon & Schuster, 2004), 72–76.

42. Ibid., 86.

43. Ibid., 85.

44. There are many reasons to doubt Paul O'Neill's assessment of President Bush's intentions with regard to Iraq, in addition to those mentioned previously. As treasury secretary, it is unlikely that O'Neill would have been at all of the meetings at which policy toward Iraq was discussed. For instance, O'Neill was absent at the meeting with outgoing Secretary of Defense William Cohen, Donald Rumsfeld, Condoleezza Rice, and Colin Powell ten days before inauguration at which policy toward Iraq was discussed (Woodward, *Plan of Attack*, 9–10). Additionally, O'Neill's very bitter break with the administration after severe disagreements over policy suggest the importance of keeping the motivations of the writer in mind while reading *The Price of Loyalty*.

45. Chaim Kaufmann, "Threat Inflation and the Failure of the Marketplace of Ideas," *International Security* 29, no. 1 (Summer 2004): 5.

46. Woodward, *Plan of Attack*, 11.

47. "PSRA/Newsweek Poll, October 11–12, 2001." AEI Studies in Public Opinion: "Public Opinion on the War on Terrorism, the War with Iraq, and America's Place in the World," 32.

48. Though the war on Afghanistan is not the focus of this work, an excellent overview of the decision-making leading to that war is contained in Bob Woodward's *Bush at War*.

49. "Brit Hume Goes One-on-One With First Lady Laura Bush," September 10, 2002 [www.foxnews.com] (accessed February 5, 2005).

50. "Mr. Bush's New Gravitas," *New York Times*, October 12, 2001, A24.

51. Fred Greenstein, "Leadership Style of George W. Bush," 11; Eric Quinones, "Greenstein: Bush a 'Less Sure-Footed' Leader in Iraq War, Despite His Post-Sept. 11 Growth," *Princeton Bulletin* 92, no. 21 (March 31, 2003).

52. John Lewis Gaddis, *Surprise, Security, and the American Experience* (Cambridge: Harvard University Press, 2004), 82.

53. Bill Sammon, "Attacks of September 11 Defined Bush Presidency," *Washington Times*, September 11, 2002.

54. An exception to this view is Alexander Moen, who asserts that there was no transformation, because "if he [Bush] had to accumulate all his skills and talents in the few days after September 11, he would have failed miserably." However, this is an overly defensive interpretation of the very idea of a transformation. In fact, Bush's skills, values, and ideology were in place before 9/11, as Moen claims. However, the idea of a transformation refers to the hypercharged sense of mission, of purpose that Bush was imbued with after September 11. The transformation did not furnish President Bush with any new skills, or dramatically change his personality or worldview; but that does not make it any less of a dramatic transformation. See Alexander Moen, *The Foreign Policy of George W. Bush: Values, Strategy and Loyalty* (London: Ashgate Press, 2004), 140.

55. Stanley A. Renshon, *In His Father's Shadow: The Transformations of George W. Bush* (New York: Palgrave MacMillan, 2004), 137.

56. Bill Sammon, "Bush Rates Progress High After 180 Days," *Washington Times*, July 27, 2001, A1.

57. David Frum, *The Right Man: The Surprise Presidency of George W. Bush* (New York: Random House, 2003), 274.

58. Quoted in Milbank, "For Bush, War Defines Presidency," A01.

59. Greenstein, "The Leadership Style of George W. Bush," 11.

60. Woodward, *Plan of Attack*, 12.

61. Gordon, "Bush's Middle East Vision," 160.

62. Condoleezza Rice, "Promoting the National Interest," *Foreign Affairs* 79, no. 1 (January/February 2000): 61.

63. Ibid.

64. James Risen, David E. Sanger, and Thom Shanker, "In Sketchy Data, Trying to Gauge Iraq Threat," *New York Times*, July 20, 2003.

65. "President Bush Meets with Prime Minister Blair," January 31, 2003 [www.whitehouse.gov] (accessed February 5, 2005). (Emphasis added.)

66. Jervis, *Perception and Misperception in International Politics*, 300.

67. "Letter Accompanying NSS 2002" [www.whitehouse.gov] (accessed February 5, 2005).

68. Ibid.

69. Much of the literature and commentary on the NSS 2002 has made reference to the "doctrine of pre-emption." However, I agree with Robert Jervis, who called it "violence to the English language," to refer to the Bush doctrine as "pre-emptive," when it is, in fact, based on "preventive" action. Jervis, "Understanding the Bush Doctrine," 369ff.

70. Lawrence Freedman, *Deterrence* (London: Polity Press, 2004), 84.

71. Ibid., 105.

72. "West Point Commencement Address," June 1, 2002 [www.whitehouse.gov] (accessed February 5, 2005).

73. For a more detailed exposition of the reasons why nuclear deterrence requires stable, "mature" states with a culture of accountability, and some minimum level of technological capacity, see Karl Kaiser, "Non-Proliferation and Nuclear Deterrence," *Survival* 31, no. 2 (March/April 1989): 123–136.

74. Schelling, *Arms and Influence*, 39.

75. Jervis, "Understanding the Bush Doctrine," 369.

76. Gaddis, *Surprise, Security and the American Experience*, 70–71.

77. Robert Pape has recently argued for the "strategic logic" of suicide terrorism. Pape's conclusions are based on his view that, in the past, terrorism had been moderately successful at achieving political goals. However, while leaders of terrorist organizations might be "rational" in the conventional sense of the word, those who carry out suicide attacks do not necessarily share that quality. Moreover, even Pape seems to acknowledge that "deterrence" of suicide terrorism is difficult to achieve, and instead suggests that the best course of action is to make suicide terrorist attacks as difficult to carry out as possible, by improving domestic security. Surely this is a reasonable suggestion, but taken alone it is unlikely to appeal to a leader given to forceful, proactive solutions. See Robert Pape, "The Strategic Logic of Suicide Terrorism," *American Political Science Review* 97, no. 3 (August 2003): 1–19.

78. Many noted political scientists have stated that they believed Saddam to be deterrable or containable. However, the difference of opinion even among academics who specialize in issues of war and peace, threats and security, etc., shows the extent to which the matter relies on individual perception. See Nicolas Lemann, "The War on What?" *New Yorker*, September 16, 2002; John J. Mearsheimer and Stephen M. Walt, "Can Saddam Be Contained? History Says Yes" (Occasional Paper, Belfer Center for Science and International Affairs, International Security Program, November 2002).

79. "The National Security Strategy, 2002," 15.

80. Robert Jervis, for instance, argues that the administration's main concern was not deterrence per se, but rather "extended deterrence": deterring Saddam from coercing or attacking Kuwait and Saudi Arabia with the leverage of WMD.

However, I would argue that while this was one of Bush's concerns, his main concern—the possibility of which could not be ignored after September 11—was another terrorist incident on U.S. soil. As Jervis is right to point out, the possibility of such an attack, sponsored or aided in some way by Saddam Hussein, was unlikely, but people are willing to pay a high price to decrease the probability of a danger from slight to none. This is especially understandable given the terrible consequences of such an attack, which might make living with even a slight risk seem unbearable. Robert Jervis, "The Confrontation between Iraq and the US: Implications for the Theory and Practice of Deterrence," *European Journal of International Law* 9, no. 2 (June 2003): 318, 320–321.

81. "West Point Commencement Address."

82. Ibid.

83. For instance, see David Stout, "Bush Calls Iraqi Vow a Trick," *New York Times*, September 18, 2002; Richard Stevenson, "Bush Says Iraq Isn't Complying With Demands to Disarm," *New York Times*, January 21, 2003.

84. "West Point Commencement Address."

85. "National Security Strategy, 2002," 5.

86. Moen, *The Foreign Policy of George W. Bush*, 147; and Colin Powell, "A Strategy of Partnerships," *Foreign Affairs* 83, no. 1 (January/February 2004): 22.

87. Woodward, *Bush at War*, 49.

88. Ibid., 61.

89. Ibid., 81.

90. Ibid., 83.

91. Ibid., 87–91.

92. Ibid., 99.

93. Ibid., 107.

94. Franks, *American Soldier*, 268.

95. John Tatom, "Iraqi Oil Is Not America's Objective," *Financial Times*, February 13, 2003, 17.

96. Daniel Yergin, "Gulf Oil: How Important Is It Anyway?" *Financial Times*, March 22, 2003, 1.

97. "What Will Happen to Oil after Saddam?" *Times* (London), December 12, 2002, 31.

98. Daniel Yergin, "Oil Shortage Conventional Wisdom Says that Oil Can Bail Out Iraq ..." *Boston Globe*, May 25, 2003, 10.

99. James Cox, "Victory in Iraq Likely Would Bring Cheaper Oil—Eventually." *USA Today*, February 25, 2003, 1.

100. "Crude Oil and Total Petroleum Imports Top 15 Countries," U.S. Energy Information Administration [www.eia.doe.gov/pub/oil_gas/petroleum/data_publications/company_level_imports/current/import.html]; "United States Country Analysis Brief," US EIA [www.eia.doe.gov/emeu/cabs/usa.html].

101. Cox, "Victory in Iraq Would Bring Cheaper Oil—Eventually," 1.

102. Anthony Sampson, "Oilmen Don't Want Another Suez," *Guardian*, December 22, 2002, 17.

103. Joshua Chaffin and Andrew Hill, "The Rush to Secure Contracts to Rebuild Iraq and the Awarding of the First Waves of Deals is Causing as Much Debate as the Decision to Wage War," *Financial Times*, April 28, 2003, 19.

104. Woodward, *Plan of Attack*, 104, 111, 205, 258, 322–324.

105. Ibid., 51.

106. That war plans against Iraq had not been updated during his entire tenure as president provides further evidence that Bill Clinton's enunciated policy of regime change was more rhetorical than actual.

107. Franks, *American Soldier*, 328–330; Woodward, *Plan of Attack*, 59.

108. "President Delivers State of the Union Address," January 29, 2002 [www.whitehouse.gov] (accessed February 5, 2005).

109. Frum, *The Right Man*, 225–245.

110. Franks, *American Soldier*, 366–369; Woodward, *Plan of Attack*, 96–98.

111. "U.S.-Pakistan Affirm Commitment Against Terrorism," February 13, 2002 [www.whitehouse.gov] (accessed February 5, 2005).

112. Franks, *American Soldier*, 376.

113. Woodward, *Plan of Attack*, 111.

114. Ibid., 113–114. Interestingly, Franks' own memoirs place the date much later. Franks recalls in his memoirs that, as late as September 2002, war was neither "inevitable" nor "imminent." (Franks, *American Soldier*, 404).

115. Franks, *American Soldier*, 389.

116. Woodward, *Plan of Attack*, 168–171.

117. David E. Sanger, "Bush Presses U.N. to Act Quickly on Disarming Iraq," *New York Times*, September 13, 2002, A1.

118. Todd S. Purdham and Elisabeth Bumiller, "Bush Seeks Power to Use 'All Means' to Oust Hussein," *New York Times*, September 19, 2002, 1.

119. For more on the difference between "inspections-as-verification" and "inspections-as-discover," see Moen, *The Foreign Policy of George W. Bush*, 178–179.

120. Joseph Curl, "Inaction on Iraq 'Not an Option,'" *Washington Times*, September 5, 2003.

121. Franks, *American Soldier*, 338.

122. Mann, *Rise of the Vulcans*, 348.

123. "House Vote on Iraq Resolution," *New York Times*, October 12, 2002, A13.

124. "Congress Says Yes to Iraq Resolution," *CBS News Online*, October 11, 2002 [www.cbsnews.com] (accessed February 5, 2005).

125. Elizabeth Neuffer, "Resolution on Iraq Passes Security Council Vote Unanimous," *Boston Globe*, November 9, 2002, A1; Woodward, *Plan of Attack*, 224–226; Mann, *Rise of the Vulcans*, 347–348.

126. Julia Preston, "Iraq Tells the U.N. Arms Inspections Will Be Permitted," *New York Times*, November 14, 2002, A1.

127. Woodward, *Plan of Attack*, 234–235; Julia Preston, "U.S. Is First to Get a Copy of Report on Iraqi Weapons," *New York Times*, December 10, 2002, A1.

128. Eric Schmitt, "Buildup Leaves U.S. Nearly Set to Start Attack," *New York Times,* December 8, 2002, 1; Woodward, *Plan of Attack,* 233–234.

129. Woodward, *Plan of Attack,* 240.

130. "Iraq is in 'Material Breach' of U.N. Measure, Powell Says," *Wall Street Journal,* December 19, 2002, 1; Steven R. Weisman and Julia Preston, "Powell Says Iraq Raises Risk of War By Lying on Arms," *New York Times,* December 20, 2002, A1.

131. Woodward, *Plan of Attack,* 250.

132. Ibid., 254.

133. Ibid., 256; "President Bush Discusses Tuesday's Economic Speech," January 6, 2003 [www.whitehouse.gov] (accessed February 5, 2005).

134. For instance, see Woodward, *Plan of Attack,* 258 and "Remarks by President Bush and Polish President Kwasniewski in Photo Opportunity," January 14, 2003 [www.whitehouse.gov] (accessed February 5, 2005).

135. Woodward, *Plan of Attack,* 261.

136. Ibid., 271.

137. Julia Preston, "U.N. Inspector Says Iraq Falls Short on Cooperation," *New York Times,* January 28, 2003, 1.

138. Mann, *Rise of the Vulcans,* 354; Woodward, *Plan of Attack,* 297. It is worth noting here that—despite the oft-repeated charge of President Bush as an arrogant unilateralist—at least in this case, Bush halted the push toward war for an important coalition partner.

139. It is not within the scope of this book to fully address the questions later raised regarding the accuracy of Secretary Powell's claims. For instance, the aluminum tubes detailed in his presentation were later found to be "innocuous," and the Iraqi Survey Group asserted that they had probably been sold off to be used as drainpipes. For the purposes of this book, what is important is the extent to which Powell, and the rest of the White House administration, believed the larger claim—that Iraq was pursuing WMD. Additionally, Powell—whose integrity is widely acknowledged—stood by his claims at the United Nations. David Rennie, "Weapons Hunters Dismiss Powell's WMD Claims," *Chicago Sun-Times,* October 27, 2003, 43; Alan Beattie, "Powell Blames Media For WMD 'Firestorm,'" *Financial Times,* June 9, 2003, 2; Jimmy Burns, Guy Dinmore, Stephen Fidler, Mark Huband, and Mark Turner, "Did Intelligence Agencies Rely Too Much on Unreliable Data from Iraqi Exiles?" *Financial Times,* June 4, 2003, 19. The most comprehensive survey and analysis of this set of issues found no evidence of WMD in Iraq, but a clear intent to pursue the development of such weapons. See "Key Findings," *Comprehensive Report of the Special Advisor to the DCI on Iraq's WMD (The Duelfer Report),* September 30, 2004 [www.cia.gov] (accessed May 18, 2005).

140. Steven R. Weisman, "Powell, in U.N. Speech, Presents Case to Show Iraq Has Not Disarmed," *New York Times,* February 6, 2003, 1; "Powell's Address, Presenting 'Deeply Troubling' Evidence on Iraq," *New York Times,* February 6, 2003, 18.

141. Woodward, *Plan of Attack*, 301.

142. Richard W. Stevenson, "Bush Gives Hussein 48 Hours, and Vows to Act," *New York Times*, March 18, 2003, 1; "President Says Saddam Must Leave Within 48 Hours," March 17, 2003 [www.whitehouse.gov] (accessed February 5, 2005).

143. John F. Burns, "As Baghdad Empties, Hussein Is Defiant," *New York Times*, March 19, 2003, 1; David E. Sanger and John F. Burns, "Bush Orders Start of War on Iraq," *New York Times*, March 20, 2003, 1.

144. "President Bush Interview with Diane Sawyer," December 16, 2003.

145. David Stout, "Bush Calls Iraqi Vow a Trick," *New York Times*, September 18, 2002.

146. Ibid.

147. See, for instance, Deborah Orin, "Bush: World's Better Off since I Took Out 'Madman' Saddam," *New York Post*, October 10, 2003, 6.

Chapter 7

1. Randall L. Schweller, "Domestic Structure and Preventive War: Are Democracies More Pacific?" *World Politics* 44, no. 2 (January 1992): 242.

2. Eden, *Full Circle*, 521.

3. Nutting, *No End of a Lesson*, 17.

4. Ibid., 18.

5. Eden, *Full Circle*, 474.

6. Perlmutter, *The Life and Times of Menachem Begin*, 13.

7. Quoted in Judith Miller, "U.S. Officials Say Iraq Had Ability to Make Nuclear Weapons in 1981," *New York Times*, June 9, 1981, A9.

8. Eisenhower, *Mandate for Change*, 144.

9. Ibid.

10. Perlmutter, Handel, and Bar-Joseph, *Two Minutes over Baghdad*, xviii.

11. "A Report to the President Pursuant to the President's Directive of January 31, 1950 (NSC 68)," *FRUS*, 1950, vol. I, 281.

12. Quoted in Coll, "Assault on Pakistan Gains Favor in India," A25.

13. Perlmutter, Handel, and Bar-Joseph, *Two Minutes over Baghdad*, 69.

14. Eden, *Full Circle*, 509.

15. "Report to the National Security Council by the Chairman of the National Security Resources Board (Symington)," State Department, *FRUS*, 1951, vol. I, 11.

16. Morgenthau, "The Conquest of the United States by Germany," 25.

17. Schnabel, *History of the Joint Chiefs of Staff*, vol. I, 128.

18. Eisenhower, *Mandate for Change*, 446.

Epilogue

1. For a dissenting opinion, see Dan Reiter, "Preventive Attacks Against Nuclear Programs and the 'Success' at Osiraq," *Nonproliferation Review* 12, no. 2 (2005), 355–356.

Bibliography

Acheson, Dean. 1969. *Present at the Creation: My Years in the State Department.* New York: W. W. Norton.

Adams, James. 1990. "Pakistan 'Nuclear War Threat.'" *Sunday Times* (London), May 27.

Adamthwaite, Anthony. 1988. "Suez Revisited." *International Affairs* 64 (3): 449–464.

Ahmed, Firdaus. 2003. "The Sole 'Lesson' of the Iraq War." Institute of Peace and Conflict Studies. April 28 [www.ipcs.org].

Albright, David. 1993. "India and Pakistan's Nuclear Arms Race: Out of the Closet but Not in the Street." *Arms Control Today* 23 (5): 11–16.

Allen, Henry. 1988. "The Sunset Side of Ronald Reagan." *Washington Post,* November 7, B1.

Allen-Mills, Tony. 2001. "Pakistan Panics over Threat to Arsenal." *Sunday Times* (London), November 4.

Arend, Anthony Clark. 2003. "International Law and the Preemptive Use of Military Force." *Washington Quarterly* 26 (2): 89–103.

Art, Robert J., and Robert Jervis, eds. 1973. *International Politics: Anarchy, Force, Imperialism.* Boston: Little, Brown.

Asghar, Raja. 2001. "Kashmir Fears; Rivals Talk Nukes." *Herald Sun* (Australia), December 26, 53.

Astorino-Courtois, Allison. 2000. "The Effects of Stakes and Threat of Foreign Policy Decision-Making." *Political Psychology* 21 (3): 489–510.

Bajpai, K. Shankar. 2003. "Untangling India and Pakistan." *Foreign Affairs* 82 (3): 112–120.

Barber, James David. 1972. *The Presidential Character: Predicting Performance in the White House.* New Jersey: Prentice-Hall.

Beattie, Alan. 2003. "Powell Blames Media for WMD 'Firestorm.'" *Financial Times* (London), June 9, 2.

Beaumont, Peter. 2003. "Countdown to Conflict: Last Days of Saddam." *Observer*, February 23, 17.

Ben-Gurion, David. 1970. *Memoirs: David Ben-Gurion.* New York: World.

————. 1971. *Israel: A Personal History.* New York: Funk and Wagnall's Press.

Benjamin, Milton R. 1978. "How to Keep Atom Bombs Out of Regional Wars." *Washington Post*, December 8, A16.

————. 1980. "France Plans to Sell Iraq Weapons-Grade Plutonium." *Washington Post*, February 28, A29.

————. 1982. "India Said to Eye Raid on Pakistani A-Plants." *Washington Post*, December 20, A1.

Benoit, Kenneth. 1996. "Democracies Are Really More Pacific (in General): Reexamining Regime Type and War Involvement." *Journal of Conflict Resolution* 40 (4): 636–657.

Berkowitz, Bruce D. 1985. "Proliferation, Deterrence, and the Likelihood of Nuclear War." *Journal of Conflict Resolution* 29 (1): 112–136.

Bernstein, Barton J. 1974. "The Quest for Security: American Foreign Policy and International Control of Atomic Energy." *Journal of American History* 60 (4): 1003–1044.

————. 1989. "Crossing the Rubicon: A Missed Opportunity to Stop the H-Bomb." *International Security* 14 (2): 132–160.

Betts, Richard K. 1986–1987. "A Nuclear Golden Age? The Balance before Parity." *International Security* 11 (3): 3–32.

————. 2001. "Striking First: A History of Thankfully Lost Opportunities." *Ethics and International Affairs* 17 (1): 17–24.

Bhimaya, Kotera M. 1994. "Nuclear Deterrence in South Asia: Civil-Military Relations and Decision-Making." *Asian Survey* 34 (7): 647–661.

Black, Chris, and Brian McGrory. 1996. "U.S. Launches Second Attack on Iraq." *Boston Globe*, September 4, A1.

Black, Ian, and Benny Morris. 1991. *Israel's Secret Wars: A History of Israel's Intelligence Services.* New York: Grove Press.

Blechman, Barry M., and Tamara Cofman Wittes. 1999. "Defining Moment: The Threat and Use of Force in American Foreign Policy." *Political Science Quarterly* 114 (1): 1–30.

Bothe, Michael. 2003. "Terrorism and the Legality of Pre-emptive Force." *European Journal of International Law* 14 (2): 227–240.

"Both Parties Back Truman Arms Call." 1950. *New York Times*, September 3, 11.

Brands, H. W. 1989. "The Age of Vulnerability: Eisenhower and the National Insecurity State." *American Historical Review* 94 (4): 963–989.

Broder, John M., and Stanley Meisler. 1992. "India, Pakistan Were on the Brink of Nuclear War." *Chicago Sun-Times*, January 26, 18–19.

Brodie, Bernard. 1959. *Strategy in the Missile Age.* New Jersey: Princeton University Press.

Brooks, Stephen G. 1997. "Dueling Realisms." *International Organization* 51 (3): 445–477.

Buhite, Russell D. 1990. "War for Peace: The Question of an American Preventive War against the Soviet Union, 1945–1955." *Diplomatic History* (14): 367–385.

Bundy, McGeorge. 1982. "Early Thoughts on Controlling the Nuclear Arms Race: A Report to the Secretary of State, January 1953." *International Security* 7 (2): 3–27.

Bunn, M. Elain. 2003. "Preemptive Action: When, How, and to What Effect?" *Strategic Forum* (200): 1–8.

Burka, Paul. 1999. "The W. Nobody Knows." *Texas Monthly*, June 1.

Burns, Jimmy, Guy Dinmore, Stephen Fidler, Mark Huband, and Mark Turner. 2003. "Did Intelligence Agencies Rely Too Much on Unreliable Data from Iraqi Exiles?" *Financial Times* (London), June 4, 19.

Burns, John F. 2001. "Iraq Defiant as U.S. Lobbies Arabs on Shift in Sanctions." *New York Times*, February 25, 4.

———. 2001. "Pakistan Is Reported to Have Arrested Militant Leader." *New York Times*, December 31, A3.

———. 2002. "Pakistan Is Said to Order an End to Support for Militant Groups." *New York Times*, January 2, A1.

———. 2003. "As Baghdad Empties, Hussein Is Defiant." *New York Times*, March 19, 1.

Burrows, William E., and Robert Windrem. 1994. *Critical Mass: The Dangerous Race for Superweapons in a Fragmenting World.* New York: Simon & Schuster.

Burton, John, and Stephen Fidler. 2001. "Seoul Sides with Moscow on US Missile Defence Plan." *Financial Times* (London), February 28, 1.

Byman, Daniel, and Matthew Waxman. 2002. *The Dynamics of Coercion: American Foreign Policy and the Limits of Military Might.* Cambridge: Cambridge University Press.

Carlton, David. 1989. *Britain and the Suez Crisis.* New York: Basil Blackwell.

Castano, Emanuele, Simona Sacchi, and Peter Hays Gries. 2003. "The Perception of the Other in International Relations: Evidence for the Polarizing Effect of Entativity." *Political Psychology* 24 (3): 449–468.

Chaffin, Joshua, and Andrew Hill. 2003. "The Rush to Secure Contracts to Rebuild Iraq and the Awarding of the First Waves of Deals is Causing As Much Debate As the Decision to Wage War." *Financial Times* (London), April 28, 19.

"Challenge to Soviets." 1956. *New York Times*, April 23, 26.

Chan, Steve. 1984. "Mirror, Mirror on the Wall . . . Are the Freer Countries More Pacific?" *Journal of Conflict Resolution* 28 (4): 617–648.

Chari, P. R., Pervaiz Iqbal Cheema, and Stephen Philip Cohen. 2003. *Perception, Politics, and Security in South Asia: The Compound Crisis of 1990.* New York: RoutledgeCurzon.

Chellaney, Brahma. 1991. "South Asia's Passage to Nuclear Power." *International Security* 16 (1): 43–72.

———. 2000. "New Delhi's Dilemma." *Washington Quarterly* 23 (3): 145–153.

Clad, James. 1991. "India: A World at War with Itself." *Washington Post*, March 31, B3.

Claiborne, William. 1981. "Begin Criticizes Weinberger, Assails Critics of Bombing." *Washington Post*, June 15, A16.

———. 1981. "Begin's Raid Tied Hands of U.S., Astonished His Own Cabinet." *Washington Post*, June 14, A29.

———. 1981. "Begin Threatens to Destroy Any Reactor Menacing Israel; Begin Says Raid Was 'Legitimate Self-Defense.'" *Washington Post*, June 10, A1.

———. 1982. "India Denies Plan to Hit Pakistani Nuclear Plants." *Washington Post*, December 21, A10.

Clark, William. 1986. *From Three Worlds: Memoirs.* London: Sidgwick and Jackson.

Cody, Edward. 1980. "Israel Angered as French Send Uranium to Iraq." *Washington Post*, July 20, A15.

Cohen, Stephen P. 1984. *The Pakistan Army.* Los Angeles: University of California Press.

———. 1992. "A Way Out of the South Asia Arms Race." *Washington Post*, September 28, A17.

———. 2002. "The Nation and the State of Pakistan." *Washington Quarterly* 23 (5): 109–122.

Coll, Steve. 1990. "Assault on Pakistan Gains Favor in India." *Washington Post*, April 15, A25.

Constable, Pamela. 1999. "Pakistan Aims to 'Avoid Nuclear War.'" *Washington Post*, July 13, A14.

Cordesman, Anthony H. 2002. *Weapons of Mass Destruction in India and Pakistan.* Washington, DC: Center for Strategic and International Studies (CSIS).

Cottam, Martha L. 1994. *Images and Intervention: U.S. Policies in Latin America.* Pittsburgh, PA: University of Pittsburgh Press.

Cottrel, Robert, Stephen Fidler, Andrew Gowers, and Andrew Jack. 2001. "Putin Hits at US Decision to Pull Out of ABM Treaty." *Financial Times* (London), December 14, 1.

Cox, James. 2003. "Victory in Iraq Likely Would Bring Cheaper Oil—Eventually." *USA Today*, February 25, 1.

Crawford, Neta C. 2002. "The Best Defense: The Problem with Bush's 'Pre-Emptive' War Doctrine." *Boston Review* 28 (1): 20–23.

———. 2003. "The Slippery Slope to Preventive War." *Ethics and International Affairs* 17 (1): 30–36.

Curl, Joseph. 2003. "Inaction on Iraq 'Not an Option.'" *Washington Times*, September 5.

Das, Runa. 2003. "Postcolonial (In)Securities, the BJP and the Politics of Hindutva: Broadening the Security Paradigm between the Realist and Anti-Nuclear/Peace Groups in India." *Third World Quarterly* 24 (1): 77–96.

Dayan, Moshe. 1976. *Moshe Dayan: The Story of My Life.* New York: William Morrow.

Dean, Gordon. 1954. "Tasks for the Statesmen." *Bulletin of Atomic Scientists* 10 (1): 11.

Deming, Angus. 1981. "Two Minutes over Baghdad." *Newsweek*, June 22, 22.

———. 1981. "What Israel Knew." *Newsweek*, June 22, 25.

Devroy, Ann, and Barton Gellman. 1993. "U.S. Allied Jets Batter Iraq's Air Defense." *Washington Post*, January 19, A1.

DiManno, Rosie. 2002. "World's Powder Keg Is Not in Afghanistan." *Toronto Star*, January 7, A2.

Dittmer, Lowell. 2001. "South Asia's Security Dilemma." *Asian Survey* 41 (6): 897–906.

Doerner, William R. 1987. "Knocking at the Nuclear Door." *Time* 129 (13): 42–43.

Eban, Abba. 1977. *An Autobiography.* New York: Random House.

"Echoes of War." 1990. *Economist* 314 (7639): 33.

Eden, Anthony. 1960. *Full Circle: The Memoirs of Anthony Eden.* Boston: Houghton Mifflin.

Eisenhower, Dwight D. 1960. *Public Papers of the Presidents of the United States: Dwight D. Eisenhower, 1953.* Washington, DC: U.S. Government Printing Office.

———. 1963. *The White House Years: Mandate for Change, 1953–1956.* New York: Doubleday.

———. 1965. *The White House Years: Waging Peace, 1956–1961.* New York: Doubleday.

Erskine, Hazel Gaudet. 1963. "The Polls: Atomic Weapons and Nuclear Energy." *Public Opinion Quarterly* 27 (2): 155–190.

Evera, Stephen Van. 1984. "Causes of War." PhD diss., University of California, Berkeley.

———. 1984. "The Cult of the Offensive and the Origins of the First World War." *International Security* 9 (1): 58–107.

Farnham, Barbara. 1990. "Political Cognition and Decision-Making." *Political Psychology* 11 (1): 83–111.

Farouk-Sluglett, Marion, and Peter Sluglett. 2001. *Iraq Since 1958: From Revolution to Dictatorship.* London: I.B. Tauris Press.

Feaver, Peter D. 1992–1993. "Command and Control in Emerging Nuclear Nations." *International Security* 17 (3): 160–187.

Feaver, Peter D., Scott Sagan, and David J. Karl. 1997. "Proliferation Pessimism and Emerging Nuclear Powers." *International Security* 22 (2): 185–207.

Feldman, Shai. 1982. "The Bombing of Osiraq—Revisited." *International Security* 7 (2): 114–142.

Ferrell, Robert H., ed. 1981. *The Eisenhower Diaries.* London: W. W. Norton.

Fidler, Stephen, and Roula Khalaf. 2001. "Arab Resistance Rises to Meet Bush's Tough New Line on Iraq." *Financial Times* (London), April 19.

Fineman, Howard. Web Exclusive. "Bush Studied '67 Pre-emptive Strike," October 9, 2002 [*Newsweek*].

Fineman, Mark. 1990. "India's Leader Warns of an Attack by Pakistan." *Los Angeles Times*, April 15, A7.

Finlay, David J., Ole R. Holsti, and Richard R. Fagen, eds. 1967. *Enemies in Politics.* Chicago: Rand McNally Press.

Ford, Peter S. 2004. "Israel's Attack on Osiraq: A Model for Future Preventive Strikes?" MA diss., Naval Postgraduate School.

Foyle, Douglas C. 1999. *Counting the Public in: Presidents, Public Opinion, and Foreign Policy.* New York: Columbia University Press.

Franck, Thomas M. 1970. "Who Killed Article 2(4)? Or: Changing Norms Governing the Use of Force by States." *American Journal of International Law* (64): 809–837.

Frank, Katherine. 2002. *Indira: The Life of Indira Nehru Gandhi.* New York: Houghton Mifflin.

Franks, Tommy. 2004. *American Soldier.* With Malcom McConnell. New York: Regan Books.

Freedman, Lawrence. 2003. "Prevention, Not Pre-emption." *Washington Quarterly* 26 (2): 105–114.

———. 2004. *Deterrence.* London: Polity Press.

Friedberg, Aaron L. 1988. *The Weary Titan: Britain and the Experience of Relative Decline, 1895–1905.* Princeton: Princeton University Press.

Frum, David. 2003. *The Right Man: The Surprise Presidency of George W. Bush.* New York: Random House.

Gaddis, John Lewis. 1982. *Strategies of Containment: A Critical Appraisal of Postwar American National Security Policy.* Oxford: Oxford University Press.

———. 2002. "A Grand Strategy of Transformation." *Foreign Policy* (133): 50–55.

———. 2004. *Surprise, Security, and the American Experience.* Cambridge: Harvard University Press.

Ganguly, Sumit. 2001. *Conflict Unending: India-Pakistan Tensions since 1947.* New York: Columbia University Press.

Ganguly, Sumit, and Kent L. Biringer. 2001. "Nuclear Crisis Stability in South Asia." *Asian Survey* 41 (6): 907–924.

Ganguly, Sumit, and Rodney W. Jones. 2000. "Correspondence: Debating New Delhi's Nuclear Decision." *International Security* 24 (4): 181–189.

Geller, Daniel S. 1990. "Nuclear Weapons, Deterrence and Crisis Escalation." *Journal of Conflict Resolution* 34 (2): 291–310.

Gellman, Barton. 1998. "U.S. Planes Hit Iraqi Site after Missile Attack." *Washington Post*, December 29, A1.

George, Alexander. 1969. "The 'Operational Code': A Neglected Approach to the Study of Political Leaders and Decision-Making." *International Studies Quarterly* 13 (2): 190–222.

———. 1974. "Assessing Presidential Character." *World Politics* 26 (2): 234–282.

Giles, Gregory F. 1993. "Safeguarding the Undeclared Nuclear Arsenals." *Washington Quarterly* 16 (2): 173–186.

Gilpin, Robert. 1981. *War and Change in World Politics*. Cambridge: Cambridge University Press.

Glad, Betty. 1983. "Black-and-White Thinking: Ronald Reagan's Approach to Foreign Policy." *Political Psychology* 4 (1): 33–76.

Gladstone, Arthur. 1959. "The Conception of the Enemy." *Journal of Conflict Resolution* 3 (2): 132–137.

Glaser, Charles L. 1997. "The Security Dilemma Revisited." *World Politics* 50 (1): 171–201.

Gordon, Michael R. 1994. "South Asian Lands Pressed on Arms." *New York Times*, March 23, A5.

Gordon, Philip H. 2003. "Bush's Middle East Vision." *Survival* 45 (1): 155–165.

Greenstein, Fred, ed. 2003. *The George W. Bush Presidency: An Early Assessment*. Baltimore: Johns Hopkins University Press.

Guhin, Michael A. 1972. *John Foster Dulles: A Statesman and His Times*. New York: Columbia University Press.

Gulick, Edward Vose. 1955. *Europe's Classical Balance of Power: A Case History of the Theory of One of the Great Concepts of European Statecraft*. New York: W. W. Norton.

Hagerty, Devin T. 1995–1996. "Nuclear Deterrence in South Asia: The 1990 Indo-Pakistani Crisis." *International Security* 20 (3): 79–114.

———. 1998. *The Consequences of Nuclear Proliferation*. Cambridge: MIT Press.

Hagerty, Devin T., and Steve Fetter. 1996. "Correspondence: Nuclear Deterrence and the 1990 Indo-Pakistani Crisis." *International Security* 21 (1): 176–185.

Harrison, Selig S., Paul H. Kreisberg, and Dennis Kux, eds. 1999. *India and Pakistan: The First Fifty Years*. Cambridge: Cambridge University Press.

Hendrickson, Paul. 1979. "Reagan: The Cause, the Prize and the Rendezvous." *Washington Post*, November 13, B1.

Hermann, Margaret G., and Paul A. Kowert. 1997. "Who Takes Risks? Daring and Caution in Foreign Policy Making." *Journal of Conflict Resolution* 41 (5): 611–637.

Hermann, Margaret G., Thomas Preston, Baghat Korany, and Timothy M. Shaw. 2001. "Who Leads Matters: The Effects of Powerful Individuals." *International Studies Review* 3 (2): 83–131.

Hermann, Richard K., and Michael P. Fischerkeller. 1995. "Beyond the Enemy Image and Spiral Model: Cognitive-Strategic Research after the Cold War." *International Organization* 49 (3): 415–450.

Hersh, Seymour M. 1993. "On the Nuclear Edge." *New Yorker* 69 (6): 57–73.

Horne, Alistair. 1988. *Harold Macmillan Volume 1: 1894–1956.* New York: Viking Press.

Housego, David. 1990. "India Urged to Attack Camps in Pakistan over Strife in Kashmir." *Financial Times* (London), April 9, 6.

"House Vote on Iraq Resolution." 2002. *New York Times,* October 12, A13.

Houweling, Henk W., and Jan G. Siccama. 1988. "The Risk of Compulsory Escalation." *Journal of Peace Research* 25 (1): 43–56.

Hubbell, Stephen. 1998. "The Containment Myth: US Middle East Policy in Theory and Practice." *Middle East Report* (208): 8–11.

Huntington, Samuel P. 1957. "To Choose Peace or War: Is There a Place for Preventive War in American Policy?" *United States Naval Institute Proceedings* 83 (4): 359–369.

Hutcheson, Ron. 2003. "Bush Risks All in Iraq Stance." *Philadelphia Inquirer,* March 9.

Huth, Paul, and Bruce Russett. 1984. "What Makes Deterrence Work? Cases from 1900 to 1980." *World Politics* 36 (4): 496–526.

———. 1993. "General Deterrence between Enduring Rivals: Testing Three Competing Models." *American Political Science Review* 87 (1): 61–73.

Ignatieff, Michael. 2003. "Why Are We in Iraq? And Liberia? And Afghanistan?" *New York Times,* September 7, A6.

Immerman, Richard H., and Robert R. Bowie. 1998. *Waging Peace: How Eisenhower Shaped and Enduring Cold War Strategy.* New York: Oxford University Press.

"India Issues Warning if Pakistan Intervention." 2003. *Milwaukee Journal Sentinel,* April 11, 9.

"Iraq Is in 'Material Breach' of UN Measure, Powell Says." 2002. *Wall Street Journal,* December 19, 1.

"Israeli General Sees Iraq Near Nuclear Capacity." 1977. *Washington Post,* July 30, A13.

"Israelis Cite Quotations by Iraqi Aides to Stress Perils of a Baghdad Bomb." 1981. *New York Times,* June 21, 3.

Jehl, Douglas. 1993. "Did India and Pakistan Face Atomic War? Claim Is Debated." *New York Times,* March 23, A3.

Jervis, Robert. 1976. *Perception and Misperception in International Politics.* Princeton: Princeton University Press.

———. 1978. "Cooperation under the Security Dilemma." *World Politics* 30 (2): 167–214.

———. 1988. "War and Misperception." *Journal of Interdisciplinary History* 18 (4): 675–700.

———. 1992. "Political Implication of Loss Aversion." *Political Psychology* 13 (2): 187–204.

———. 2003. "The Confrontation between Iraq and the US: Implications for the Theory and Practice of Deterrence." *European Journal of International Law* 9 (2): 315–337.

———. 2003. "Understanding the Bush Doctrine." *Political Science Quarterly* 118 (3): 365–388.

Johnman, Lewis, and Anthony Gorst. 1997. *The Suez Crisis.* London: Routledge.

Kaarbo, Juliet, and Ryan K. Beasley. 1999. "A Practical Guide to the Comparative Case Study Method in Political Psychology." *Political Psychology* 20 (2): 369–391.

Kahnneman, Daniel, and Amos Tversky. 1979. "Prospect Theory: An Analysis of Decision under Risk." *Econometrica* 47 (2): 263–292.

Kaiser, Karl. 1989. "Non-Proliferation and Nuclear Deterrence." *Survival* 31 (2): 123–136.

Kamen, Al. 1990. "Tension over Kashmir Called Strongest in Decade." *Washington Post*, April 21, A21.

Kanwal, Gurmeet. 2001. "India's Nuclear Doctrine and Policy." *Strategic Analysis* 24 (11): 1707–1731.

Kaplowitz, Noel. 1976. "Psychopolitical Dimensions of the Middle East Conflict: Policy Implications." *Journal of Conflict Resolution* 20 (2): 279–318.

———. 1990. "National Self-Images, Perceptions of Enemies, and Conflict Strategies: Psychopolitical Dimensions of International Relations." *Political Psychology* 11 (1): 39–82.

Kapur, Ashok. 2001. *Pokhran and beyond: India's Nuclear Behavior.* New York: Oxford University Press.

Karabell, Zachary. 2003. *Parting the Desert: The Creation of the Suez Canal.* New York: Alfred A. Knopf.

Karl, David J. 1996–1997. "Proliferation Pessimism and Emerging Nuclear Powers." *International Security* 21 (3): 87–119.

Kelly, Michael. 2002. "A Chronology of Defiance." *Washington Post*, September 18, A29.

Kelman, Herbert C., ed. 1965. *International Behavior: A Social-Psychological Approach.* New York: Holt, Rinehart and Winston.

Kennan, George F. 1967. *Memoirs: 1925–1950.* Boston: Little, Brown.

Kissinger, Henry. 1955. "Military Policy and Defense of the 'Grey Areas.'" *Foreign Affairs* 33 (3): 416–428.

———. 1994. *Diplomacy.* New York: Simon & Schuster.

———. 2004. "America's Assignment—Pre-emption." *Newsweek*, November 8.

Kogan, Nathan, and Michael Wallach. 1964. *Risk Taking: A Study in Cognition and Personality.* New York: Holt, Rinehart and Winston.

Koven, Ronald. 1981. "Many Nations Ready to Break into Nuclear Club; About 15 Nations Ready to Break into Five-Member Nuclear Club." *Washington Post*, June 15, A1.

Kreidie, Lina Haddad, and Kristen Renwick Monroe. 1997. "The Perspective of Islamic Fundamentalists and the Limits of Rational Choice Theory." *Political Psychology* 18 (1): 19–43.

Krepon, Michael, and Mishi Faruqee, eds. 1994. *Conflict Prevention and Confidence-Building Measures in South Asia: The 1990 Crisis.* Washington, DC: The Henry L. Stimson Center.

Krosney, Herbert, and Steve Weissman. 1981. *The Islamic Bomb: The Nuclear Threat to Israel and the Middle East.* New York: Times Books.

Kyle, Keith. 2003. *Suez: Britain's End of Empire in the Middle East.* London: I.B. Tauris.

Larson, Deborah Welch. 1985. *The Origins of Containment: A Psychological Explanation.* Princeton, NJ: Princeton University Press.

———. 1997. "Trust and Missed Opportunities in International Relations." *Political Psychology* 18 (3): 701–734.

Laurence, William L. 1948. "How Soon Will Russia Have the A-Bomb?" *Saturday Evening Post* 221 (10): 23, 181–182.

Lawren, William. 1988. *The General and the Bomb: A Biography of General Leslie R. Groves, Director of the Manhattan Project.* New York: Dodd, Mead.

Lebow, Richard Ned. 1984. "Windows of Opportunity: Do States Jump through Them?" *International Security* 9 (1): 147–186.

Legro, Jeffrey W. 1994. "Military Culture and Inadvertent Escalation in World War II." *International Security* 18 (4): 108–142.

———. 1997. "Which Norms Matter? Revisiting the 'Failure' of Internationalism." *International Organization* 51 (1): 31–63.

Lemann, Nicolas. 2002. "The War on What?" *New Yorker*, September 16.

LeMay, Curtis E. 1968. *America Is in Danger.* New York: Funk & Wagnalls.

Lemke, Douglas, and Suzanne Werner. 1996. "Power Parity, Commitment to Change, and War." *International Studies Quarterly* 40 (2): 235–260.

Leviero, Anthony. 1953. "To Build Military." *New York Times*, May 1, 1.

Levy, Jack S. 1987. "Declining Power and the Preventive Motivation for War." *World Politics* 40 (1): 82–107.

———. 1988. "Domestic Politics and War." *Journal of Interdisciplinary History* 18 (4): 653–673.

———. 1992. "An Introduction to Prospect Theory." *Political Psychology* 13 (2): 171–186.

———. 1997. "Prospect Theory, Rational Choice, and International Relations." *International Studies Quarterly* 41 (1): 87–112.

Litwak, Robert S. 2002–2003. "The New Calculus of Pre-Emption." *Survival* 44 (4): 53–80.

Lloyd, Selwyn. 1978. *Suez 1956: A Personal Account.* New York: Mayflower Books.

Lloyd, T. O. 1996. *The British Empire, 1558–1995.* Oxford: Oxford University Press.

Louis, Wm. Roger, and Roger Owens, eds. 2003. *Suez 1956: The Crisis and Its Consequences.* Oxford: Oxford University Press.

Luce, Edward. 2001. "Pakistan Helped Organize Bombers, Says India." *Financial Times* (London), December 17, 8.

———. 2002. "Death Sentence for Terror Gang." *Financial Times* (London), December 19, 10.

———. 2002. "Indian Hardliner Dares Pakistan to Fight 'Face to Face.'" *Financial Times* (London), December 2, 10.

———. 2002. "India's Peaceable Premier." *Financial Times* (London), January 5, 11.

———. 2003. "We'll Talk Only When Terror Ends, India's Leader Tell UN." *Financial Times* (London), September 26, 11.

Luce, Edward, and Farhan Bokhari. 2003. "Observers Taken Aback by India's Change of Heart." *Financial Times* (London), May 3, 13.

Luostarinen, Heikki. 1989. "Finnish Russophobia: The Story of an Enemy Image." *Journal of Peace Research* 26 (2): 123–137.

Macdonald, Scot. 2000. *Rolling the Iron Dice: Historical Analogies and Decisions to Use Military Force in Regional Contingencies.* Westport, CT: Greenwood Press.

"The Makings of a Bloody, Old-Fashioned War." 1990. *London Economist* 315 (7651): 35.

Makiya, Kanan. 1989. *Republic of Fear: The Politics of Modern Iraq.* 2nd ed. Berkeley: University of California Press.

Malhotra, Inder. 1989. *Indira Gandhi: A Personal and Political Biography.* Boston: Northeastern University Press.

Malik, Mohan. 2003. "High Hopes: India's Response to U.S. Security Policies." *Asian Affairs* 30 (2): 104–109.

Mandelbaum, Michael. 1995. "Lessons of the Next Nuclear War." *Foreign Affairs* 74 (2): 22–37.

Mann, James. 2004. *Rise of the Vulcans: The History of Bush's War Cabinet.* New York: Viking.

Marwah, Onkar. 1981. "India and Pakistan: Nuclear Rivals in South Asia." *International Organization* 35 (1): 165–179.

Matinuddin, Kamal. 2002. *The Nuclearization of South Asia.* New York: Oxford University Press.

"Matthews Favors U.S. War for Peace." 1950. *New York Times,* August 26, 1.

Mazarr, Michael J. 1995. "Going Just a Little Nuclear: Non-Proliferation Lessons from North Korea." *International Security* 20 (2): 92–122.

Mazzetti, Mark, and Thomas Omestad. 2002. "Ready. Aim. Fire First." *U.S. News and World Report* 133 (13): 26.

McCarthy, Rory, and Luke Harding. 2002. "India Acts on Kashmir Massacre." *Observer,* May 19, 23.

McCrary, Ernest. 1979. "Iraq's Oil Ploy to Gain Nuclear Knowhow." *Business Week,* 62.

McCullough, David. 1991. *Truman.* New York: Simon & Schuster.

Mearsheimer, John J. 1990. "Back to the Future: Instability in Europe after the Cold War." *International Security* 15 (1): 5–56.

———. 1994–1995. "The False Promise of International Institutions." *International Security* 19 (3): 5–49.

Mearsheimer, John J., and Stephen M. Walt. 2002. "Can Saddam Be Contained? History Says Yes." Occasional Paper, Belfer Center for Science and International Affairs, International Security Program.

Meisler, Stanley, and John M. Broder. 1992. "Terrifying Pursuit of Nuclear Arms." *Los Angeles Times,* January 19, 1, 4.

Meraj, Zafar, and David Housego. 1990. "Indian Premier Warns of Danger of Kashmir War." *Financial Times* (London), April 11, 6.

Milbank, Dana. 2003. "For Bush, War Defines Presidency." *Washington Post,* March 9, A1.

Miller, Judith. 1981. "U.S. Officials Say Iraq Had Ability to Make Nuclear Weapons in 1981." *New York Times,* June 9, A9.

———. 1981. "Was Iraq Planning to Make the Bomb? Debate By Experts Seems Inconclusive." *New York Times,* June 19, A11.

Moen, Alexander. 2004. *The Foreign Policy of George W. Bush: Values, Strategy and Loyalty.* London: Ashgate Press.

Moore, John Bassett. 1906. *A Digest of International Law Volume II.* Washington, DC: U.S. Government Printing Office.

Moore, W. B., and David Alan Rosenberg. 1981–1982. "Smoking Radiating Ruin at the End of Two Hours: Documents on American Plans for Nuclear War with the Soviet Union, 1954–1955." *International Security* 6 (3): 3–38.

Moran, Charles McMoran Wilson. 1966. *Winston Churchill: The Struggle for Survival, 1940–1965; Taken from the Diaries of Lord Moran.* Boston: Houghton Mifflin.

Moravscik, Andrew. 1997. "Taking Preferences Seriously: A Liberal Theory of International Politics." *International Organization* 51 (4): 513–553.

Morgenthau, Hans J. 1946. *Scientific Man vs. Power Politics.* Chicago: University of Chicago Press.

———. 1950. "The Conquest of the United States by Germany." *Bulletin of Atomic Scientists* 6 (1): 21–26.

———. 1967. *Politics among Nations: The Struggle for Power and Peace.* New York: Alfred A. Knopf.

"Mr Bush's New Gravitas." 2001. *New York Times,* October 12, A24.

Munthe, Turi, ed. 2002. *The Saddam Hussein Reader.* New York: Thunder's Mouth Press.

Murray, Allan. 2003. "Bush Seeks to Remake World with Much Help, Discussion." *Wall Street Journal,* June 3.

Murray, Shoon Kathleen, and Jonathan A. Cowden. 1999. "The Role of Enemy Images and Ideology in Elite Belief Systems." *International Studies Quarterly* 43 (3): 455–481.

Nakdimon, Shlomo. 1987. *First Strike: The Exclusive Story of How Israel Foiled Iraq's Attempt to Get the Bomb*. Translated by P. Kidron. New York: Summit Books.

Neuffer, Elizabeth. 2002. "Resolution on Iraq Passes Security Council Vote Unanimous." *Boston Globe*, November 9, A1.

Niou, Emerson, and Peter D. Feaver. 1996. "Managing Nuclear Proliferation: Condemn, Strike, or Assist?" *International Studies Quarterly* 40 (2): 209–233.

Nitze, Paul H. 1989. *From Hiroshima to Glasnost: At the Center of Decision, a Memoir*. New York: Grove Weidenfeld.

"The Nuclear Edge." 1990. *Washington Post*, February 3, A24.

Nutting, Anthony. 1967. *No End of a Lesson: The Story of Suez*. New York: Clarkson N. Potter.

Oberdorfer, Don. 1984. "Pakistan Concerned about Attack on Atomic Plants." *Washington Post*, October 12, A28.

Offner, Arnold A. 2002. *Another Such Victory: President Truman and the Cold War, 1945–1953*. Palo Alto, CA: Stanford University Press.

"Omar for Pre-Emptive Strikes against Militants." 2001. *Hindu*, October 1.

Oren, Michael B. 2002. *Six Days of War: June 1967 and the Making of the Modern Middle East*. Oxford: Oxford University Press.

Orin, Deborah. 2003. "Bush: World's Better Off since I Took Out 'Madman' Saddam." *New York Post*, October 10, 6.

Orme, John. 1987. "Deterrence Failures: A Second Look." *International Security* 11 (4): 96–124.

Pajak, Roger F. 1983. "Nuclear Status and Policies of the Middle East Countries." *International Affairs* 59 (4): 587–607.

"Pak Fitter Case for Pre-Emptive Strike: Sinha." 2003. *Times of India*, April 10.

"Pakistani Quoted as Citing Nuclear Test in '87." 1993. *New York Times*, July 25, 12.

Pape, Robert. 2003. "The Strategic Logic of Suicide Terrorism." *American Political Science Review* 97 (3): 1–19.

The Parliamentary Debates (Hansard): House of Commons, Volume 446. 1948. London: His Majesty's Stationary Office.

Paul, T. V. 1995. "Nuclear Taboo and War Initiation in Regional Conflicts." *Journal of Conflict Resolution* 39 (4): 696–717.

Peleg, Ilan. 1987. *Begin's Foreign Policy, 1977–1983: Israel's Move to the Right*. New York: Greenwood Press.

Peres, Shimon. 1995. *Battling for Peace: A Memoir*. New York: Random House.

Perlmutter, Amos. 1987. *The Life and Times of Menachem Begin*. New York: Doubleday.

Perlmutter, Amos, Michael I. Handel, and Uri Bar-Joseph. 2003. *Two Minutes over Baghdad*. 2nd ed. London: Frank Cass.

Petersen, Walter J. 1986. "Deterrence and Compellence: A Critical Assessment of Conventional Wisdom." *International Studies Quarterly* 30 (3): 269–294.

Post, Jerrold M., and Robert S. Robins. 1993. *When Illness Strikes the Leader: The Dilemma of the Captive King*. New Haven, CT: Yale University Press.

Potter, Pittman B. 1951. "Preventive War Critically Considered." *American Journal of International Law* 45 (1): 142–145.

Powell, Colin. 2004. "A Strategy of Partnerships." *Foreign Affairs* 83 (1): 22–34.

Powell, Robert. 2003. "Nuclear Deterrence Theory, Nuclear Proliferation and National Missile Defense." *International Security* 27 (4): 86–118.

"Powell's Address, Presenting 'Deeply Troubling' Evidence on Iraq." 2003. *New York Times*, February 6, 18.

Preston, Julia. 2002. "Iraq Tells the U.N. Arms Inspections Will Be Permitted." *New York Times*, November 14, A1.

———. 2003. "U.N. Inspector Says Iraq Falls Short on Cooperation." *New York Times*, January 28, 1.

Prial, Frank J. 1991. "U.N. Team Finds Chemic Arms 4 Times Greater than Iraq Claims." *New York Times*, July 31, A1.

Purdham, Todd S., and Elisabeth Bumiller. 2002. "Bush Seeks Power to Use 'All Means' to Oust Hussein." *New York Times*, September 19, 1.

Puri, Luv. 2003. "India Has Right to Pre-Emptive Strike." *Hindu*, April 7.

Quester, George H. 1973. *Nuclear Diplomacy: The First Twenty-Five Years*. 2nd ed. New York: Cambridge University Press.

———. 1988. "Crises and the Unexpected." *Journal of Interdisciplinary History* 18 (4): 701–719.

Quinones, Eric. 2003. "Greenstein: Bush a 'Less Sure-Footed' Leader in Iraq War, Despite His Post-Sept. 11 Growth." *Princeton Bulletin* 92 (21): 1.

Rabb, Theodore K., and Robert I. Rotberg, eds. 1989. *The Origin and Prevention of Major Wars, Studies in Interdisciplinary History*. New York: Cambridge University Press.

Rajmara, Sheen. 1997. "Indo-Pakistani Relations: Reciprocity in Long-Term Perspective." *International Studies Quarterly* 41 (3): 547–560.

Raser, John R. 1966. "Deterrence Research: Past Progress and Future Needs." *Journal of Peace Research* 3 (4): 297–327.

Rashid, Ahmed. 1990. "Pakistan Fears Indian Attack over Kashmir." *Independent* (London), April 2, 12.

Rearden, Steven L., and Kenneth W. Thompson, eds. 1990. *Paul H. Nitze on National Security and Arms Control*. Vol. 14, *W. Alton Jones Foundation Series on Arms Control*. New York: University Press of America.

Reiter, Dan. 1995. "Exploding the Powder Keg Myth: Preemptive Wars Almost Never Happen." *International Security* 20 (2): 5–34.

———. 2005. "Preventive Attacks Against Nuclear Programs and the 'Success' at Osiraq." *Nonproliferation Review* 12 (2): 355–371.

Rennie, David. 2003. "Weapons Hunters Dismiss Powell's WMD Claims." *Chicago Sun-Times*, October 27, 43.

Renshon, Stanley. 2004. *In His Father's Shadow: The Transformations of George W. Bush*. New York: Palgrave Macmillan.

Rhode, David. 2003. "Fighting in Kashmir Revives Rancor in Pakistan and India." *New York Times*, September 28, 8.

Rice, Condoleezza. 2000. "Promoting the National Interest." *Foreign Affairs* 79 (1): 45–62.

Riddell, Peter. 1991. "Nuclear Arms Plan Admitted by Iraq." *New York Times*, July 9, 18.

Risen, James, David E. Sanger, and Thom Shanker. 2003. "In Sketchy Data, Trying to Guage Iraq Threat." *New York Times*, July 20.

Rosati, Jerel A. 2000. "The Power of Human Cognition in the Study of World Politics." *International Studies Review* 2 (3): 48–75.

Rosenberg, David Alan. 1979. "American Atomic Strategy and the Hydrogen Bomb Decision." *Journal of American History* 66 (1): 62–87.

———. 1983. "The Origins of Overkill: Nuclear Weapons and American Strategy, 1945–1960." *International Security* 7 (4): 3–71.

Russell, Bertrand. 1946. "The Atomic Bomb and the Prevention of War." *Bulletin of Atomic Scientists* 2 (7–8): 19–21.

"Russell Urges West to Fight Russia Now." 1948. *New York Times*, November 21, 4.

Sagan, Scott D. 1994. "The Perils of Proliferation: Organization Theory, Deterrence Theory and the Spread of Nuclear Weapons." *International Security* 18 (4): 66–107.

———. 2001. "The Perils of Proliferation in South Asia." *Asian Survey* 41 (6): 1064–1086.

Sammon, Bill. 2001. "Bush Rates Progress High after 180 Days." *Washington Times*, July 27.

———. 2002. "Attacks of September 11 Defined Bush Presidency." *Washington Times*, September 11.

Sampson, Anthony. 2002. "Oilmen Don't Want Another Suez." *Guardian*, December 22, 17.

Sanger, David E. 2001. "After ABM Treaty: New Freedom for U.S. in Different Kind of Arms Control." *New York Times*, December 15, 8.

———. 2002. "Bush Presses U.N. to Act Quickly on Disarming Iraq." *New York Times*, September 13, A1.

Sanger, David E., and John F. Burns. 2003. "Bush Orders Start of War on Iraq." *New York Times*, March 20, 1.

Sanger, David E., and Julia Preston. 2002. "Bush to Warn U.N.: Act on Iraq or U.S. Will." *New York Times*, September 12, 1.

SarDesai, D. R., and Raju G. C. Thomas, eds. 2002. *Nuclear India in the Twenty-First Century*. New York: Palgrave Macmillan Press.

Schafer, Mark. 1999. "Cooperative and Conflictual Policy Preferences: The Effect of Identity, Security, and Image of the Other." *Political Psychology* 20 (4): 829–844.

Schafer, Mark, and Michael D. Young. 1998. "Is There Method in Our Madness? Ways of Assessing Cognition in International Relations." *Mershon International Studies Review* 42 (1): 63–96.

Schelling, Thomas C. 1966. *Arms and Influence.* New Haven, CT: Yale University Press.

Schlesinger, Arthur, Jr. 2002. "The Immorality of Preemptive War." *New Perspectives Quarterly* 19 (3): 41–42.

Schmitt, Eric. 2002. "Buildup Leaves U.S. Nearly Set to Start Attack." *New York Times,* December 8, 1.

Schnabel, James F. 1996. *History of the Joint Chiefs of Staff.* Vol. 1, *The Joint Chiefs of Staff and National Policy, 1945–1947.* Washington, DC: Office of the Joint Chiefs of Staff.

Schofield, Victoria. 2003. *Kashmir in Conflict: India, Pakistan and the Unending War.* London: I.B. Tauris Press.

Schweller, Randall L. 1992. "Domestic Structure and Preventive War: Are Democracies More Pacific?" *World Politics* 44 (2): 235–269.

Sciolino, Elaine. 1991. "Iraqi Report Says Chemical Arsenal Survived the War." *New York Times,* April 20, A1.

Sevak, Amith, and Michael Krepon, eds. 1995. *Crisis Prevention, Confidence Building, and Reconciliation in South Asia.* New York: St. Martin's Press.

Shales, Tom. 1984. "Battle Hymn of the Republicans." *Washington Post,* August 24, B1.

Sharon, Ariel. 1989. *Warrior: The Autobiography of Ariel Sharon.* New York: Simon & Schuster.

Shipler, David K. 1981. "Begin's Aides Say Much More Was at Stake than Election." *New York Times,* June 14, 3.

———. 1981. "Prime Minister Begin Defends Raid on Iraqi Nuclear Reactor; Pledges to Thwart a New 'Holocaust.'" *New York Times,* June 10, A1.

Shlaim, Avi. 1997. "The Protocol of Sevres, 1956: Anatomy of a War Plot." *International Affairs* 73 (3): 509–530.

Shuckburgh, Evelyn. 1986. *Descent to Suez: Diaries, 1951–1956.* New York: Random House.

"Significance of the H-Bomb and America's Dilemma." 1950. *Newsweek,* February 13, 20.

Silver, Eric. 1984. *Begin: The Haunted Prophet.* New York: Random House.

Sipress, Alan. 2001. "U.S. Favors Easing Iraq Sanctions." *Washington Post,* February 27, A1.

Slocombe, Walter B. 2003. "Force, Preemption and Legitimacy." *Survival* 45 (1): 117–130.

Smith, J. P. 1978. "Evidence Indicates Iraq Encourages Terrorism." *Washington Post,* August 6, A21.

———. 1978. "Iraq Emerging as Formidable Middle East Power." *Washington Post,* August 6, A1.

———. 1978. "Iraq's Nuclear Arms Option." *Washington Post,* August 8, A14.

Snyder, Glenn H. 2002. "Mearsheimer's World–Offensive Realism and the Struggle for Security." *International Security* 27 (1): 149–173.

Snyder, Jack. 1984. "Civil-Military Relations and the Cult of the Offensive, 1914 and 1984." *International Security* 9 (1): 108–146.

Snyder, Jack, and Edward D. Mansfield. 2002. "Incomplete Democratization and the Outbreak of Military Disputes." *International Studies Quarterly* 46 (4): 529–549.

Snyder, Jed C. 1983. "The Road to Osiraq: Baghdad's Quest for the Bomb." *Middle East Journal* 37 (4): 565–593.

Sofaer, Abraham D. 2003. "On the Necessity of Pre-Emption." *European Journal of International Law* 14 (2): 209–226.

Sofer, Sasson. 1988. *Begin: An Anatomy of Leadership.* New York: Basil Blackwell.

Spector, Leonard S. 1988. *The Undeclared Bomb.* Cambridge, MA: Harper & Row.

———. 1990. *Nuclear Ambitions: The Spread of Nuclear Weapons, 1989–1990.* San Francisco: Westview Press.

Steinberg, James. 2005–2006. "Preventive Force in US National Security Strategy." *Survival* 47 (4): 55–72.

Stenbruner, John. 1976. "Beyond Rational Deterrence: The Struggle for a New Conception." *World Politics* 28 (2): 223–245.

Stevens, Austin. 1950. "General Removed over War Speech." *New York Times,* September 2, 1.

Stevens, William K. 1984. "India Worried by U.S. Links to Pakistanis." *New York Times,* October 21, 7.

Stevenson, Richard. 2003. "Bush Gives Hussein 48 Hours, and Vows to Act." *New York Times,* March 18, 1.

———. 2003. "Bush Says Iraq Isn't Complying with Demands to Disarm." *New York Times,* January 21.

Stoessinger, John G. 1981. *Nations in Darkness: China, Russia and America.* 3rd ed. New York: Random House.

Stout, David. 2002. "Bush Calls Iraqi Vow a Trick." *New York Times,* September 18.

Strasser, Steven. 1981. "A Risky Nuclear Game." *Newsweek,* June 22, 20.

Stuart, Douglas, and Harvey Starr. 1981–1982. "The 'Inherent Bad Faith Model' Reconsidered: Dulles, Kennedy, and Kissinger." *Political Psychology* 3 (3–4): 1–33.

Suskind, Ron. 2004. *The Price of Loyalty: George W. Bush, the White House and the Education of Paul O'Neill.* New York: Simon & Schuster.

Taliaferro, Jeffrey W. 2000. "Security Seeking under Anarchy." *International Security* 25 (3): 128–161.

———. 2004. *Balancing Risks: Great Power Intervention in the Periphery.* Ithaca, NY: Cornell University Press.

Tannenwald, Nina. 1999. "The Nuclear Taboo: The United States and the Normative Basis of Nuclear Non-Use." *International Organization* 53 (3): 433–468.

Tatom, John. 2003. "Iraqi Oil Is Not America's Objective." *Financial Times,* February 13, 17.

Taubman, Philip. 1984. "Worsening India-Pakistan Ties Worry U.S." *New York Times*, September 15, 2.

Taylor, A.J.P. 1954. *The Struggle for Mastery in Europe, 1848–1918.* Oxford: Clarendon Press.

Taylor, Terence. 2004. "The End of Imminence?" *Washington Quarterly* 27 (4): 57–72.

Tellis, Ashley J. 2001. *India's Emerging Nuclear Posture: Between Recessed Deterrent and Ready Arsenal.* California: RAND Press.

Tiwari, Rajiv. 1990. "India: Ominous Sabre-Rattling with Pakistan." *IPS-Inter Press Service*, April 12.

Tobin, Elayne. 2002. "Dubyaspeak." *Nation* 275 (5).

Trachtenberg, Marc. 1988–1989. "A 'Wasting Asset': American Strategy and the Shifting Nuclear Balance, 1949–1954." *International Security* 13 (3): 5–49.

———. 1989. "Strategic Thought in America, 1952–1966." *Political Science Quarterly* 104 (2): 301–334.

———. 1991. *History and Strategy.* Princeton, NJ: Princeton University Press.

Truman, Harry S. 1956. *Memoirs by Harry S. Truman.* Vol. 2, *Years of Trial and Hope.* New York: Doubleday.

"US Alarmed by India's War Threats." 2003. *Straits Times* (Singapore), April 13.

U.S. Department of State. 1972. *Foreign Relations of the United States, 1946.* Vol. 1. Washington, DC: U.S. Government Printing Office.

———. 1976. *Foreign Relations of the United States, 1949. Vol. 1, National Security Affairs; Foreign Economic Policy.* Washington, DC: U.S. Government Printing Office.

———. 1976. *Foreign Relations of the United States, 1950. Vol. 7, Korea.* Washington, DC: U.S. Government Printing Office.

———. 1977. *Foreign Relations of the United States, 1950. Vol. 1, National Security Affairs; Foreign Economic Policy.* Washington, DC: U.S. Government Printing Office.

———. 1979. *Foreign Relations of the United States, 1951. Vol. 1, National Security Affairs; Foreign Economic Policy.* Washington, DC: U.S. Government Printing Office.

———. 1984. *Foreign Relations of the United States, 1952–1954. Vol. 15 (1), Korea.* Washington, DC: U.S. Government Printing Office.

———. 1984. *Foreign Relations of the United States, 1952–1954. Vol. 2 (1), National Security Affairs.* Washington, DC: U.S. Government Printing Office.

———. 1984. *Foreign Relations of the United States, 1952–1954. Vol. 2 (2), National Security Affairs.* Washington, DC: U.S. Government Printing Office.

Varble, Derek. 2003. *The Suez Crisis 1956.* Oxford: Osprey.

Varshney, Ashutosh. 1991. "India, Pakistan, and Kashmir: Antinomies of Nationalism." *Asian Survey* 31 (11): 997–1019.

Waggoner, Walter H. 1950. "U.S. Disowns Matthews Talk of Waging War to Get Peace." *New York Times*, August 27, 1.

Wagner, Abraham R. 1974. *Crisis Decision-Making: Israel's Experience in 1967 and 1973*. New York: Praeger Publishers.

Wagner, R. Harrison. 1991. "Nuclear Deterrence, Counterforce Strategies and the Incentive to Strike First." *American Political Science Review* 85 (3): 727–749.

Walker, Stephen G. 1977. "The Interface between Beliefs and Behavior: Henry Kissinger's Operational Code and the Vietnam War." *Journal of Conflict Resolution* 21 (1): 129–168.

Waltz, Kenneth. 1962. *Man, the State and War: A Theoretical Analysis*. New York: Columbia University Press.

———. 1979. *Theory of International Politics*. 1st ed. New York: Random House.

———. 1981. "The Spread of Nuclear Weapons: More May Be Better." *Adelphi Papers*.

———. 1993. "The Emerging Structure of International Politics." *International Security* 18 (2): 44–79.

Warner, Geoffrey. 1979. "'Collusion' and the Suez Crisis of 1956." *International Affairs* 55 (2): 226–239.

Weisman, Steven R. 2003. "Powell, in U.N. Speech, Presents Case to Show Iraq Has Not Disarmed." *New York Times*, February 6, 1.

Weisman, Steven R., and Julia Preston. 2002. "Powell Says Iraq Raises Risk of War by Lying on Arms." *New York Times*, December 20, A1.

"Why Iraq Won't Deal with Israel: An Interview with Saddam Husayn, Iraq's Strong Man." 1977. *U.S. News and World Report*, May 16, 96.

Wilson, Richard. 1991. "Nuclear Proliferation and the Case of Iraq." *Journal of Palestine Studies* 20 (3): 5–15.

Winner, Andrew C., and Toshi Yoshihara. 2002. "India and Pakistan at the Edge." *Survival* 44 (3): 69–86.

Wirsing, Robert G. 2003. *Kashmir in the Shadow of War: Regional Rivalries in a Nuclear Age*. New York: M. E. Sharpe.

Wohlstetter, Albert. 1959. "The Delicate Balance of Terror." *Foreign Affairs* 37 (2): 211–234.

Woodward, Bob. 2002. *Bush at War*. New York: Simon & Schuster.

———. 2004. *Plan of Attack*. New York: Simon & Schuster.

Yergin, Daniel. 1992. *The Prize: The Epic Quest for Oil, Money and Power*. New York: Free Press.

———. 2002. "What Will Happen to Oil after Saddam?" *Times* (London), December 12, 31.

———. 2003. "Gulf Oil: How Important Is It Anyway?" *Financial Times*, March 22, 1.

———. 2003. "Oil Shortage Conventional Wisdom Says that Oil Can Bail Out Iraq..." *Boston Globe*, May 25, 10.

Index

Acheson, Dean, 64, 65
Analogies: Appeasement, 33–34, 35, 40, 145; Hitler, 33, 40, 51, 115, 116, 145, 154; Holocaust, 44, 51–52, 56, 57–58; Rhineland, 33

Balance of Power, 3, 4, 7, 15, 21, 24, 39, 41, 59, 99–100, 102, 151, 164
Begin, Menachem: 15–16, 44, 50, 113, 147; bad faith image of Arabs, 152; Early life, 50–51; Osiraq decision, 54–55; timing of attack, 55–56, 155; worldview, 51–52, 143–144
Belief that War is Inevitable Factor, 18, 154–155
Bharatiya Janata Party (BJP), 91, 92, 93, 100–101, 145, 155
Bhutto, Benazir, 91
Black-and-White Thinking Factor, 19–20, 158–159
Bohlen, Charles E., 70
British decline, 24, 28–30
Bush Doctrine, xi, 1, 2, 108, 125, 141, 161
Bush, George W.: 1, 15, 147; and "State of war" with Iraq, 154; and time pressure, 157; as a leader, 112–115, 144; as primary decision-maker, 108–109; early foreign policy, 110–112; early policy towards Iraq, 109–110; impact of September 11, 119–122; National Security Strategy (2002), 122–127; on Saddam Hussein, 115, 153–154; worldview of, 108, 115–117, 123

Cheney, Richard, 1, 109, 118, 122, 128, 130, 132, 135, 136, 137
Churchill, Winston, 33, 52, 68–69, 114
Coercion, 8
Cold War, xi, 10, 21, 61–62, 102, 110–111, 140, 153, 158; Bush and, 111, 117, 123, 124, 125, 126
"Collusion," Suez Case, 36–37
Credibility, 9

Declining Power Factor, 16, 148–151
Deterrence, 8–9, 82–83, 12, 124, 125, 126, 132, 138–139, 161–162, 164, 165
Deterrence, nuclear, 10, 22, 100, 105

Eden, Anthony: 23, 25, 40, 147; background of, 30; belief that war was inevitable, 154; collusion, 36–37; decisiveness, 144; declining power factor, 150; economic pressure, 28; perception of Nasser, 25, 29, 33, 152; time pressure, 156; use of analogies, 33, 35

Eisenhower, Dwight D.: advantage of the offensive, 157; and Cold War, 76–77; declining power factor, 150; image of Soviet Union, 84–85, 152–153; "New Look" National Security Strategy, 76–77, 144; and preventive war, 78–80, 147–148; and pre-emption, 81–82, 86; on U.S. superiority, 75; Suez, 24, 28, 33, 38; time pressure, 156

France: nuclear cooperation with Iraq, 46, 47–48, 52, 54; Suez, 34, 36

Freedman, Lawrence, 3, 123–124

Gaddis, John Lewis, 112, 117, 120, 125, 167n2

Gandhi, Indira: 91, 104, 145; image of Pakistan, 153; on possible pre-emptive strike, 88–90, 156

Gandhi, Rajiv, 90, 91

Gates, Robert, 92–94

Gazit, Shlomo, 47

Hagerty, Devin T., 94, 95

Hersh, Seymour, 94

Huntington, Samuel, 3, 5, 59–60

Hussein, Saddam: and the United States, 108, 126–127, 131, 138, 140; incendiary rhetoric, 47; rise to power, 45–46. See also Iraq.

Imminence, 2, 3

Inherent Bad Faith Factor, 17–18, 151–154

International Atomic Energy Agency (IAEA), 52–53, 57, 88–89

International law, xi, 3, 11, 12, 27, 37, 40, 52–53; and Saddam Hussein, 108, 138

Iraq: and "Caramel" fuel, 49–50; choice of nuclear reactor, 47; early Nuclear Program, 44–45; importance of oil, 45; purchase of Uranium, 49; relationship with Israel, 42; reprocessing plant, 49. See also Hussein, Saddam.

Italy, 46, 49, 53–54

Kargil War, 95–96, 99, 105

Kennan, George, 61–62

Kissinger, Henry, 23, 29, 59

Leadership psychology, 15–16, 143–146

Levy, Jack, 4, 7, 15, 24, 40, 148, 150

Methodology, 20–22

Morality, 37, 64–65, 77, 78, 147

Motivations of leaders, 7

Musharraf, Pervez, 96, 99, 101, 105

Nasser, Gamal: 23, 25, 35; and Aswan High Dam, 25–26; seizure of Canal, 26

National Security Council (NSC), 61, 77, 80–81, 121, 127–128, 134

Nitze, Paul, 62, 66, 83–84

NSC-68, 63, 64–67, 85, 154

Nutting, Anthony, 26, 27, 29, 31, 32, 33, 36–37, 152

Oakley, Robert, 92

Oil: Iraq, 46, 49; Suez, 23, 25, 29, 30–32, 37, 174n45; United States, 129–131

O'Neill, Paul, 117–119, 191n44

Peres, Shimon, 15, 54, 55, 57, 143, 155

Powell, Colin, 97, 110, 128, 134, 136, 137
Pre-emption, definition of, 3
Prevention: and aggression, 6–8; and coercion, 8–10; and nuclear deterrence, 10–11; and regime type, 147; and reputation, 148; and risk-taking, 14, 146–147; definition of preventive action, 3, 4; legality of prevention/preemption, 11–14; types of preventive action, 6
Proliferation optimist/pessimism, 10
Prospect Theory, 14

Rumsfeld, Donald, 109, 110, 118, 127, 128, 129, 132, 135, 137, 138, 191n44
Rusk, Dean, 71–72

Schelling, Thomas, 74, 83, 102, 124
Security Dilemma, 5, 9, 17
Self-image, 30, 39–40
Sevres Conference, 23, 37–38
September 11, 2001, xi, 2, 22, 96, 98, 108–112, 115, 117, 119–122, 124, 125, 127–129, 139–141, 147, 154, 163, 165
Simla Accords, 91
Singh, V.P., 91, 92
Sinha, Yashwant, 97
Situation that Favors the Offensive Factor, 18, 157–158
Solarium project, 79, 81
Soviet Union: atomic test, 63; conventional superiority of, 60
Suez Canal: 23, 25; importance of, 29, 31; seizure of, 26–27; Suez Canal Company, 27

Trachtenberg, Marc, 62, 66–67
Transition Periods, 10, 15
Truman, Harry, 62, 63

Ul-Haq, Zia, 90, 101
United Nations, 11–14, 53, 69, 109, 119, 133, 135, 137, 138, 196n139

Window Thinking Factor, 18, 155–157
Woodward, Bob, 109, 118, 121, 131

About the Author

JONATHAN RENSHON holds a master's degree in international relations from the London School of Economics and Political Science. He has served on the editorial board of the *Millennium Journal of International Relations.*